SWIM, JUMP, FLY

A guide to changing your life

First published in Great Britain in 2022

Copyright © Charlotte Sheridan 2022

www.swimjumpfly.com

ISBN: 978-1-3999-3004-8

001

All cartoons and illustrations by Simon Pearsall.
Printed and bound in Great Britain by Blissetts.

Introduction

Welcome. Bienvenue. Willkommen. Bienvenido. I'm glad you're here.

Perhaps you are uncertain thinking, "Is this book right for me?" I get it. There are a lot of books out there about improving our lives, in fact too many to choose from. How do you know whether you'll like this one? It isn't much fun dive-bombing a pool when the water is freezing. By dipping your toe into this introduction, you can test us out (the book and me).

You're probably asking: "Who are you, Charlotte? And, if I read *Swim, Jump, Fly*, what will I get? What will change for me?" You ask good questions.

I'm Charlotte Sheridan and I'm an occupational (organisational) psychologist, coach and writer. During 2019 and 2020 I interviewed 108 people who were going through shifts in their lives, be it health, career, relationship, or other types of change. You can find out more about this research in Appendix D.

> It has been cathartic just telling somebody the whole story.
> — Kathryn (interviewee)

> I don't really ask that anyone listens to me, so I'm usually not listened to. For me, it's so great to just be able to speak about this."
> — Gina (interviewee)

When I started this research, I was going through a career change myself, wondering what to do next. I was curious to find out how people made successful shifts in their work. What started as a handful of conversations about careers snowballed into a huge research project about different types of change. By the time I'd finished (after 75 hours of interviews), I had identified a number of themes about how to make positive shifts. I'll be sharing these throughout *Swim, Jump, Fly*.

Here are some examples of the stories I gathered:

Orla's lung suddenly collapsed and she had to have emergency surgery. But it went wrong and for the last twelve years she has been quite unwell. Despite life changing dramatically she doesn't want to go back. "I feel like I've evolved. I understand so much more about life, about kindness, about people. And how

1

being the best at something doesn't matter a jot. Like being clever, working hard. None of that matters. I didn't know that before all of this happened."

Anne is French and lives in Ireland. In the past when her partner said things she disagreed with, she kept quiet and thought, "I'm just going to pretend I haven't heard it." Whilst this went on for years, one day she just ran out of steam. She got to the point where she couldn't ignore it. "I need to stop pretending like everything is fine. I disagree with what he says. I need to stop pretending and hiding my emotions." Anne remembers the day well because it was when she decided, "I can't stay with him. It's not possible, our values are so different." So, she decided she had to go. But then it took her six months to pluck up the courage to move to action.

Jinhai works in Hong Kong, where he didn't fit in with his colleagues or the company's work culture. "I felt like I had to put on an act for them. I had to be this professional guy who's doing a good job, but at the end of the day, the work wasn't something that I cared about. I had to convince people to do certain things that I didn't really believe in myself." It wasn't helped by a micro-managing boss who got on his nerves. Over time all of this started to impact his health. "Physically I got sick quite often and I was stressed out. There was a lot of pressure and I wasn't sleeping well. That definitely took a toll on me, both physically and mentally, and at that point I felt I had to make a change."

Rob went through some dark times when he left his family home and children, then went through a separation with his partner. He was suicidal and at one point he "was really close to checking out." He says, "It's just been a voyage of discovery for the last three and a half years. My story may sound sad to some people. But I think that what I've worked out is that it's never too late." Life is better for Rob who says, "I'm single now. But, where I felt alone my whole life, I don't feel alone anymore. I'm still a work in progress. I do feel I'm finally putting all the pieces of me together. I'm reaching an interesting time in my life."

When I spoke to these people, I found interesting patterns. Things they thought, felt, or actioned that helped them work through changes in their lives. There were also activities they wouldn't do again. Over 18 months I wrote these into a weekly blog called *Spoon-by-Spoon*[1]. Readers of the blog said it was useful to hear what other people were going through and they felt less alone. Now I'm turning these themes into a book to help you.

Who would benefit from reading *Swim, Jump, Fly*? If you're contemplating a change in your life, then it's for you. You might be switching roles or addressing your physical or mental health, or general wellbeing. Perhaps you want to start or finish a relationship or friendship, or you're contemplating somewhere new to live. If you don't have a clue where to begin, it'll be great for you too.

> I knew I wanted a change but didn't know what to change to. I just didn't know where to start. I was going around in circles in my head, not actually making any progress. — Maeve (interviewee)

I've based this book on two foundations: the science of change plus lived experiences of people going through shifts in their lives. My writing is underpinned by:

- Lessons I learned as a professional Change Management Consultant helping others shift, including change management models.[2]
- Knowledge of psychology and human behaviour – I've been a Chartered Occupational Psychologist for 25 years. This includes the science of adult learning, how we can gain skills, practice behaviours and how to make change stick.
- Experience as a Coaching Psychologist supporting individuals at crossroads in their lives, coaching them through their own personal shifts.
- Stories, quotes and themes gathered from the 75 hours of interviews. These were people from 27 countries who were going through change. I've also included some of the 77,000 words I wrote in my *Spoon-by-Spoon* blog that covered many of these themes.
- I ran the research and wrote the blogs during the 2020/21 global pandemic. For many people it was a wake-up call, an emotional and life audit, a time to face up to changes they had wanted to make for years.

Now to your other questions, which I haven't forgotten. "What will I get if I read *Swim, Jump, Fly*? What will change for me?" For starters you'll find out more about your own change, where you are now and where you want to go. I'll include ideas from business, psychology, coaching, philosophy and other thinking that will support you. There will be plenty of exercises to work through, which will help you better understand yourself and what you want. Building your self-awareness is important before you go through change. It's hard to make progress if you don't know who you are, what's important to you or where you're heading.

Once you've got that sorted, I'll guide you through simple steps to work out how to start the process, how to progress and stay motivated when the going gets tough. You'll hear stories from the people I spoke to, plus I'll share some of my experiences of shifting too. As a Management Consultant I used to fly around the world in a power suit with shoulder pads. I now run a coaching, writing and photography business. The suits are gathering dust.

> "I hate the rat race. I'm 30 and my friends are getting married and having babies and I want to go and travel the world and live in a camper van. I just want to elope. It would be really cool. I spend a lot of time on Pinterest looking at camper vans. — Emily (interviewee)

I would like the book to feel like coaching, but for a fraction of the cost. A collaboration where you are the expert on you, and I offer ideas and frameworks that might help, plus some companionship along the way. I'm simply a guide with information on the different paths you might choose to reach your destination. Together we'll walk through the ups and downs that come with change and you'll hear what 108 people learned throughout the process. By the end of *Swim, Jump, Fly* you'll:

- Know where you are now and where you want to go.
- Be clear about the steps you can take to get there.
- Have tried a number of experiments to see what works best.
- Understand what may be blocking you from shifting.
- Know how you can keep on track and stay motivated.
- Be clear you're not alone, mad or misguided.
- Understand you can make this change, whatever you need it to be.
- Have the tools to successfully change in other parts of your life.

Some additional thoughts before we get going. Our lives aren't perfect and we all want to shift a few things around. If we make the effort to go through change then it's likely we will want it to stick. In short, we want sustainable change. A word to the impatient (that's also me by the way): sustainable change takes a bit of time and energy. It won't happen overnight. Despite knowing there are no free lunches, we are still drawn to these types of claims: *Get Rich in Four Weeks! Develop Amazing Abs in Three Days! Lose 100 pounds in an Afternoon!*

We know they don't work, but we're ever hopeful. The problem is that fast change is like elastic: unless you hold it tight, it will ping right back to where it came from. Forcing things to shift too quickly means it won't be sustainable in the long term. So, if you think changing won't take any effort, please stop reading *Swim, Jump, Fly* right now. Say, "No thanks" to sustainable change and slide this book back onto the shelf.

❝ Real change, enduring change, happens one step at a time. — Ruth Bader Ginsburg (Lawyer and US Supreme Court Associate Justice)

You might be wondering what tips I have for reading *Swim, Jump, Fly*. Firstly, throw yourself in. There are exercises to help you learn more about yourself and the actions you might take. Do them wholeheartedly and you'll get more bang for your buck (pound, euro, dollar, rupee). There is also scientific evidence that working with a bit of pace means your change will be more successful. I'll explain this later, but for now try to read the book (and do the exercises) in less than three months.

Taking in information in multiple ways helps us learn more easily, as does pacing the learning, by taking breaks. I will offer different ways to engage with the content, along with time to reflect. Making meaningful and personal connections between the material and your own life will be key.

> " I realised one day that I didn't recognise myself. I started to not see anything of the person I used to be and who people were drawn to.
> I just didn't feel that person existed anymore. — Jacqui (interviewee)

If you're someone who loves to munch on detail, there is more at the back of the book in the appendices, plus on the *Swim, Jump, Fly* website (swimjumpfly. com). There are also references in each chapter to books, websites, articles, and some of the 70,000+ words of my coaching blog. If you prefer to start with a more top-down/big picture approach, then you can read the end of chapter summaries first. There will also be opportunities to apply all of this to your own change, through exercises, quizzes, surveys, reflections and actions.

Brené Brown is a well-known academic, writer and researcher. She suggests building on your learning by indexing ideas that resonate or stand out for you. She calls it *integration work*.[3] Highlight the word/phrase, note down the page number and write this in a relevant index category that you've created. She uses categories like *I don't get it, I want to work on this, read more* or *quotes*. You can create your own category titles, they could be named after your pets, if you like. It's up to you.

In terms of other tips, I'd say hold all this information lightly, since this book will have limitations. People might say I place too much emphasis on some areas and that I miss other information out. I'm not suggesting my approach is a golden set of rules you have to follow. It's not a theory of everything that will transform your life overnight. It will take time and effort. I prefer to see *Swim, Jump, Fly* as a library full of information, exercises and ideas. Some will resonate, others you'll dislike. Whilst I'd suggest following each step in the 5-Step Process, whether you use all the other material is up to you. Pick and choose from the menu, eat the things that sound tasty, ignore the ones that don't. Only you will be able to work that out.

It's also useful to remember you already have many skills, experiences, and resources that you need to make this change. John Whitmore[4] was a British leadership/organisational change thinker and writer who said we are "like an acorn, which contains within it all the potential to be a magnificent oak tree. We need nourishment, encouragement, and the light to reach toward, but the oaktreeness is already within."

What's holding you back may not be a lack of skills or opportunities. It may be a lack of confidence or a negative voice in your head that repeats on a loop. Or you might need reminding of successful change you've made in the past. Maybe you're not making full use of the resources you already have around you. Or perhaps you don't feel in control or have permission to change; you often have more agency than you believe you do, and other people (generally) want you to be happy.

Right, that's enough of that. It's time to face the changes in your life. Are you ready to dive in?

Chapter 1

Change is a funny thing. We want it and we don't want it, all at the same time. We would like some things to stay the same, whilst preferring others to shift. We want the world to stop spinning when we're happy and to speed up when we're not.

Take a friendship that's going well. We enjoy our friend's company and we like how they make us feel. But one evening over a drink they tell us they are moving to Tokyo. We feel sad, since neither of us lives in Tokyo right now. As the conversation continues, we start to realise this is making us feel a bit annoyed. Our friend is shifting the dynamics and we're losing control. More than ever, we want to press pause so that things can stay the same.

Or what if our work is going well? It's close to home. We like the people and it makes us feel stretched and fulfilled. But then on one morning we get an email: "Good news, we want you to run the Argentina project." But we don't want a bigger workload, we were just fine as we were THANK YOU VERY MUCH.

Perhaps we're on a holiday with friends or family. We're having a lovely time. The weather is great, the food is delicious, we're relaxed at last. But tomorrow is our last day. Out here, in this amazing place, we don't want this trip to end.

There is the opposite of course when we aren't so fine and dandy. When we wish life would hurry up. Perhaps we're on a walk and we look up at the sky. The clouds are dark and foreboding. It starts to rain. Soon it becomes a downpour and we don't have a coat. In our mind we fast-forward, seeing ourselves back home in the warm and dry.

Or perhaps we've been feeling down for a day, or a week, or, if we're unfortunate, much longer. We wish our lives were different, somewhere in the future, feeling better. When our mood eventually lifts, or the rain finally stops, our hand is hovering over the pause button again. We're back where we started, wishing the world would stay the same.

Don't worry if this is you. This is what it's like to be human. We all feel like this from time to time – hoping things would stay the same whilst wishing other things would change. *Swim, Jump, Fly* will help you to work out what is in your gift to change and what is not. British philosopher and Buddhist, Alan Watts,[5] was teaching in the 1950s and 60s, and said that the more resistance we have to change, the more pain it will bring us. We need to stop craving permanence for particular situations in our lives and just get on with living.

————

I mentioned that during 2019/2020 I talked to 108 people in 27 countries. One week I chatted with Dhaval from Gujarat, Ruby in San Diego, Jinhai from Hong Kong and Kira in Toronto. The next week I had virtual stopovers in Norway, Greece, Brazil, France and Australia. I enjoyed leaping from the west of the globe to the east. It was exciting talking to people around the world.

What they had in common was change. These folks were moving between cities or countries, getting divorced, shifting their career, or dealing with unexpected changes in their physical or mental health. The youngest was 28 and the oldest was 68, yet whoever I spoke to, or wherever they were from, they all talked about the same sorts of topics. You can read more about this research in Appendix D at the back of *Swim, Jump, Fly*.

I'll be using stories throughout the book. This is because we feel less alone when we hear stories about others going through similar shifts. Equally, finding out about other people's successes can be motivating and help us work through our own change projects.

Here are some more of their stories to get us going: Bill worked for a large international organisation but was unhappy. He went through many changes in just a few years, including moving to another country and planning a transformation in his career. Looking back, he says, "Don't be afraid of change. Don't feel that you have to stay with something you don't enjoy because sometimes making change is a lot of fun." Whilst it can be challenging and difficult, "You learn a lot about yourself and what you're capable of. You can end up in a much better situation… somewhere you're more comfortable a lot sooner."

Misha found her life wasn't going the way she'd hoped. "I was stressed and working long hours and my health was so bad. My mental health wasn't great either." She found herself searching for quick fixes and remedies to stop her thinking about the stresses in her life. "To get comfort I'd go shopping and buy jewellery or drink alcohol." But she got through to the other side and now she says, "I have found a completely different definition for my life, a humble, simple way of looking at things."

Mary wanted to change a lot of things. Her relationship, where she lived and her work… all at once. She didn't want to do things by halves! The challenge for her was that she kept it all to herself. "I was really good at playing the part. I didn't tell anyone else." So, she had to work through many changes on her own. We'll cover how to help ourselves by sharing plans with friends or family and having the right resources to support us through our shift.

Others have had change thrust on them, they had to ride the wave when it crashed over their heads. Jitesh went through significant and sudden change. "We've got to do it very quickly, otherwise you'll lose the use of your right leg." Urgent advice from his surgeon and a momentous event that had small beginnings, picking up a box. You can find out more about what he went through later.

Change happens all the time, whether we like it or not. So, where we put our energy is important. The trick is to work out what's in our control and what is not. However, we often focus on the things we can't influence, which doesn't leave much time or energy for the things we can control.

❝❝ The only constant is change. — Heraclitus (Greek philosopher 500 BC)

In broad terms, the driver at the heart of our desire to change is a yearning for happiness. The social psychologist and Harvard Professor, Daniel Gilbert, wrote a whole book about this topic, called *Stumbling on Happiness*[6]. He says we want to be happy and much of what we do is a means to that end. Whether we're running away from sadness, or regret, or sprinting towards pleasure or joy. In fact, happiness was the number one theme in all my interviews. During the research, I ran a *Thematic Analysis.* This is just a fancy name for identifying the themes. From the top 18 themes, happiness came in at number one, showing up 248 times. And don't forget there were only 108 interviewees! Find out more about the research in Appendix D.

Happiness showed up in a number of themes that I identified. These included 'finding pleasure in small things', 'being grateful', 'having fun' and 'in a sense of belonging' (plus its reverse, 'not belonging'). It appeared in these topics too: 'challenging ourselves', 'enjoying work', 'having passion, meaning and purpose', 'being fulfilled' or 'making a difference', 'recognition and appreciation', 'empathy and respect' and through 'collaborating and helping others'.

We are all constantly shifting in our lives, often going through life transitions. This could be leaving our family home for the first time, becoming a parent, hitting a significant birthday, buying a house, becoming unwell, or many other changes. These can all give us increased levels of uncertainty and anxiety, unsure how we can move forward, where we are in the process or even who we are anymore.

In addition, we might have a number of selves we could be, or might be, or may never be. Social Psychologists Hazel Rose Markus and Paula Nurius[7] say that we have *possible selves,* a set of ideal selves we would like to be. They talk about the successful version of ourselves, the rich one, the thin self, the admired self or the loved self. However, we also have selves that we are afraid of becoming, the alone self, the incompetent one, the depressed self, the unemployed version of ourselves or even the bag lady self.

I also like this distinction from Existential Psychologists. They talk about *necessity*, things that are unavoidable in our lives, the things we do not choose, that we just have to live with. This is different to *possibility*, which is our freedom to choose how we define ourselves, relate to our lives, and the way we see the world. You can work out which are your own possibilities shortly. So, let's get back to you.

Do you want to make some changes in your life? I'm presuming that's a "yes" if you're reading *Swim, Jump, Fly!* Are you unhappy with things as they are? You can start making sense of what to change by trying this next exercise. You'll discover if you're hitting your head against a wall or not. I'm a psychologist and I'm qualified to tell you that bashing your head generally hurts. Instead of wasting time on the wrong things, try this exercise instead. People find it an eye-opener.

Exercise 1: Spans of control (or circles of influence)

1) Get three pieces of papers and label them **one, two** and **three**. If you're tempted to do this on a computer, I suggest you don't. There's benefit from physically working on this, crossing things out, starting again, creating something yourself. Plus, it gets you away from your tech for a bit.

Think about all the things that you want to change in your life. Write a list of them on **page one**. Write as much as you can, include all the little things that annoy you. Find another piece of paper if you need to. Keep going until you run out of irritations.

2) On **page two** draw three columns. Label the first one *In my control* i.e. you can resolve it without needing anyone else's help. Label the second one *I can influence* i.e. you have some control over it, but will need others to help you. Or it might be that some of it is outside of your gift. For the third one, write: *Outside my control/influence.*

Now review your list on **page one**. Take each item you identified and fit them into one of the columns on **page two**. If you change your mind about the column, just cross it out and move it to another column.

IN MY CONTROL	I CAN INFLUENCE	OUTSIDE MY CONTROL/ INFLUENCE

Diagram 1: Review of spans of control

3) On **page three** draw a large circle, then draw a smaller circle inside this larger one. Inside the smaller circle write these words: *In my control.* Inside the bigger circle write: *I can influence.* Outside the bigger circle write: *Outside my control/influence.*

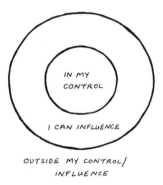

Diagram 2: Spans of control

4) Now take each item on **page two** and place it on its corresponding circle on **page three** – the circles *In my control, I can influence* or *Outside my control/ influence.*

5) Spend a bit of time reviewing **page three**. Then ask yourself some of these questions:

- What do I notice?
- Are there any items in the *Outside my control/influence* space?
- How much time do I spend worrying about these things? What effort do I expend trying to change them?
- What actions do I need to stop because I have no control? How can I accept things that are not in my control?
- What about the *I can influence* space? Am I clear that I don't have full control on these?
- Who do I need to help me with the items in the *I can influence* space? These might be behaviours, actions, attitudes, outlook, or decisions, for example.
- Now look at the *In my control circle*. What do I have influence or control over? What actions can I start?
- Ultimately, much of our life is really just about this – working out what is in our gift and what is not.

Why not share what you've discovered with a trusted friend, partner, or family member? Talking about change with others can really help kick-start the process. We often get caught up in mind loops, thinking too much and going round and round inside our heads. Why not get your friend, partner or family member to try this exercise too? They might find it enlightening.

 If you don't like something, change it. If you can't change it, change your attitude. — Maya Angelou (American writer and civil rights activist)

Clients who have tried this exercise often keep their lists close at hand. For example, on a board in the kitchen or on their phone. They find it useful to review the list every few weeks as it reminds them what to stop, start or continue.

Life is short and we have too much to do. So, an important part of making successful change is to focus on where we will see the most difference. Are you a bit clearer now about where you can put your effort? Will you stop head-butting the wall? It will hurt less if you do. Plus, you'll have more energy and time for the important (and fun) things in life.

Now we need to look at two more aspects: why we want to make the change in the first place and the character of the change we want to make. Being clear about the nature of the shift, and the distance we need to travel to get there, will increase how successful our change will be.

As my coaching clients and readers of the *Spoon-by-Spoon* blog will know, I'm fond of saying, "Why cook up a feast when we all we need is a sandwich?" Knowing why we want to change and how much of a shift we want to go through is key. There's no point putting in more effort than is needed if we only need to adjust a bit. This is where the idea of *Swim, Jump, Fly* comes in. Using this concept will help you focus your efforts on the right things, whether that's small iterations or going for radical change in your life.

One thought to share. If you're seeking a hopeless change project, then pick one that requires you to change somebody else. We have very little control in this space and will be disappointed by the lack of results. The only thing we can truly work on is our own life, so it's better to work on changing ourselves, rather than trying to change others.

Let's go back to the research participants for a moment, as they can bring some of these ideas to life. I'll start with the career changers. Many wanted a radical shift, something utterly different. Accountants who wanted to be actors, marketeers who wanted to be mid-wives, teachers who wanted to walk the tightrope. OK, I made that last one up.

There was a second group who liked parts of their work but really disliked the rest. Some aspects of their roles were like comfortable jeans, others like wearing someone else's shoes: not so nice. There was a third group who quite liked their work but needed a few tweaks. Perhaps they were bored and needed a change. Or maybe the WHAT of their work was fine, but the HOW was a bad fit. Introverts who had to talk most of the day, forestry consultants who were chained to their laptops and would rather be outside. Mavericks and entrepreneurs who were tied to rule-bound institutions.

One day I was coaching a client who was working on her career change. She needed to shift but didn't know where to start. I asked: "Do you need to shimmy a little, or would you prefer to jump into a different role? Or maybe it's bigger; a launch into a totally new career?" She paused and sighed. I asked it in a different way: "Do you need to Swim, Jump, Fly?" This unlocked a whole new conversation, and we were on our way.

The point is not to throw the baby out with the bathwater. We don't need to toss out skills that we've acquired over the years, as they might come in handy. Knowing the character of the change and the distance we need to travel: can save us time. Why go down wildly different paths if a few small adjustments here and there might work? Or why prance about on the side lines, if only radical change is what you need?

I tried this approach with a number of other clients. For example, one was having problems with her relationship, another was unhappy with his health and weight. I found that this idea worked very well across different types of change. Whether to Swim, Jump, or Fly? It seemed to be a useful question that helped my clients to focus, avoid overwhelm and concentrate effort in the right place. From this I created a 5-Step Process which gets great results.

———

Now let's turn to you and focus on your own change. The first step is to ask yourself WHY. If you don't know the purpose of your change then it's unlikely you'll maintain it. Sometimes we know our motivations, but we just don't follow them because we are sociable. We hate feeling left out, so try to fit in and mirror how others behave. This means we end up walking down unexpected paths. Not following our WHY can make us very uncomfortable.

I watched an interesting TED Talk by neuroscientist Dr Alan Watkins[8] in which he discusses the *disease of meaning*. He says many of us stay stuck in the state of a nine-year-old. We're basically adhering to rules around education, society and work and it takes a crisis, or an intense event, for us to start questioning our meaning, purpose and the role we play in the world.

I ran a podcast called *Tyranny of the Shoulds* where I interviewed guests about different *shoulds* in their lives It was based on a concept by Karen Horney, a German/American psychotherapist who said there were two types of self; a real self, and an ideal self. The ideal self is one that we will never reach, because perfection is not realistic. What other people want for us is much harder to sustain. All these *shoulds* that we carry around can often make us unhappy. If you'd like to listen to the podcast, you can find it on the website: swimjumpfly. com.

> ❝ ❝ I need to stop comparing myself and doing what other people think is the right thing. Just do what I think is the right thing. — Gina (interviewee)

Kira is originally from Russia but now lives in Canada, and she agrees. "I was brought up not to think about myself, to think about what others think. So, there are always requirements. Then also I was the only child in the family." What her parents wanted drove many of her choices. "So, with the university it was 'take the safer path and get accepted somewhere instead of not being accepted where you want to be. What are you going to do for a year now?'"

There were other choices she made that everyone agreed with. "Moving to Israel on the other hand, I'm Jewish and they felt passionate about Israel. The economic situation was very bad in Russia at that time, and it was easy to move on to Israel." She's not alone. Many of us are driven by the expectations of others. So, getting clear about WHY you want to change in the first place is key. Is this shift something you want to do? Or are you doing it for others?

A second part of my approach focuses on the distance you'll need to go to create a successful shift in your life. This is where the idea of *Swim, Jump, Fly* comes in. How far will you want to travel? A short distance to something similar? Or do you need to jump in order to make a change, or to fly far away to another place? To bring these types of movement alive, I've attached an animal to each one. The fish swims, the grasshopper jumps and the bird... well you get the picture. I'm a simple soul at heart.

To start with, we'll get a sense of which might fit the shift you need to make. Over time you can change your mind and move to a different distance/animal, since we all swim, jump and fly at different periods in our lives. Later I'll tell you about how I shifted from a bird to a fish and then a grasshopper, all in a short period of time.

Exercise 2: Dipping your toe into the 5-Step Process

First pick a change you want to make. It's better to focus on one, as it'll be easier to manage. Change can be hard if we try to do too many things at once, especially when we're starting out. We become confused and overwhelmed and give up. Select a change you'd like to work on and ask yourself this:

1) How far do I need to travel? How big does the change need to be? Think about whether you are a fish that needs to swim somewhere close by, such as starting a new hobby. Or do you need to increase the degree of change? Do you want to jump further away, like starting a new relationship? If this is the case, then you currently might be a grasshopper. Perhaps you want to shift dramatically and fly somewhere far away, like the other side of the world. This could be physically or metaphorically. Do you need to go through radical change in your life? In which case (at the moment) you're probably a bird. Don't worry if you're not sure about this yet. We'll spend a lot more time working it out over the next few chapters.

2) The next step is the type of change. Ask yourself: Do I need to focus on WHAT I'm doing or HOW I'm doing it? In terms of WHAT, is this a significant relationship that's not going well? Perhaps it's where you live, you want to be in a different part of the country. Or perhaps your WHAT is your mental health, which needs some work.

When it comes to HOW, this is the way in which you're doing those things. For example, perhaps you sit at a desk but you'd rather be doing something physical for work. Or is it the people you work with? Perhaps you have to have to run meetings with large groups, but you'd rather just be on your own. Or is it the way you are losing weight? Eating fewer calories but also doing less exercise? If this is the case, then exercise would be the area to build on.

Let's focus on the getting fit scenario for a moment. Perhaps you are exercising well enough, but dislike going to a gym, preferring to be in nature. It will be hard exercising below street level, in a room with no windows. Your senses are full of other people's sweat and grunts and you'd rather be out walking through fields with the wind in your hair. In his book *Atomic Habits*[9], James Clear writes that many people going through change think it's hard because they lack motivation but what they're actually missing is clarity. They don't know when and where to take action. This is what much of *Swim, Jump, Fly* is about.

———

If you're not clear on this yet, that's totally fine as there are quite a few chapters devoted to exercises so you can work this out. This is just a quick summary to share some ideas.

Right, that's it, the end of the chapter. Just before we wrap up, here is what we covered:

- Change is all around us, whether we like it or not.
- Being clear about what is in your control and what is not, so that you focus on areas of your life where things are more likely to change.
- Sharing what you've learned with someone else can help you see things more clearly.
- Stories of change from my interviewees, which were quite different and varied, showing how you, too, can make changes in many areas of your life.
- Plus, the number one topic in my interviews, which was 'happiness'.
- A quick summary of some of the steps in the 5-Step Process – which we'll cover in much more detail soon.
- The central theme of swim, jump and fly – that the size of your change is key.

Next, we'll spend time with some of the people we met earlier. We'll find out more about how they have changed. But first, why not take a break?

Chapter 2

In this chapter we'll meet some of the participants and their stories. This will help you understand the central themes of the book, that successful change has two things at its heart. In the last chapter I eased you into talking about the first area, the size of the change you need to make/the distance you need to travel, whether it's a tweak or iteration (fish), a bigger jump to something else (grasshopper) or a need to fly much further away in our change (bird).

Now I'm going to add in another piece to this puzzle. The second part of which animal you are, your appetite for change. Let's say you know you need to make a large shift, but you're a little risk averse. Your experience tells you that you're better off taking small steps. The way you tend to go through change is a bit like the accelerator pedal in the car. Some people like to take their foot off the gas and go slower ('fish' types). Others prefer to press all the way down ('birds').

We've got plenty of time to get our heads around which animal you are. So, for now, sit back, relax, eat some popcorn and enjoy the show. Right, let's jump in.

1) The Fish:
A fish way of changing is slow and in increments. A sideways shimmy, a flick of the fin here, a sweep of the tail there. When people swim like fish, they make small changes over time, not radical shifts. It's not the kind of 'give up your job, sell all the contents of your house and move to a small island in the middle of nowhere' kind of change. But people in this group still want to move their life on a bit.

Anupa's family is from Kenya and she is an example of a fish. Some years ago she had pains in her feet, but was busy with her life and didn't think much about them. Anupa's mother became very unwell and then unfortunately died. Anupa's pains got worse, possibly down to the stress of caring for her mother whilst she was ill. Anupa says, "I guess I wasn't really paying attention to myself. I didn't realise that my health was suffering. I thought I was OK."

The doctors said it was early onset arthritis and suggested "aggressive treatment which had a lot of side effects." Anupa wanted something less harsh and identified an alternative treatment plan, following Ayurvedic principles. She saw an Ayurvedic[10] doctor who gave her herbal medicines and a diet to follow, plus she went on an Ayurverdic retreat and came back "feeling very healthy and detoxed."

When we spoke, Anupa said she was still following this way of eating. "It makes my body light and balanced and I feel a lot of energy. I used to feel a lot of fatigue, pain and stiffness in the morning. I don't have that anymore. I feel great and since then the last few years have been pretty good. I feel that this is the path for me." For her, making slow and incremental changes suited the change she wanted to make and her personality.

———

Gunther is 50. He's British, but with a German mother. He's a music manager and in the past his work has included a lot of tour management. Three things happened to Gunther in quick succession. First, he had terrible back pain which took a very long time to diagnose, followed by a hip operation. Then, his father died. "That was horrific. He had a heart operation and I wasn't expecting it. I thought he was going for a routine stent replacement, but he died in the operation. Then that was that." A year later his mother was diagnosed with bipolar disorder. "She went into a mental institution. Men in white coats locked her in there for three months." Each one of these would have been difficult, but the three together were more challenging.

Gunther decided to speak to his boss about taking time off to re-group and have "a bit more time for me." He had started writing a book about his German grandfather, which he wanted to finish, and also to do more "motorcycling which fuels my mental health, my physical health. It was about having more time to do those things." He organised a day off every other week which suits him really well. This is not a dramatic change in his life, but this small shift is making a big difference, giving him time to relax and do the things he loves.

Fish can make bigger shifts. They just need to take it step by step. Gunther and his partner wanted to spend more time outdoors. So, after the work changes had bedded in, they moved closer to the countryside. I asked how it was going. "It is incredible. I feel rejuvenated, re-spiritualised, just reconnected with the earth. I love being out in nature. We've got a bit of civilisation and a community and it's a lovely sort of bohemian vibe to the town. And in two minutes I'm in fields, so it just couldn't be more idyllic for me." Gunther ended up in a different place mentally, physically and geographically. But it took some time as he didn't want to make all those changes at once.

———

Mel is in her 40s and works for a large organisation in the Human Resources team. She likes it because the work is interesting, and she gets on with the people. But then she was asked to take on a new role that wasn't such a good fit. It didn't take long before she knew it wasn't right for her. "I wasn't doing the kind of stuff that was adding any value at all. I was just mopping up after everyone and putting little things right all the time." Mel says, "I was just basically being the fixer for lots of things."

So, what did she do? She knew she didn't want to leave the company. She wanted to make some changes, but not throw everything up in the air. Instead, she found a way to swim a bit further, but without leaving the waters she was in. She organised a conversation with her boss and was honest, saying, "This is not very fulfilling. This role is not what I wanted it to be and it's really going off in a very funny direction." No drama, just a grown-up conversation about how she was feeling.

The conversation was well timed since "they were already thinking about the way they structured the team." In the ensuing discussions Mel got to talk about what she wanted, and her boss shared some different roles that might be a good fit. When we spoke, she'd only been in this new role for a few months. "I'm loving it so far, I've got to be honest. It has been really interesting." Why? Because she knew she was making a difference.

———

"De grão em grão enche a galinha o papo." These are the first words Madelana said to me before we'd started our conversation. "It roughly means 'grain by grain the chicken fills its gizzard, or stomach.' So, it says every step goes forward towards something bigger." That sums up her way of making change, step by step. Madelana is Portuguese but grew up in South Africa. "I always

had a sense of not belonging because even though I'm Portuguese I was born in South Africa. When I moved to Portugal, I didn't speak the language. So, I always felt like an outsider even after picking up the language and integrating."

More recently Madelana has been unhappy again. "I think it's because I turned 40 and found my life was stuck. I had nowhere to go. I thought, 'This is not what I dreamt when I was a kid.' I just wanted to be able to have the courage that I've lost many, many, many decades ago, to just find myself." She has nearly burned out a few times over the past few years. "I never listened to advice to look after myself." She felt stressed much of the time and wanted things to change.

As a 'fish', Madelana has now made small sideways moves to address her unhappiness and stress. She has tried Social Tango, worked with a personal trainer and also runs because she feels "so relaxed afterwards. Whatever is pesky in my mind, it just melts away." She has therapy too, "I think that, in conjunction with exercise, has helped."

I asked Madelana if she could go back in time, what advice she'd give herself. "Don't be so scared. Just try out things." Fear had stopped her from making changes. "I think being scared of failing stopped me from trying." Being honest has also helped. "You have to open up. You have to be vulnerable. And in way to move on is to be vulnerable. Trust people more." She feels her life is much better, from taking small steps, changing bit by bit.

2) The Grasshoppers:
Now we'll focus on the grasshoppers. They make bolder moves than the fish, bounding into new areas, travelling far enough that it feels different. Grasshoppers take more risks, jumping as they do in quick succession, taking on more in a shorter period of time. However, they do still take calculated risks, depending on the context.

Tim has been acting like a grasshopper. He has recently made a number of changes. Career, health, relationship and more. He went through a messy break-up, lost his job and then comfort-ate to deal with his unhappiness. "Those two years were mega unhappy. I can see this now. But at the time I didn't know that I was self-medicating by eating. It was pizza, chocolate and God knows what." He said he "was just eating a lot of terrible food. By January I was not in good shape."

So, Tim decided to make quite a few changes. His background was accounting, but he had never enjoyed it. In fact, he'd studied psychology at university and wanted to develop people instead. So, Tim booked himself onto an introduction to coaching programme in Switzerland, where he was living. One of the other participants, a German woman, became a good friend. He enjoyed the course so much that over many months he went on to train to be certified as a coach. And what of his friend? "Long story short, we made a great connection, spent thousands of hours on the phone through lockdown and now we're a couple. I'm talking to you from her apartment in Basel right now."

Tim then spent a year building "self-awareness and looking inward, learning about myself. This has very much continued" and he is now managing a successful coaching practice supporting other people going through change. He put time into working on his relationship, which was "unexpected and wonderful and a fast start."

But what does Tim mean by a fast start? "We became expectant parents three months after we met. And then moved in together during the pandemic and did all that get to know you stuff during a lockdown. That was really tough." Of parenthood he says their "entry was early. It was planned, it was just about two years earlier than we thought it would be." Tim made quite a few changes in a short period of time, moving faster and taking more risks than a fish would. This is an example whereby change happened to Tim, rather than him being fully in control. We talk about this in chapter three. We'll cover plans, planning and how we often need to pivot when things turn out differently than expected.

———

Yasmeen wanted to be creative when she was growing up in Kuwait. "I started doing plays in high school, but my dad had a huge problem with it. In that part of the world, they don't really celebrate women being on stage. He said, 'I prefer my daughter to be somebody who is valued for how she thinks, what she can say and her intelligence.'" So, Yasmeen took a Bachelor's degree, then a Masters in Library Sciences. "I don't think my dad understood that creativity is a form of intelligence. He wanted me to be a lawyer."

Yasmeen moved to Canada and then for years she worked in education. "The people were great, but they were very different from me." What stopped her from moving into something more creative? "I think I just kind of forgot myself." She chased opportunities she could do "not necessarily what I wanted to do" and lost track of her purpose and direction. But one day she woke up and realised she'd been living "the same life for 10 years at the same job. How the heck did I end up here?"

Whilst others thought Yasmeen was doing well at work, she "felt like a failure internally because I knew that what I wanted for myself was very different from what people expected of me." Over time she became very stressed and eventually "went nuclear and lost it at work. I yelled at an assistant about something that was not her fault." Yasmeen packed her things, left the office and drove to the mountains to think.

Soon afterwards she quit her work and since then she's been trying to be more creative. "I went travelling, I engaged in travel memoirs and talked to different people. I met drag queens, just sort of experimenting in what I wanted to do creatively." She took classes in writing and acting. "I found the theatre tribe. It was just a mind-blowing revelation because they are so much like me." She kept telling herself, "If it's creative and it's scary, it's something I should do." This is more of a grasshopper approach, hopping here and there, trying things out.

———

Walter trained and then worked as a butcher, but his wife's family were successful business people and he felt he couldn't keep up with them. He worried his wife would think, "I've married a duff one here. The rest have got these big flash houses. I'm not going to get that." One day Walter's brother-in-law rang him up with a job offer. His brother-in-law was very persuasive. He said, "Jack your job in, we'll give you a company car, laptop. Drive around the country, meet all the project managers, find out what they do. Bosh, you're done. We'll give you £30,000 a year."

Walter knew it wouldn't be a good fit, "I didn't know what to do, because I knew how it would make me feel. But then what an opportunity? And I ummed and ahhhed, and then just said, 'Yeah.'" He worked as a project manager for a decade but really disliked it. "I always felt a bit of a charlatan in the role. Like I was going to get found out. I've never felt like I fitted in with the people, really." He got more and more anxious as the years went by. "Pressure, pressure, pressure. Being in a job where the workload is so much that it's impossible to succeed. You had to be able to handle continual small failures. Let fires burn and just deal with the biggest one. You're dealing with fallout all the time."

Eventually Walter was signed off with stress. He took some time to find his feet again. But now he has set up on his own and it's working out really well, since he has turned two of his hobbies into successful businesses – dog walking and pet portraiture photography. The photography business is growing so quickly that he needs to close the other one down. Despite his earlier fears, his wife is really proud of him.

Grasshoppers jump from place to place, but it's not radical change. Walter hopped sideways, a career shift that uses his project management skills but also means he can plough his own furrow. He really enjoys the work and it fits him much better. Success also means something different for him now. "You don't have to follow this expectation of what you should do through life. It could be in a very different form. And it's better if it's something that fits you." In a later chapter we'll talk about success, about other people's expectations and how it can make us very unhappy.

3) The Birds:
Going through change like a bird means travelling a greater distance, landing over here, flying off there, travelling further. At times it can even be a long-distance route that transforms a person in the process. Cecilia is in her 30s and has worked as a corporate lawyer for 13 years. "It wasn't a job I ever wanted to do. It was the path I ended up on due to my parents thinking it was a good idea. A lot of people go into a job, love it but then fall out of love. I never loved what

I did. I was never doing what I wanted."

If she'd been a fish Cecilia would have tried small changes. But as a bird she flew away… literally, to Amsterdam, then Singapore. She tried to make it work by "moving countries, moving companies, moving industry, going from private practice to in-house. Hoping that something would click so I could say, 'now I'm doing what I love.'" Instead, for years she resigned herself to being unhappy. "I came to accept it and just thought, well that's life. You know, it's work. You don't have to love it." She was always surprised when she met people who enjoyed their work. She assumed "they were lying because how can anyone enjoy what they do?"

Cecilia wondered if she was the problem. "For years I thought I was a bit broken, that there was some stuff that was a bit wrong with me. I think I always assumed that was the case." The final straw was a promotion to the top role of General Counsel. "It was the pinnacle of my career, but the idea of taking it made me feel physically sick. Ironically, it was what led me to resign." Now she understands she "wasn't really living an authentic life. I was having to battle against this, every single day. No wonder I was exhausted." It is obvious why she burnt out. "That's a very emotionally, mentally and physically draining environment to be in. Now I realise there is nothing really fundamentally wrong or broken with me."

After resigning, everything else in her life started to unwind too. "My relationship started to struggle and ended. And all my belongings were in storage because I'd been living in my partner's apartment. They all burnt in a fire." It sounds like the plot of a film, but Cecilia is quite philosophical. "The universe is saying you need to change what you're doing because you're not living the life you're meant to be living."

So where is Cecilia now? When we last spoke, she had packed up her life and was about to fly to Indonesia for dive master training, followed by yoga teacher training. She says this won't be her final destination since birds don't sit still in one place for long. Her plan is to "focus on doing things that give me pleasure and enjoyment. Seeing if that could lead into a career. Or it might just be a way to meet people who can open my eyes to different ways of life, different ways of living, different priorities."

———

Remember Jitesh, from chapter one? His surgeon said, "We've got to do it very quickly, otherwise you'll lose the use of your right leg." But what led up to such urgent advice? Jitesh was working for a consulting firm in Qatar, in the Middle East and "the client had sent a huge box of files and things. It was a Saturday and we were working late. I foolishly picked up the box." Then his back gave way.

After a few weeks the pain subsided so he carried on as before. Then it happened again. "Things just broke and I had to take time out. I had a spinal blister. The spinal fluid leaked and was pressing my sciatic nerve. They had to operate to remove the blister and stabilise my back." Then a third time, but by then things had reached a critical point. "That's when I paid attention, but it was too late to do anything without surgery. The nerve had pretty much died."

The problem was that Jitesh's work was so stressful. He worked very long hours, was trying to get promoted to partner, ate all the wrong things at the wrong times of day and didn't exercise. He says with "hindsight, I could have prevented it getting to that level, but I didn't really do anything. I didn't pay much attention." I heard this often in other conversations. We fail to notice soon enough. Catch it in time and we get to decide the outcome. Leave it too late and it's not ours to choose anymore. "It got to a point where I had no choice. I ended up with a fusion of the lower vertebrae."

So how is Jitesh now? He's doing well, having made many different shifts in his life, all at once. He has flown far from where he started. He does stretches and exercises at home, regularly goes hiking and does yoga. He cooks himself proper meals, is eating healthily and keeping his weight under control. He also decided to change his work and career. "I'd had enough. I was no longer interested in partnership."

Jitesh is enjoying this role. "I'm no longer in the rat race. I don't have to prove myself to anyone." He says that, "Frankly I have no regrets leaving. On the day, I felt a big lead weight lifted off my shoulders. I suddenly felt a great sense of freedom. I would never go back to that environment again." His thoughts on reflecting back? "Work was the focus at that time and that drove everything. That needed changing." His advice to us is to "Get a balance between work, health and other things. Get your priorities set out clearly… re-focus and re-prioritise other things in life." Birds sometimes change many things at once, so they end up further away.

———

Mary is a food process engineer and wanted to change a lot of things. Her work, her relationship and where she lived. If she had been a fish, she would have taken these one at a time, over many years. But that wasn't her way. The problem was that her partner was keen to get married, but she was "hemming and hawing, I didn't want to do that, we were like friends."

Her social life was based around her partner and they were known in many of the same pubs and restaurants. "It was a smallish town. It wasn't like I could live the other side of it and not bump into people." Work was a big factor too because Mary was the first female engineer at her organisation. "Every second person in town I'd meet would be someone I knew from work. I just couldn't really extricate myself from any of it without leaving."

Mary handed in her notice at work, sold her house and moved, all at once. She didn't tell her parents until it was all done because she was concerned about how they would react. "They would have been worried I was giving up a permanent pensionable job. Having come through the 80s and the early 90s, knowing how hard things were and that jobs were so valued."

Happily, Mary was surprised by her parents' reaction. "I ended up going to visit them for a week between handing in my notice and the time I finished the job. My mum told me much, much later 'I knew you'd made the right decision. You never stopped singing all the time you were here!' I didn't realise I was singing. But I knew I felt lighter." We'll go on to cover how living a life that fits our purpose, values and skills can make us truly happy.

That's the end of this chapter and the stories of participants who are fish, grasshoppers and birds. Here's a short summary before we head off to the next chapter:

- We covered four stories in the fish group. Anupa worked on her physical health, Gunther wanted more balance in life, changed his work and later on he moved to the countryside.
- We also met Mel who wanted to shift her role a little, but not leave her organisation, plus Madelana, who was stressed and needed to find ways to work on her mental health.
- In the grasshopper group we heard from Tim who was making more changes at once, his health, relationship and career. We met Yasmeen

who changed her role and thoroughly explored her creative side.
- We also heard from Walter who made a large shift around his mental health and wellbeing, and changed his career from project management to setting up and running two successful businesses.
- Then, in the bird group, we heard about Cecilia, who gave up 13 years of high-flying law career, to explore becoming a diving and yoga instructor, whilst leaving a long-term relationship, losing all her possessions and changing country.
- We also found out how Jitesh turned his life around from health, to cooking, to exercise and a change in career.
- Finally, we heard from Mary who changed her work, relationship and home, all at once.

The next chapter is all about our purpose and our direction.

Chapter 3

If you've read books on how to improve your golf swing, or watched chefs cooking on a TV show, then you'll know that being told something isn't the same as doing it yourself. It's hard to flip a pancake without holding the pan. That's why I've designed the next few chapters for you to try it out yourself; working on your change that is, rather than tossing pancakes.

This is where my 5-Step Process comes in. It's easy to use, as I like to keep things simple. We make change more complicated than it needs to be. We tell ourselves it'll be difficult which raises our blood pressure before we've even begun. We get lost in the process, not knowing which way is up. This is where the 5-Step Process can help. It's my own creation but I've borrowed ideas from people like Professor Stephen Palmer, an academic, coaching psychologist and Director of the *Centre for Coaching*, who developed the *PRACTICE*[11] model to help people work through change. Find out more about this in Appendix B.

I've also built on some of the concepts of the *transtheoretical model of behavior change* (TTM), which was developed in the 1970s by psychologists James Prochaska and Carlo Diclemente. You can read more about TTM in Appendix B. TTM looks at how ready someone is to change their behaviour and I use this concept in my 5-Step Process. TTM's approach guides people through change, focusing on insight and contemplation first, only later moving to action. Here are the TTM stages:

1) Pre-contemplation (not ready)
2) Contemplation (getting ready)
3) Preparation (ready)
4) Action (changing)
5) Maintenance (continuing)

Back to you. Do you think you're ready to make a change? Research on TTM has shown that if you're not ready, then you're unlikely to succeed. How much we progress tends to be a function of which stage we are in so if you're not ready, nothing much will happen. If you want to shift, you'll need to contemplate your change properly by building your self insight, thinking through the impact of your current behaviours, why you'd like to change and reflecting on what the future might look like. Without insight you're unlikely to move to action. That's why so much of the focus at the start of this book is on getting to know yourself!

❝ How prompt we are to satisfy the hunger and thirst of our bodies, how slow to satisfy the hunger and thirst of our souls! — Henry David Thoreau (naturalist, essayist, poet, and philosopher)

John Norcross is an American professor of psychology, psychiatry, and is a clinical psychologist. Along with other academic researchers, Norcross[12] gathered evidence about TTM via people going through change. For example, they monitored the success in cardiac patients who were contemplating giving up smoking. The goal was to not be smoking six months after they had been through a smoking cessation programme. They found those who were most likely to hit this goal were the ones who were ready for action. Only a small number of *pre-contemplators* gave up smoking, but nearly double the number of *contemplators* were able to do so. The most successful group were people who were prepared for action as they were nearly 3.5 times more likely that *pre-contemplators* (and 1.75 times more likely than *contemplators*) to give up smoking.

How does this relate to you? Well, one way for you to move from contemplator to planner to action is to read *Swim, Jump, Fly* quite quickly. I suggest you do this in less than three months. Therefore, you might like to:

- Read the introduction, plus chapters 1 – 7, in a month and do the exercises.
- Then read chapters 8 – 14 in the next month.
- In the third month read chapters 15 – 22, including doing the exercises.

Here is some advice from Maeve, one of my interviewees: "I would say just really try and keep momentum going. Once you start doing something about it, set yourself weekly tasks to try and keep momentum going… And small steps are better than no steps."

Now to a different way to think about change from the world of business. The role of a professional Change Manager, like me (or at least the old me), is working for organisations who want to persuade their people to change. They sometimes use this equation[13]: D x V x F > R

D stands for dissatisfaction and V is for vision (of the future). F stands for first practical steps and R is for resistance. The first three need to be bigger than resistance if you're going to move, otherwise, nothing will change.

Here is a gearshift from Management Consulting into Buddhism. Thich Nhat Hanh was a Vietnamese Buddhist monk, prolific author and peace activist and is often referred to as the father of mindfulness. "People have a hard time letting go of their suffering. Out of a fear of the unknown, they prefer suffering that is familiar." If you prefer, switch out the word *suffering* and replace it with *dissatisfaction*. We'll cover resistance further on, but for now why not take the *Am I ready for change?* quiz in Appendix A. It will help you decide whether to throw yourself in, or just throw in the towel.

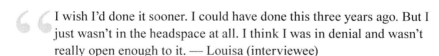

I wish I'd done it sooner. I could have done this three years ago. But I just wasn't in the headspace at all. I think I was in denial and wasn't really open enough to it. — Louisa (interviewee)

Now we'll spend some time on the 5-Step Process, as it's the heart of *Swim, Jump, Fly*. Think of it as a framework, something to hold onto whilst you're making your way through change. Some people picture it like stabilisers on a bike. Others think of inflatable armbands, keeping them afloat whilst they learn to swim. Whatever comes to mind is just fine with me.

I'd like to introduce you to my 5-Step-Process. Process, say "Hello" to the lovely reader. Reader, say "Hello" to my process. You're going to get to know each other over the next few weeks.

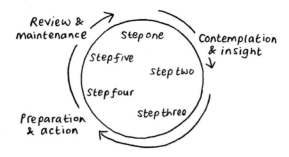

Diagram 3: The 5-Step Process

Here are the five steps in the process:

Step one: WHY and WHERE (purpose and destination)
Step two: WHICH (animal i.e. the distance to travel)
Step three: WHAT and HOW (the type of change)
Step four: WHO and WHEN (planning action and experimentation)
Step five: HOW MUCH and HOW WELL (reviewing and evaluating progress)

Steps one to three are about contemplating your change process, building insight about yourself, why you want to change and where you'd like to end up. You'll spend time thinking about the impact of your current behaviour, plus what life will be like in the future if you don't change.

Step one is WHY and WHERE; step two focuses on the size of the change you need to make/the distance you travel, the WHICH part of the process, the animal that reflects your change. Then, step three, focusing on WHAT or HOW.

It's important to build your self-insight via steps one to three, otherwise you won't have the right foundations for making a shift. When I was reviewing the themes from my interviews, the concepts of Clarity and Direction came up 298 times. Find out more about the research in Appendix D.

Clarity showed up through these topics: 'looking back over time', or 'through distance from a problem', or via 'travelling and being away from the change'. It appeared as 'advice participants would give to their younger selves', 'standing back and looking at their lives as a whole', and 'taking in different perspectives'. It was also getting a better understanding of who they were and where they wanted to go.

Direction appeared in these topics: 'a lack of direction', 'feeling stuck or trapped,' 'being confused'. It was about 'falling into action' without thinking it through, 'leaving relationships, situations and roles without planning,' having no 'obvious path ahead'. It was also through 'procrastination', sitting on things for years (sometimes decades), or not leaving a difficult situation early enough.

Back to the 5-Step Process. When you're ready, it will be time for action in step four – WHO and WHEN. This is the planning piece; where you're going to be trying out experiments to see what works best. In the last step, number five, you'll be looking at HOW MUCH and HOW WELL, reviewing progress, finding out which actions had impact, and which are destined for the trash-can. Finally, I've included ideas, exercises and resources to help you maintain your momentum, because your motivation will dip from time to time. That's completely normal and an expected part of any change you'll be going through.

Step One: WHY and WHERE

Did you read Lewis Carroll's books when you were younger? If you know *Alice's Adventures in Wonderland*[14] you might remember the Cheshire Cat, who happens to be a talking cat. At one point in the story, Alice strikes up a conversation with the cat and their conversation goes like this:

"Would you tell me, please, which way I ought to go from here?'
'That depends a good deal on where you want to get to,' said the Cat.
'I don't much care where—' said Alice.
'Then it doesn't matter which way you go,' said the Cat."

Knowing WHY you want to change (your motivation) will give you impetus to get going. Friedrich Nietzsche was a German philosopher who said having a 'why' means we can bear almost anything in our life. Focusing your efforts and actions on those things that bring meaning and purpose will make for a better life. That's why you need to be clear about what matters to you.

Knowing WHERE you want to end up also means you'll head in the right direction, otherwise you'll go round and round in circles and will feel very sick. Focusing on purpose can ground you when everything else is shifting around. Gina was one of my interviewees who struggled with WHY. In the organistion she worked in they said, "Website traffic numbers are very important in the work." But this didn't give her a WHY. "It was always really weird and confusing how seriously people took everything." She felt no-one would care if the product or website disappeared. "I always struggled with feeling I wasn't doing any meaningful work, wasn't contributing to society or doing any good in the world."

Emily is 30 and worked in aerospace engineering. She ended up in programme management which wasn't a good fit. "It's really knocked my confidence and I haven't felt like I can add any value. I feel without purpose. I've gone through cycles of being quite depressed and quite anxious." Work is important to her so, "I've had counselling and I know the career portion of my life is important. Even if the rest of my life has been perfectly lovely, I've really struggled to have any purpose and feel any worth."

 I spent most of my time feeling under-appreciated and like a cog in a machine. I just felt like I was a drone working there.
— Bez (interviewee)

A useful concept around WHY is *Ikigai*. It's a Japanese idea that means *a reason for being*, having a sense of purpose, or more generally something that brings pleasure or fulfilment. It's about where our passions and talent overlap with what the world needs/is willing to pay for. There's more about *Ikigai* in an excellent book by Héctor García and Francesc Miralles[15].

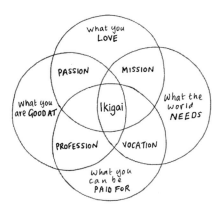

Diagram 4: Ikigai adapted from García and Miralles

Dr Scott Barry Kaufman is a cognitive scientist and humanistic psychologist and founder of the *Center for the Science of Human Potential*. His work is based on Abraham Maslow's theory of *Self-Actualisation and Human Motivation*.

Maslow's theory says we need to fulfil basic needs like food, safety, love and a sense of belonging. But we also have an inborn desire to be *self-actualised*; this means using our talents, feeling fulfilled and being the best we can be. Kaufman has developed an updated version of Maslow's theory to help people who are feeling unfulfilled, so they can find a life that works for them. Having a deeper purpose, being connected to something bigger than ourselves can be so important in our lives. You might like to read Kaufman's book on the topic called *Transcend: The New Science of Self-Actualization*[16].

Exercise 3: Knowing your WHY

1) First identify a single change you'd like to make. Change gets harder if we shift too many things at once, so pick one. The mediator, writer and speaker Diego Perez[17] agrees. He says trying to overhaul everything at the same time will feel overwhelming and suggests we pick one or two, focus on them and give them time to take hold.

If you need prompting just go back to exercises 1 and 2 from the first chapter. Review what you wrote and select a change you'd like to manage. Make sure you pick one from the *in my control group*, otherwise you'll be making your climb steeper than it needs to be.

2) The next part can be done in a number of ways, depending on your preferences. Either a) grab a piece of paper or a notebook and reflect on your own, or b) work with someone else who can ask you the questions and discuss them, then take down your answers, or c) use your smartphone to record yourself talking about it. I often make notes this way whilst I'm on a walk. One thing to mention is that sharing how you're feeling with someone else can help. Journaling is useful too, a way of getting your feelings out onto paper. In fact, just try any method that feels right for you!

3) If you're taking the writing route, try to do this physically with pen and paper, rather than a laptop or computer. In 2014 American[18] research found that typing into a laptop impaired learning because it resulted in shallower processing. Plus, in 2020, researchers in Norway[19] found there was greater brain activity in children and young adults who were handwriting/drawing than when they were typing using a keyboard. When you are writing by hand it's likely you'll develop a better understanding of the content, because it's slower, plus it boosts learning and insights. It's also just a great way to use less technology!

Steve is in his early 50s and has decades of experience leading engineering projects and operations. He has also recently studied for a Masters degree in behavioural change. "I had a book for reflecting on my coaching and a book for reflecting on this whole thing about changing my outlook. There's definitely something very powerful about writing it down. There's lots of research on this topic and it certainly had a big impact on me."

 Every time you state what you want or believe, you're the first to hear it. It's a message to both you and others about what you think is possible. Don't put a ceiling on yourself. — Oprah Winfrey

4) Ask yourself these questions (or get another person to ask you):

- What's so important about working on this problem? What concerns me about my situation? What is my motivation to shift? What are the benefits I hope to get and what are the costs/what will I lose if I change?
- Spend time reflecting on the underlying causes of your situation or behaviour. What led to it/what maintains it now? What are the consequences of your behaviour (positive and negative)? This can be the impact on you and on others. Think about what might help you shift, what needs to be different. Visualise what life will be like in a year once you have made all the changes. Imagine what it'll be like if you haven't.
- Try not to focus on the surface aspects. It's more powerful to reflect on what's below the surface of the presenting issue, what others can't see. We often do things to get rid of, stop, or block unwanted thoughts and feelings. So, behaviours like drinking too much, overeating, not speaking up, procrastinating, spending too much time on social media, and a multitude of other behaviours might be about suppressing challenging feelings about ourselves or our lives.
- Anna has experienced this: "I would definitely recommend having some therapy or coaching to really get underneath what it is you're dissatisfied with and where it comes from." She says otherwise it'll just be a "temporary fix." She spent time getting to the heart of her challenge. "I associated a lot of my stress and anxiety with my job, but I still get stressed and anxious now" despite leaving her marketing role. "There's something deeper going on for me. It almost doesn't matter what job I do. I am predisposed to doing it in a certain way." Anna got a lower paid role so she wouldn't worry so much. "It's a little local job, ten minutes down the road. How difficult can that be? Yet I get stressed about it. So, there is that realisation of, 'oh so it's actually in my head.'"

- This may leave you concerned because you can't afford therapy or coaching. Working through all the exercises in this book will help you to start to uncover blockers and understand your drivers on your own. So, why not start this yourself now?

- Ask yourself what are your feelings at the heart of this challenge? How does the problem make you feel about yourself? For example, are you unhappy because you're lonely? Are you feeling trapped or claustrophobic in a relationship? Are you scared about losing control? Do you feel you'd like to belong somewhere, but don't have roots? Are you anxious about being vulnerable? Will this course of action help you alleviate those things?

- Paying attention to your feelings is an important part of change. But, if you're finding this hard, you might like to try using metaphors to encourage you to open up. There's more about these types of exercises in Appendix A.

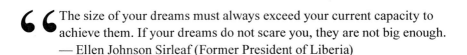

> The size of your dreams must always exceed your current capacity to achieve them. If your dreams do not scare you, they are not big enough.
> — Ellen Johnson Sirleaf (Former President of Liberia)

- Now focus on your confidence levels in making this change. You can use a scale of 1 (not at all confident) to 10 (extremely confident). Ask yourself, how confident am I that I will successfully make this shift? Also, what made me choose that number? Then think about what might help you to move closer towards 10.
- Then ask WHY NOW? If this has been a long-standing issue or challenge in your life, what is different this time? Why is it important to work on it now? What have you tried so far/how did that go? What helped/didn't help? What has shifted since then? If you've tried to make a change and it didn't work,

why is now a better time to do this?

- Finally, you will feel more resistant if other people (me included) try to convince you to change. None of us can fix this for you. You are the only one who can do it. So why not take the *Am I ready for change?* quiz. It's in Appendix A. Another option is to go back to the first exercise and pick another change project you'd like to work on. Select one that you really believe you can achieve, as that may be more motivating.

5) An activity you might like to try is connecting with your body:

- Close your eyes (as long as you're safe to do so) and breathe slowly for a few moments. You might be able to sense the WHY somewhere in your body.
- Does it feel like an ache in your chest or a fluttering in your stomach? Is it in the clenching of your hands or a tightness in your jaw? Being able to locate it in your body can be useful since we often spend too much time in our heads.
- Try and put it into words. If that's hard to do, take a moment or two. The more challenging it is for you to locate or describe it, the more pausing, reflecting and focusing/staying with it will help.
- Gestalt therapists often help clients to slow down, pay attention, focus on the present and what is happening for them in the moment. They talk about the dangers of staying so busy that we lose contact with how we feel. This exercise is an opportunity to re-connect with yourself and work out what is going on at a deeper level.

Finally, someone asked me, "Can I use this book if I'm not choosing a change? If it's change that's been forced on me from outside?" The answer is yes. Non-intentional change is when your partner runs off to join the circus. Or when your work organisation decides to shut up shop and move to Canada. That's fine if you'd like to work in Canada. Not so much if you don't.

Triggers for change came up 56 times in my *Thematic Analysis* research. Sometimes people had choice about the shifts they went through, but in many instances, it was something outside of themselves, for example health issues, relationships breaking down, or a sudden loss of a role. So, the answer is yes, this approach works for non-intentional change as the same steps apply. You'll still have a WHY if you discover you have a stomach ulcer and you want to get better. If you're caught up in the middle of a family dispute you can still work out what's in your gift to change and what is not. It might be a lot more frustrating, because you didn't elect to start out on this journey, but you're still going through a change.

Exercise 4: Knowing your WHERE

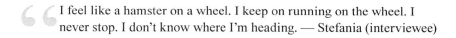

> I feel like a hamster on a wheel. I keep on running on the wheel. I never stop. I don't know where I'm heading. — Stefania (interviewee)

In his book, *The 7 Habits of Highly Effective People*[20], Stephen Covey suggests that we begin with the end in mind. The next step is to ask yourself WHERE you'd like to end up. This could be what you want to feel, think, or do differently once you've made the change. You may find your WHERE is less of a specific destination, it may be more a vision of the direction in which you want to travel. It's less about outputs, more about outcomes.

Here is an example from Leah who felt that "it suddenly crept up on me and I thought, 'am I just getting a bit stale? Is this best for me?' That's where I thought I'm a bit lost. It's the age-old question: which direction do you go in or what avenues have you got?"

It's useful to ask yourself what will have shifted by the end of this? How will things be different/better? How would you like things to change? WHERE is the destination or direction that you're aiming at. Creating a self-image of how you'd like to be in the future is a key part of successful change.

Here are some steps you can take to help with this:

1) Visualise your WHERE, by playing a show-reel of your new life in your head. Where are you, what is going on around you? What can you see or hear? How are you feeling? Imagine what will be different or better. Create an image of your new self in the future. Perhaps even think about what this might look

like in a year, two years or five years-time? You may identify a number of possible futures. If you have a few that's fine too. Just pick the one that feels right for you to work on now.

Professional athletes use visualisations and imagery. They run through a future race, imagining WHERE they will end up, how they'll feel, think and behave when they have successfully made it onto the podium. Research shows that imagining your actions means you're more likely to complete them in the future, but conversely, the more we imagine failure and the obstacles we'll hit, the more doubt we have in ourselves. Then we are more likely to give up. In Appendix A there are visualisation and guided imagery exercises that might help you.

2) You can also use metaphors and stories to visualise your future life. I use something I've developed called *Liminal Muse Conversation Cards* created from my photographs, many of them abstract, which are all printed on double sided cards. These help people identify metaphors about the future and bring their desires to life. You can read more about metaphors in Appendix A.

3) You could try using the *Miracle Question*[21]. This is something coaches use in sessions with clients. Imagine that, overnight as you sleep, a miracle happens. The miracle is that the things you are trying to change in your life have magically taken place. How would you know that the miracle has happened and that your challenges have been addressed? What would be the first sign? What are you seeing, thinking, doing differently? What has changed?

4) We've been focusing on the internal sense of your destination and now it's good to also think about the external WHERE – what others might see has changed. If you wrote *feel confident* for example, how would that manifest itself

to the people around you? Would it be a healthier you who is able to play in the park with your kids more easily? Or would it be that you were fit enough to join the five-a-side on a Saturday morning? Try and be specific.

5) Finally, we need to set goals that will help you reach your WHERE, your destination. If we can work towards meaningful goals then it will give us a sense of direction, purpose, and meaning in life. One way to set goals is to use SMART, which stand for **S**pecific, **M**easurable, **A**chievable, **R**ealistic and **T**ime based.

It's easy to say, "I want to be an astronaut" but what if there is zero chance of this happening? A more achievable goal could be learning about the European Space Agency and its space programme (specific), with enough knowledge to tell others about it (measurable), during a ten-minute presentation with questions at the end (achievable and realistic), in two months (time based). All of the above is more likely to happen than becoming an astronaut. By the way, teaching others about a subject is a great way to get to grips with a topic yourself.

Psychologists Dr Edwin Locke and Dr Gary Latham[22] developed the *Goal Setting Theory of Motivation* which has shown over hundreds of studies that it can help people achieve their goals. The theory outlines five principles that increase our chances of success when goal setting: clarity (clear goals, e.g. SMART), challenge (making it difficult, but attainable), commitment (buying into/accepting the goals) and feedback (gauging how well we're doing).

A quick word about intrinsic versus extrinsic goals before we cover SMART goals. An intrinsic goal relates to ourselves, for example personal growth, health, or relationships with ourselves or others. Extrinsic goals are things like money, fame, status or anything that requires validation from others. There has been a huge amount of research on this and studies find that people who place a high importance on extrinsic goals are less likely to be satisfied with life, have higher drug and alcohol use and generally have lower levels of wellbeing. So, aiming to become the first billionaire in your family may back-fire.

It's also useful to create SMART goals because you'll be able to assess progress, be more encouraged by it and know when you've reached your target. SMART goals are also useful because you can share them with other people, as accountability can help you reach your destination. So, I'd suggest telling friends and family what you're planning. I'll just offer one more thought that it's better to set positive oriented goals. So, instead of focusing on giving up smoking (negative), set a goal to become healthier (positive).

> The only limit to the height of your achievements is the reach of your dreams and your willingness to work for them. — Michelle Obama[23]

My last reflection on WHERE is that you may start out with a specific destination in mind. Over time this may become more of a direction of travel and that's OK. You may need to pivot or shift the end point a little, that's fine. As long as you have a vision of where you want to end up, it will take you in the right direction.

Why not spend some time reflecting on this now? Or you could record yourself, so you can listen back to what you said. Some of you might want to discuss what you've discovered with another person. My husband will tell you I'm one of these *talking it through* types. He'll sit quietly nodding, saying nothing (he's an introvert), listening patiently to me (an extrovert) talking on and on. At the end I'll say, "Great, that was really helpful." He will smile wisely, knowing I just needed an audience.

If you'd like more help articulating your goals and future vision, your WHY and WHERE, then look at the *Letter from the Future* exercise in Appendix A.

―――

That's it for this chapter. There are more exercises for you to do in the next one. But before that, here is a summary of the key themes:

- We've covered how to select the change you want to make, picking one or two so you don't overwhelm yourself, making sure it's in your control.
- We've gone through the first step in the 5-Step Process – your WHY and WHERE.
- Knowing WHY you want to change is vital. If you're not clear, then you'll end up focusing on the wrong course of action. You'll be disappointed when nothing much ends up shifting.
- Understanding your WHERE, your destination, is key to creating successful change. Not knowing where you want to end up will mean you're Alice in your own Wonderland.
- We've covered how you see yourself changing, along with what others observe. It helps to visualise what the future might look like too, as that makes it more likely to happen.
- Finally, we discussed SMART goals and how they help you plan the change and make it achievable.

Chapter 4

In the last chapter we covered WHY and WHERE. WHY is our purpose around change and what it will bring us in terms of benefits. WHERE is the place we want to end up, the destination we'd like to reach. Now it's the turn of step two, the WHICH part of the puzzle. We're still in the contemplation and insight part of the process, getting clear about ourselves.

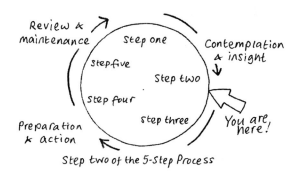

Step two of the 5-Step Process

Diagram 5: Step two of the 5-Step Process

Step one: WHY and WHERE (purpose and destination)
Step two: WHICH (animal, i.e. the distance to travel). We are here.
Step three: WHAT and HOW (the type of change)
Step four: WHO and WHEN (planning action and experimentation)
Step five: HOW MUCH and HOW WELL (reviewing and evaluating progress)

Step Two: WHICH

I selected three animals to represent the heart of this book: a fish, a grasshopper and a bird. I chose them to represent the size of the change you might want to make and the distance you might need to travel. A steady forward motion, with tweaks and iterations here and there, will enable you to swim to nearby waters. This means you are following the course of a 'fish'. If you're a 'grasshopper' you'll jump further away (physically or metaphorically), whilst retaining a few elements of your current situation. However, if you want to make a much bigger shift, you'll be flying much further away, so the 'bird' way of making change is for you. You'll try things out, fly over there, land over here, take off to go somewhere else. A bird can also fly a long way from home, which means there's opportunity for change, reinvention, even a new life.

Identifying your WHICH will be driven by a combination of:
a) Your personality, your style and your appetite for risk
b) Your context, how big the change needs to be/the distance you need to travel

Diagram 6: The Animal spectrum

Let's start with personality. Think about how you generally approach change in your life. Does it make you feel anxious? Are you a little risk averse? Do you test the water out before you swim? Let's say you want to learn Karate. You might watch it on TV, talk to people who practice it, try a one-hour taster session, rent the jacket and trousers/pants before you decide to commit. You'll also have a money back guarantee in your back pocket... just in case. You like to take small steps.

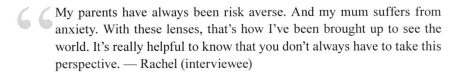 My parents have always been risk averse. And my mum suffers from anxiety. With these lenses, that's how I've been brought up to see the world. It's really helpful to know that you don't always have to take this perspective. — Rachel (interviewee)

Or are you a bit bolder, taking bigger decisions and making more change? In the Karate scenario you might invest money in a longer course or buy all the kit before you've started. You're up for trying new things, jumping slightly further away from home. You're unlikely to throw everything up in the air all at once though, that would be too much.

Avoid too much risk
Incremental change
Test a few things slowly

Enjoy more risk
Dynamic change
Try many things quickly

Diagram 7: Personality and risk taking on the Animal Spectrum

Perhaps you like to take risks or enjoy change quite a lot of the time. You'll fly further to a new destination (physical or metaphorical) just to stir up life a bit. In the Karate example you'll sign up for an all-singing-all-dancing three-month camp in Japan where they confiscate your mobile/cell phone. You know nothing about Karate (or Japan), you just fancied a change. Your research has been minimal. You just happened to see it on TV and thought it looked fun. Of course, I'm exaggerating for effect, but I think you get my point. The first part is how you tend to deal with change, from being a little more risk averse, to jumping in with both feet.

———

The second piece of the WHICH puzzle is your context: how far your situation requires you to travel when you go through your change process. If a few tweaks here and there are sufficient in your exercise programme, then that's a fish's way. If you are unhappy where you live in a city and would rather be in the countryside, it's a further distance to jump; that's a grasshopper. Or perhaps, you need a complete financial make-over, so you're willing to try multiple things, ending up far away from where you started. In this case, it's a bird.

a small change that
can be addressed
quite easily

A very big shift, or
a large volume of
different shifts

Diagram 8: Context on the Animal Spectrum

Sometimes your personality and the size of the change are aligned, a marriage made in heaven. Let's say you've reflected on yourself over the last few chapters. You think you might approach change like a bird. The shift you want to make is also quite dramatic. If this is the case, it's aligned with the style of change you normally take.

Or perhaps you are more fish oriented in how you shift things around. You swim slowly in small increments which fits the change you need to make. Maybe your friendships are a bit stale and you'd like to meet new people. You'd like to try out a local hiking group, since you do a lot of walking already. It's not a massive change but it's enough to make a difference. Your style/personality fits the change you need to make, so this will work well.

There might be times when you need to make a more dramatic change in your life, for example like Mary in chapter two, who wanted to change her professional and personal life all at the same time. But your style may be to take things slowly. Let's say you want to completely overhaul your lifestyle. This will be harder if you're risk averse, or you like to shift things bit by bit. There will be less of a match between the way you go about change and the size of the change you want to make. It is perfectly possible to do it, it will just take a bit longer. You'll be taking smaller steps, rather than leaping and bounding to your destination.

The disconnect between our expectations and our need for change, can create a challenge if we don't have a word with ourselves. Sara was on a course about changing her career, but temporarily it made her feel worse. "I've been quite angry. I think there's been a lot of frustration because you have this idea that after the eight weeks, you're going to have a new career. I felt frustrated in my own expectations." This boiled over when she started "throwing things out of frustration, rather than actually trying to beat anyone up. I went to seek help from a therapist because something wasn't right."

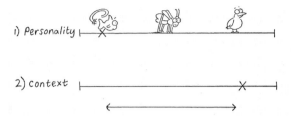

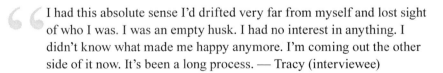

Diagram 9: Gap between personality and size of change on the Animal Spectrum

If you want a big change, but are used to taking things slowly, then you'll need to be patient. The way it can work is either, 1) stretch out your timeframe – expect things to take longer than you had initially planned, or 2) reduce the size of the initial change you want to make. Rather than a complete life make-over, make one or two sideways moves. You'll be stretching your boundaries over time, until you're in a different place. Radical change via lots of incremental steps, like the Chinese proverb *a journey of a thousand miles starts with a single step.*

> I had this absolute sense I'd drifted very far from myself and lost sight of who I was. I was an empty husk. I had no interest in anything. I didn't know what made me happy anymore. I'm coming out the other side of it now. It's been a long process. — Tracy (interviewee)

If you are a bird type you may throw yourself in and overreach at times, acting too quickly and travelling too far. Perhaps a more subtle change is needed? More time to reflect, before you shift. If you usually race to action then pausing, reassessing and make small steps, might be what you need, a counterbalance to how you normally tackle change.

Now there's an opportunity for you to work out where you are on the *Animal Spectrum*. This will be an area, rather than an exact spot. Somewhere that aligns with how you normally deal with change, along with the shift you want, or need, to make. A word of warning to the precise, to perfectionists or those who like things explained scientifically. This is more art than science.

Ultimately this exercise is about getting to know yourself and your situation better. Understanding what you can do to make this change successful and how to stay motivated along the way. If you're far apart on your personality (how you deal with change) and your context (the change you need to make), I'll share how you can make this work later in the book. So, no need to feel anxious, if you think this might be you.

Exercise 5: Knowing WHICH animal reflects your change journey

This exercise will help you discover where you might sit right now on the animal spectrum. You can do this on your own, or work with someone else so you can talk it through. Or perhaps you'd like to record your findings so you can listen back to it yourself. This can often bring further clarity or insight. You are welcome to do this whilst in a yoga headstand… if you think that will help.

1) Take a piece of paper or a notebook, and re-create the *Animal Spectrum* and write the words *Fish*, *Grasshopper* and *Bird* along the top. Then, think about how you deal with change most of the time. Do you tend to be risk averse or are you more tolerant about risk? Do you throw yourself in or bite off change in smaller chunks? Try not to overthink it, it's a general sense of where you generally sit. Now place an **X** on the first line of the spectrum, one that tends to fit your normal profile.

2) Next, ask yourself about the *context*, the second line. This is the nature of the change you want to make. Would you be happy if you just made a few adjustments here or there? Or do you need to travel a further distance, landing much further away? If you're finding this tricky you can use a scoring system, e.g. 1-10 (1 is a small change and 10 is very big). Think about the change you want to make. Is it a 4, a 6 or a 9 for example? Don't forget, we're trying to focus on one shift at a time, otherwise you may become overwhelmed. Now place an **X** on the second line on the spectrum, *context*, at the spot that feels about right for this first change project.

3) Next look at the distance between your two **X**'s. If they're close, then your style of change and the change you need to make are matched. If they are far apart then you'll need to: a) be more modest in your ambitions this time round or b), take things slowly, plan for a longer journey as this shift may take a while. If there's a gap between the two, don't beat yourself up. Managing your expectations of what you can achieve is key to staying motivated. You may need to cultivate more patience, or perhaps be a bit braver.

There's just one last thing to do. It's useful to reflect on what's come up as this will help you build your self-insight. It will also reinforce some of the learning for you. Why not take a moment to review the notes you've made? Ask yourself: what did I already know? What was surprising or new? What am I confident about? What makes me nervous about this change? What would I have to believe about myself to make this easier? What is my inner voice telling me that isn't helpful? How might I change that narrative to something more useful?

As we'll find out, contemplation, reflection and insight are all key to making successful change. For those of you into *Star Wars*, I'll leave you with a quote from one of the characters, *The Armorer*: "Persistence without insight will lead to the same outcome."

———

OK so that's this chapter done and dusted. There are more exercises to follow, but right now, let's summarise what we've covered:

- We've looked at the WHICH part of the process, the fish, grasshopper and bird.
- The two drivers for WHICH – our normal way of dealing with change, plus the amount of change we want, or need, to make, or the distance we need to travel.
- There was an exercise to find out where we are on the *Animal Spectrum*.
- We found out that when there is an alignment between the two, it will help with the process.
- If our style and the size of the change are a little less matched, we'll need to lower our expectations, reduce the size of the project, or tackle it in a different way to our usual approach.

Chapter 5

In the last chapter we looked at the WHICH step, the *Animal Spectrum* exercise, working out how far you need to travel and your normal style of change. In this chapter we'll cover the third step, the WHAT and the HOW, the final part of contemplation and insight.

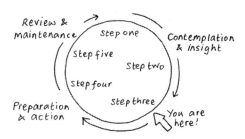

Diagram 10: Step three of the 5-Step Process

Here are the five steps in the process once more:

Step one: WHY and WHERE (purpose and destination)
Step two: WHICH (animal, i.e. the distance to travel)
Step three: WHAT and HOW (the type of change). We are here!
Step four: WHO and WHEN (planning action and experimentation)
Step five: HOW MUCH and HOW WELL (reviewing and evaluating progress)

Step Three: WHAT and HOW

WHAT is what you're doing that you want, or need, to change. This could be your friendships or relationships. Maybe it's the place you live? You're renting and you really want to buy your own property. It could be your physical or mental health that needs a boost. Or perhaps it's the work you do which you are not keen on anymore.

The good news is you have a head start on this, because in exercise one you wrote out all the aspects of your life you'd like to change. You also discovered which you have control over and which you don't. You can't fix them all at once, so pick out the most urgent, or important, one for you. The rest of the list is useful, a summary of additional areas to work on further down the line.

The HOW is the underdog of change. We're often so focused on the WHAT that much of the time we leave out the HOW altogether. Or, if we do remember it, we give it less attention than it deserves. The HOW is the runt of the litter, the small one in the corner. But successful change needs a bit of both. HOW is the way we're doing the things. If we're unclear about this, we may put our focus in all the wrong places. We may overextend ourselves thinking we needed a dramatic shift, whereas all we really wanted was a tweak.

Diagram 11: Balancing WHAT and HOW

Let's start with some examples to bring HOW alive. Take your work – HOW you're doing that can often be the key to your happiness. Are you chained to a desk all day, but would rather be doing something physical? Or is it the people you work with? Let's say you're always in large groups, but you're an introvert and you enjoy working on your own.

We can take another example of health. Maybe you need to slim down after the holidays, so you're on a diet. You're eating fewer calories and this makes you tired. The knock-on effect is now you're doing less exercise. In the end the calories in and calories out are the same as before. If this is the case then exercise is the area you need to build on, re-balancing your focus on both calories in and out. You may need to shift the type of exercise you do, perhaps to something gentler, or shorter bursts of it and more often.

Or let's say you're exercising quite often. You just dislike the HOW of your exercise regime. Perhaps you're finding it hard to keep doing it because you're a sociable person and you're exercising all on your own. What you'd really like is to join a boxing class and be with other people, but you haven't found the time to research this yet.

We met Gunther back in chapter two. He's a good example of someone trying to balance HOW and WHAT. He's a musician, loves being around music and works in the music industry. You may remember a number of challenging things happened to him in quick succession, so Gunther felt he needed to re-appraise his work and life.

It wasn't that he didn't like the industry, it was just the way he was working. He needed to shift the HOW, not the WHAT. "I love lots of elements of what I do, and I'm good at it. I've been doing it a long time... I have had great highs in that I did a lot of travelling, a lot of tour management for the artists that we look after. So I've travelled an awful lot and that was fun at first."

The problem was that it was incessant. "It was one release to the next tour, to another release, to another tour." The countries and cities started to blur. "Belgium again, is it Belgium? Yes, we're in Belgium, definitely Belgium. Is it France? No, it's Belgium." Travelling back and forth from "airport, hotel, taxi, airport, backstage, hotel. Didn't matter what city we were in.... It was just the same 'Right, great show. Phew, got the money. Let's go home.'"

Gunther has been working like this for over 18 years and throughout that time it has been "firefighting, plate spinning and just pretty much constant stress. A lot of that has been fun. But a lot of it wears you down after a while."

He's pulling back now. "I don't want to be doing this at 70, but I do want to be doing something musical for a long time. Not the intensity... the life/work has to balance." He is redefining his role by "doing a bit more supervision, delegating a little bit more than I was. I'm not doing as many hours by having Fridays off." He says it's about "re-jiggling what I enjoy, what I don't enjoy and how to readdress that balance." He's not changing WHAT he does, but he's changing HOW he does it.

Exercise 6: Knowing the difference between WHAT and HOW

If you're very clear about the difference between your WHATs and HOWs and which needs to change, then why not skip on by and we'll see you in the next chapter. If, on the other hand, you'd like some assistance, you could try this exercise:

1) First, take a piece of paper, or a notebook – again it's better to do this physically than on a laptop or computer. Draw two columns and label the first

one *List of WHATs* and the second *List of HOWs*. See the diagram below.

2) Start with the first area you want to change, your WHAT, and write this in your left-hand column. You may find it useful to go back to exercise one and check you have enough control or influence over your circumstances, that will enable you to make this shift.

3) In the second column list out all the HOWs about the area you want to change. Think about why that doesn't fit you so well. Or what makes you unhappy about it and what you'd like to change, what the difference would be. If we go back to the work example then you might write down these: a) work on my own, b) have fewer meetings, c) spend more time outside. Keep going until you've squeezed out all the HOWs you can come up with.

	List of WHATS	List of Hows
1		
2		
3		
4		
5		
6		

Diagram 12: Working out our WHATs and HOWs

4) Next, write out your second WHAT in the left column. The thing you'd like to change. It doesn't matter if you think these might be in the wrong order. You can come back later and prioritise them differently once you've done your full list.

5) Now, think about all the HOWs for that second WHAT. Reflect on the way in which you are doing those actions or how you are behaving. What would you really like to change? What doesn't fit you right now? What makes you unhappy?

Keep going until you've run out of steam. The point is to start flexing your muscles around the WHAT and the HOW — getting clear about the difference between them and identifying the specifics that need to shift. Too much focus on WHAT and not enough on HOW could mean researching how to become a high-wing artist, but forgetting you have a fear of heights. Your preferred HOW is spending time on solid ground.

6) Once you have your lists, take a second piece of paper and put your WHATs in order of priority – the ones you want to tackle first at the top, to the less important ones at the bottom. The aim is to prioritise, so you can focus your efforts in the right place. It's not a test and you won't be marked down if you change your mind. This is all gearing up to being clear about what you want.

Right, that's the end of that exercise. I suggest you do another review of this chapter and look back over your notes. Ask yourself: what am I learning about myself? What am I learning about my ideas? What was surprising or new? How does this inform my next steps? This will create a wonderful data bank on the topic called *getting to know myself.*

———

We've reached the end of this chapter, so a summary before we move on:

- We covered the topic of the WHAT versus the HOW. What we want to change and how we want to change it.
- There was a discussion about how we tend to focus on the WHAT, so the HOW gets left out. This is important as there are times when we like what we do, just not the way we do it. This nuance can often get lost in our desire to shift.
- We re-connected with the list of WHATs we want to change in our lives.
- We also did an exercise to work out the specifics, the HOWs, of what you want to change.
- Prioritising was a key part of this chapter, thinking about what we might tackle first.
- We'll also revisit WHAT and HOW once more when we get to chapter 16.

The next chapter is a very quick one, a reminder about why we're doing all this reflection before we move to action.

Chapter 6

This is a quick note for the impatient, those who are wondering why we haven't moved to action yet. Do you remember the *transtheoretical model of change* (TTM) from chapter three? There's plenty of research on TTM that shows change won't stick unless we reflect on the WHY and WHERE of change. The actions we take won't be sustainable unless we contemplate our current behaviours and the impact they have on our lives.

One of my coaching colleagues, Sarah, is a lecturer in positive psychology and also a therapist. She says this: "It's true. The reason that many public health schemes don't work that effectively is that they're trying to apply action strategies to people who need insight related strategies; even though they are still in the contemplation stage."

It must be frustrating for some of you to spend time inspecting your navel. I'm with you on this since I'm an action oriented person myself. In the past I often moved too quickly, not stopping to reflect, to think it all through, and would end up driving down the wrong road, needing to back up. Trust me, reversing at speed isn't good for your health.

We live in a world of instant gratification, wanting things to happen RIGHT NOW. But sustainable change doesn't work that way. Lasting change is a long-term journey, not a quick sprint. Building insight about yourself and your change is a better way to start. It's crazy to dive in headfirst without checking what's under the water line. We might as well launch ourselves off a cliff. I know some people do that for fun, but that's another type of crazy. Margaret Wheatley[24] is a writer, teacher, speaker, and Management Consultant, who says we spend very little time reflecting on our behaviour and lives which can create unintended consequences for ourselves.

Here are some additional thoughts from *The School of Life*, founded by a number of writers, thinkers and philosophers. This is from one of their articles titled *Self-Hatred and High-Achievement*[25]: High achievers, despite accomplishing so much, don't believe they can just be themselves. They need to demonstrate effort, achievements and awards, to feel worthy. Just being isn't enough. If they are externally validated, living off the praise from others, then they have to keep demonstrating achievements, which means constant effort and doing.

Frantic activity covers up a high achiever's underlying doubts, as being busy is reassuring. It may have been a long time since a high achiever has enjoyed a day with no commitments, but the moment they stop they become anxious. What are they missing? What actions should they be taking? Stopping to relax doesn't cut it, pausing to build insight doesn't win any prizes... if they are basing their self-worth on what others think. How can the world know they are developing or improving if they are not always working? Chasing money, power or status, are substitutes that hide all of this doubt.

Self-awareness was the second most frequent theme that came up in the interviews with the 108 participants. In fact, when I did the research on the interviews it came up 239 times. It showed itself in these topics: 'epiphanies', 'awakenings', 'transformations and rediscovering ourselves', or conversely, 'not recognising ourselves' anymore. 'Old coping mechanisms that are no longer working', being 'surprised at how we've changed' over the years, often not for the better.

Preparing will help you in your shift, because it's hard to launch yourself off without a firm foundation. Below is more evidence from TTM[26] that spending time contemplating and planning will create a more successful shift. Professor John Norcross[27], along with colleagues, researched TTM in many ways. They found contemplators were often worried about the effort it would take to change their behaviour and the losses this change would bring. Spending time on your WHY and WHERE is therefore invaluable.

The academics found that most people were in the *pre-contemplation* or *contemplation* stage, but only about 20% were *prepared for action*. Having worked on WHICH, WHAT and HOW means you've been through preparation and are now ready for action. It means you're clear there are more pros to changing than there are cons. So, you're in the *VIP Lounge of Change*. That's a special place to be.

If you're in the *contemplation* or *pre-contemplation* groups, you may think you need to move to action. However, to do this successfully you'll need to understand the impact of your behaviours on your life by building personal insight. That's why so much of this book is devoted to getting to know yourself better. Trust me, it'll help you create sustainable change.

It's important to spend time reflecting, but there is also something about pace as well. How quickly people went through stages was key too. The researchers found only 3% in the *pre-contemplation* group took action within six months. For *pre-contemplators* who moved to contemplation, 7% were active within six months. Progressing a stage in a month can therefore double your chances of taking action.

We met Anne in the introduction. She had made up her mind to leave her partner, but it took her six months to make a change. In this chapter I've been advocating how important it is to stop and reflect, to make sure we're going in the right direction. There is a balance too though as sometimes it can tip over into indecision or procrastination and we stop moving forward at all. It's therefore important to read *Swim, Jump, Fly* and do the exercises in around **three months**. Moving between stages will double the likelihood you'll get into action… so you're more likely to hit your goals. If you've engaged with the book and have done the exercises, then congratulations as you're already on a road called *Highway To Success*.

Maintaining these changes is the next hurdle. The best way to do this is to have confidence in yourself. That way you can keep going. There's much more about having faith and self-belief in a couple of chapters' time. Another area to contemplate is our patterns of thinking and ways of behaving. If we want to go through a change in our lives, it may require us to unravel some of the ways we are used to living. This takes a little time because those patterns have formed over many years, particularly if it is rewarded by the people around us.

Liane Hambly and Ciara Bomford wrote a book called *Creative Career Coaching*[28] which covers patterns of behaviour. They give an example. Let's say a family member reacts badly "when we first assert our individuality, then fear can be attached to self-expression." This will mean we learn a "script of how to behave" and will repeat this thousands of times in our lives, unless "events or self-reflection cause us to re-write the script."

We need to interrupt, unlearn these behaviours, or ways of thinking, and re-learn a different way of being. The best way to do that is through self-reflection followed by practice. The self-reflection is covered by the first three steps of the 5-Step Process, which covers contemplation and insight. Experimentation happens during step four, preparation and action. You'll find out more about this soon.

> ❝ The real voyage of discovery consists not in seeking new lands, but in seeing with new eyes. — Marcel Proust (French novelist/writer)

It might also be helpful to tell you about a type of coaching called *Solutions Focused Coaching* which helps people to solve their problems. It's particularly useful if the person is stuck in a negative cycle of thinking and are not taking action. It can also be good if they understand their problem but find it hard to move forward. Instead of thinking about all the challenges in the past, the coach helps them identify their strengths, build a vision of the future, and think about the resources they could use to reach their goal. That's why we cover resources in detail over the next few chapters.

A metaphor that works for some is thinking of climbing a mountain. The climb up the mountain is the first part of your change project. Spending time working out a little more about yourself, building self-insight, understanding what has made previous attempts come unstuck. These can be tough as we're trying to unravel long held beliefs or change behaviours that have been with us for years. The second part of the journey is more like walking down the mountain, moving to action, building momentum, picking up speed as we go.

WELL, AT BASECAMP I STARTED
To BUILD INSIGHT AND BY
CAMP THREE I KNEW MYSELF
SO MUCH BETTER...

Right, that's my *impatience* lecture over. By the way, that is also a note to myself. Here is a quick summary below of what we covered:

- This was a short chapter, one to help those who are itching to get going. Take a breath, relax, we'll get there soon!
- We discussed some more research around the TTM model of change and how we need to reflect and gain insight into why we want to make the change. We also need to focus on what will shift in the future.
- We covered pacing and how it's best to read this book and do the exercises within three months. Otherwise, we'll get stuck and give up the project.

Next, we'll be focusing quite a few chapters on resources, which are vital to any shift. But for now, why not take some time off? Water the plants, feed the cat, take a nap, watch some TV... I appreciate the focus and dedication you're giving to *Swim, Jump, Fly*. But, as they say, *all work and no play makes Jack a dull boy (or Jill a dull girl).* Why not give yourself some time to let all of that sink in?

Chapter 7

Have you ever prepared a meal but didn't have the correct ingredients? You looked for tinned tomatoes, but you'd run out. You thought about beans, but couldn't find those either. What about peas? Nope, none in the freezer. Your dinner wasn't very tasty or satisfying when you served it up in the end. It's the same when we're going through change. If we don't have the right ingredients in our cupboard, then the whole thing will be harder. Resources and giving ourselves support appeared 100 times in the *Thematic Analysis* research, so it's key to a successful change. The next few chapters are all about making life easier for yourself by getting the right resources in place before you start.

Here are some more stories from my participants and each of them found different ways to resource themselves through change. Fola lives in Nigeria and has recently had some challenging times. Both her parents died within six months of each other. She's in the middle of going through change in her life but wants to accept where she is. Fola uses imagery and metaphor to encourage herself when she's going through a difficult patch. "I imagine I'm sitting on a bench at a railway station. I'm watching the scenery, enjoying a nice sunny day, while waiting for my train to arrive. I don't know where my train is or when it will arrive, but I'm enjoying the view."

Another participant, Ruby, worked in advertising. Her first client was a non-profit Cancer Research Centre in Los Angeles. She said, "I was really excited because I thought there is a place for what I do and what advertising exists for. It can be used for good to tell important, cause or purpose-driven messages. Things that really impact humanity in a positive way." But over time Ruby's client base shifted and eventually she wound up working on a fast-food account. "I don't eat fast food and the longer I worked on it the more I thought like, 'It's just food and it's not fulfilling for me.'"

Ruby started to think, "I'm in an industry where people pat each other on the back and tell each other that they're doing great things. When in reality, maybe 10% of what is being done is good. The rest of it? We're just telling people to buy these things, consume this and that. But do they really need these things? Is it important?" Ruby felt there wasn't much meaning in her work, "There are other real problems going on in the world. We're not dealing with cancer patients or doing heart surgery on anybody. We're not dealing with people who are trying to prevent hunger." For three years she struggled on in her role, "I wasn't doing something that was going to make the world a better place. I was just really, really unhappy, feeling very stuck and not sure what to do."

So how did Ruby keep herself going? "I did other things outside of work to bring me joy and make me feel like I had a purpose. I started volunteering a lot and doing more things in the community, just to feel like I was doing something that was actually having a positive impact on people."

———

One in four of us will suffer from mental health challenges during our lives. Annette is both German and French, and she is 40. "Over six months I had a very traumatic experience which I glided into without realising, until I was right in deep. Then it was too late because I was so unwell. I had a massive nervous breakdown which totally stranded me. That was then a real turning point. That nervous breakdown was the realisation of thinking life's too short."

Of course, a key resource is counselling and therapy – Nick was in his fifties when he realised that he needed professional help. "It was all coming to a head at my last company. All the things you'd associate with stress, anxiety and lack of self-confidence." So, he booked himself 12-weeks of Cognitive Behavioural Therapy, which he found very useful.

So many of the people I interviewed sought out this type of support, from Sybille (French), Matt (American), Torsten (German), Adriana (Venezuelan), Jack and Saavi (both British) and Silvia (Australian)… there were many more, but you get my point. Professional support can be such a good resource when we're struggling.

———

Emma is 30 and lived in Germany for many years whilst working as a teacher.

She found colleagues were a great resource. "It's about working in a place where you feel supported and you're able to collaborate with people. I think it's important to be surrounded by like-minded people. Also, people who will challenge you in a supportive way."

Emma has learned that having a good sounding board is part of her ingredients list. "I was able to have conversations where we would bounce off each other." She enjoyed being open and honest. "I could say, 'actually, I'm not sure how to do this,' and they would help me. They wouldn't immediately pounce on me for saying, 'I don't know.' I could say something that was a potentially silly idea, but that might grow into a really good idea."

It wasn't always like that for Emma. "When I came back to the UK, I didn't have that sort of sounding board at the first school. I was just talking into a void. I wasn't getting anything back." She's clear that having people to collaborate with, plus being open and honest, is important to her.

Eli only discovered what his resources were when he lost them. "Something that I always wanted to do in my life was to live overseas. But in some ways, I kind of misjudged the expat experience and how it removes you from everything that you're comfortable with." Eli is a 55-year-old New Yorker who followed his wife and her new role to Sweden. "I just think that to a large degree when I moved to Sweden, I really lost touch with many of the things that I liked, and with many friends and friendships that I had. Because I also moved to a quiet village, it really was like two punches in the gut."

Eli said, "Swedish culture is very different from my own. In general, people in Northern European countries, not just here, but neighbouring countries too, are definitely people who are more into themselves." Eli has a curiosity about humanity, but he feels he has landed in a place where people are quite private. The challenge for Eli is that he's "really a people person, and I so crave that. I've always craved it. I would have long conversations with the taxi driver or with the teller at the bank, or with people who you don't normally chat with."

Eli also wonders about the rules for building new relationships. "The two areas where relationships are allowed to be made are at work and in sport. That's really about it." He says he's read about it. "I've actually gone online to see why it's so hard to make friends here… unless it's under the guise of official business (office or gym), chit chat is seen as frivolous."

Drew is American and in branding and marketing. He's also a part-time baseball coach. When we chatted on the phone, he talked about his mother who was into mindfulness 40 years ago, "Before it was a big trend in the corporate world." He started early when he was nine or ten. "I was into breathing techniques and visualisation and meditation and all that stuff. So, I brought that into the live aspects of my life, my sports being one."

I don't know much about baseball, so Drew gave me a 101 guide. He says baseball is "often characterised as a game of failure because the most successful players are considered a really great batter if they have a 30% average success rate." Drew is used to falling and picking himself up, again and again. During challenging times, particularly in situations "where you're going to struggle, my particular angle is that I will approach these with a calm mind." He breathes and "pushes the anxiety away, focusing on the moment I am in. I rely on and visualise past experiences that were successful to try to carry elements of those into my success."

Drew also translates this into his work. "I remember getting a phone call from a client who ended up being my biggest and most successful client." Drew got little notice to prepare before going in to present his ideas. "It's those moments when other people might panic, I just step away, take a deep breath, visualise what it would feel like when they award me the business." He finds this really helpful at points of stress. "I visualise walking out of the office, having done the pitch with that extra pep in my step and off to go get that post pitch drink and feel great. That is really helpful at 11.30pm the night before, when you're looking at PowerPoint and you've got another three hours worth of work to do."

———

Christine loves to be in the *Great Outdoors*. She finds it an ingredient that is restorative in her life. "As a kid although I wasn't sporty, I liked being outside. Apparently aged two the first thing I demanded every day when I woke up was 'park'. Those were my first words." One of her favourite things was a walk she made from John O'Groats to Lands End. It's no mean feat as it's 874 miles (1,407 km). From the top of Scotland to the very bottom of the UK, in Cornwall.

"Not every day was brilliant. I don't remember every day." Some were better than others and often they merged into each other. But Christine loved the trip "just in terms of exploring and freeness and really being present and being aware of what was going on around me." She never wore headphones whilst she was walking as she "just wanted to always listen to the sounds of the day unfolding. Some days I met quite a few people out walking. Some days I really didn't see anybody much."

I've been for a walk...

Many of the people I interviewed took up running as a way of resourcing themselves. Hannah is 36 and said, "I started running and that really helped me. It helped my confidence because I was able to set myself milestones, little goalposts and reach them." Her end goal was running a distance of 5 kilometres and she used a *Couch to 5K* app to get herself there. "Each week it builds you up and you do that three times a week. The next week builds on that. So, there are little milestones increasing and at the end of the app you run for half an hour." When I asked another participant, Elliott, what helped him, his answer was quite clear: "Running, running, running, running and running I think, really." That's his exact quote, word for word. It's fair to say that running is quite important to Elliott!

We met Annette earlier. She lives in Paris now but used to live in London. When she was there, she had an excellent doctor who supported her through her depression. The doctor didn't just offer antidepressants, she also asked Annette about exercise and diet. Annette used to live near a park in central London, so the doctor said, "I want you to spend every day in nature. I literally went every day to the park, which is amazing to just throw myself into nature." The doctor didn't just stop there. "She asked me what my hobby is. What I'm passionate about what makes me come alive. And for me, it's art. So, the doctor said, I want you to go to see art at least three times a week."

Annette still has what she called "dark periods" in her life which she tackles by eating healthily. "I'm finding my way in Paris, in the apartment, in the relationship and everything. I noticed that I'm eating mindlessly and I'm overeating a lot." Every year she does a dietary cleanse for a month, cutting cut out sugar, meat, wheat, dairy, fish, alcohol, coffee and tea. "It's just amazing. Every time it just resets my body. It's the addiction to sugar that's really bad for me. Once I cut it all out, I feel much better. The first week is difficult. But then after that I feel full of energy, and I need less sleep and it's really, really empowering."

———

I'll cover quite a few resources (or ingredients) in the next few chapters. The list I've pulled together isn't exhaustive so whatever has helped you in the past is a resource, something that you can rely on for your upcoming change. There's a quiz later on that will help you identify which work best for you and will help you work out what's, missing so you can plan how to fill the gap. Here is a list of the main resources that you might want to think about:

1) Mindset

The biggest resource you'll ever have is how you feel about yourself and your change. If you haven't done so, try the *Am I ready for change* quiz in Appendix A to see if you're ready to make a shift. Other mindset resources include the messages you tell yourself about this change. Whether you believe you can do it and how you talk to yourself when no one else is listening. Another topic we'll discuss is how you problem-solve and flex when roadblocks appear (which they will). Some people have a religious or spiritual faith, which gets them through, others just have faith in themselves. We'll spend some time on mindset, as it's the most important of them all.

❝ I decided I can't pay a person to rewind time, so I may as well get over it. — Serena Williams (American professional tennis player)

2) Health

If you were planning to climb a mountain, wouldn't you make sure you were fit first? That's unless you were planning on being rescued, of course. The key resources in this category are your health, mental wellbeing, what you eat, the rest you take and your sleep patterns. It includes exercise and how you pace yourself – something I've been bad at in the past. It also covers mindfulness and meditation, lowering your stress levels and taking time out.

So— what's your plan?

Get to the top - get rescued.

3) Scaffolding

A building needs scaffolding when it's having work done. And so do we. *Scaffolding* is my term for those things that will help you get through change. It can be the skills you need to manage your project and, being fleet of foot, shifting direction when new information comes in. It's also money and how you manage it, which is key if you're reducing your income, going back to study, or taking on extra costs. *Scaffolding* serves as a reality check. Being honest about how much time and energy you have available to do the work.

4) Other People

Other people can help us in so many ways. From cheering us along as we progress, to being a critical friend and sparring partner. It can be someone who can show us the errors of our ways or accountability buddies who can keep us on track. Other people include a shoulder to cry on when things get tough. It's also people with great networks who can put us in touch with others. It can be mentors who support us, or even people from history, acting as a role model to guide us on how we might like to behave.

Of course, one slice of Other People is the interviewees' stories in this book. Bill is one example: "It would feel a bit selfish if I took inspiration and motivation from other people's stories and refused to share my own. My story may help absolutely nobody, and that's fine. I really don't mind that. But at least it's out there in case somebody finds it can help them in some way."

5) Inspirations

These are all the things you can turn to for inspiration. The list is long, but here are a few ideas: books that excite you, TED talks that people suggest you watch, podcasts, websites, blogs, inspiring quotes (I like the writer Louisa May Alcott's below), articles, training courses or workshops… in fact, anything that motivates you.

> " Far away there in the sunshine are my highest aspirations. I may not reach them, but I can look up and see their beauty, believe in them, and try to follow where they lead. — Louisa May Alcott (American novelist)

Finally, have you ever watched the actor Sylvester Stallone in the film *Rocky*? If you have then you may remember he got sweaty. The character Rocky Balboa is a small-time working-class boxer from Philadelphia and for dramatic purposes he needs to fight the reigning world heavyweight champion. Unfortunately, Rocky is a drop-out. He has been drinking, fighting and failing to train. He is a weaker opponent all round.

Most of the film focuses on how Rocky gets fit for his match. His goal is to *go the distance*, making it through fifteen rounds against his opponent, Apollo Creed. There is a lot of inspirational music accompanying him jogging up and down steps or doing press-ups. To cut a long story short, he achieves his goal, just like you will, once you've read *Swim, Jump, Fly*. Think of the next few chapters about resources as a less sweaty way to get match-fit. A way of channelling *Rocky* without needing a shower.

There is quite a bit on resources, so buckle up and get ready for the ride. Mindset is such a big one that we'll cover it over two chapters, eight and nine. Then in chapter 10 we'll discuss health. In chapters 11 and 12 we'll be looking at scaffolding, other people and inspirations. Since there are so many resources you could work on, why not focus on one or two to begin with? If you try to tackle them all at once you might feel overwhelmed.

Right, now a quick summary. In the chapter the key themes were:

- The importance of having the right ingredients in our cupboard before we start. This will improve our odds considerably and make our change more successful.
- We met quite a few people from my interviews and how they all resourced themselves differently through psychotherapy, exercising, eating healthily, mindfulness and other people.
- The resources that will be coming up in the next few chapters will be mindset, health, money, skills, reality check, other people and inspirations.

Chapter 8

Psychologists love to talk about mindset because it's our window into the world. Our mindsets are an accumulation of knowledge, experience, assumptions, how we view our lives and the lives of others. It can also drive us to behave in ways that are hard to comprehend. Understanding mindset is important because it colours our experiences, skews how we feel about ourselves and shapes our internal voice and inner critic.

Mindset was the fourth highest theme in the research, showing up 202 times with these topics: 'the lenses through which we see our change' and through 'negative self-talk,' 'limiting beliefs,' 'loss of confidence,' 'imposter syndrome,' 'fear of failure,' 'getting stressed,' frustrated' and also 'anger.' Plus, there was 'trusting our intuition' (or not) and 'confidence, and courage' (having them/not having them). The topics below will help raise your awareness of your mindset and how this could influence the journey ahead.

>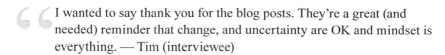
> I wanted to say thank you for the blog posts. They're a great (and needed) reminder that change, and uncertainty are OK and mindset is everything. — Tim (interviewee)

1) Why is resistance so irresistible?

I wrote a weekly coaching blog for 18 months called *Spoon-by-Spoon* and use some of it in this book. You can find my blog via the *Swim, Jump, Fly* website at swimjumpfly.com. One of my posts was about whether we're ready to change. I spent decades working in Change Management persuading people to shift their mindset and behaviours, mostly for the benefit of the organisation, although often it would help individuals too.

You'll remember the equation we covered in chapter three: $D \times V \times F > R$. The first three letters represent the drivers for change. D is level of **D**issatisfaction – I'm unhappy in my relationship, or I'm unhappy with my financial situation. Without this frustration we won't change since there's no driver. V is **V**ision of a compelling future. I want to buy my own apartment or I want to sleep better at night. Without vision we won't know where we're heading and we'll spin with no clue of where to go. That's why the WHY and WHERE are so important. F is the **F**irst practical step. Let's say we want to change career and get into bioengineering. If we don't know what skills are required or who to talk to, then it'll be difficult to start.

R is where all of this can come unstuck, **R**esistance to change. If the combined forces of D, V and F are smaller than R, nothing will shift. We could be miserable in our relationships or worried about our health, but if the cost of changing is greater than staying the same, then we won't budge. Let's turn to the interviewees again.

Stuck in the velvet rut is how Andy described 28 years working in sales. He didn't like it, but stayed, nonetheless. "It was nice and cosy. It was velvety in there because I had a pretty good salary. I was good at what I did. I was respected, was achieving, had the pension, the company car." This led him to just "bubble along for years."

Andy wanted to do something more meaningful, but instead focused on "the nice holidays we can have." If the oven broke, he'd say, "I'll just buy a new one." He felt that most people were "credit-carded up to their eyeballs and struggling. So, instead I just counted my blessings every day." Andy joined a programme during the global pandemic to force himself into action. "It unblocked certain things in my brain because I'm certainly back to being my old self again. I've completely re-engaged… despite being furloughed and the horrible things going on in the wider world. I'm thinking more clearly now."

Anna's work was unfulfilling, so she asked her dad for help. But he just said, "We can't all do what we want to do in life. We have to sacrifice something. We have to compromise. You just have to knuckle down and get on with it." This seemed to be more about him than her. "He never took a risk. He worked for the same company for his entire life. He never changed job once. He had the same commute, got the same train, walked to the same office for 40 years." Anna didn't want that life.

This is Rob again, who we met in the introduction when he was going through a huge amount of change. "If I had done this 20 years ago, I would have saved myself a lot of pain. Twenty years ago, my network was so much closer, and you don't have the added responsibilities of life, work, kids, distance." Part of being stuck is how we feel about change, which for many people is being afraid. Adeola is from Nigeria: "Breaking free is the most difficult thing... It requires a real shift in your mind-set. There is a whole fear around sticking with what you know."

2) A prophecy we can predict (a cousin of resistance)

Telling ourselves we won't achieve a goal is a great way to scupper our plans. Sociologists William Thomas and Dorothy Swaine Thomas identified *Self-Fulfilling Prophecy* in 1928. This is our predilection for prediction. We anticipate what will happen and then demonstrate that we were right all along. We might say, "I'm useless at passing tests" so there's no point in studying. We then fail our exams. Or "I've never been good at changing" and then we give up. We're creating future worlds inside our heads. We're really clever and quite daft all at the same time.

 If I keep on saying to myself that I cannot do a certain thing, it is possible that I may end by really becoming incapable of doing it. On the contrary, if I have the belief that I can do it, I shall surely acquire the capacity to do it even if I may not have it at the beginning.
— Mahatma Gandhi

Having faith (the belief, not the George Michael song) brings the upside of *Self-Fulfilling Prophecy* – we believe we can, so therefore we achieve. Faith comes in many different guises, from religious faith and belief in a higher purpose, to simply believing in ourselves. Professor Tanya Luhrmann is an anthropologist at Stanford who wrote a book about faith[29]. In it she talked about research that has repeatedly shown that people of faith report they feel better and are healthier. This is all types of faith... from pagans, Zoroastrians, Catholics, Santería Initiates, Orthodox Jews through to Evangelical Christians. In chapter 20 we'll hear about John, one of my interviewees whose faith encouraged him to believe he would be absolutely fine.

❝ ❝ Whether you think you can or whether you think you can't, you're right. — Henry Ford (industrialist and founder of Ford Motor company)

Believing in our ability to be able to change and then working in alignment with that, makes us much more likely to hit our goals. We're more likely to maintain momentum if we trust we can overcome the obstacles in our way. Just setting goals isn't enough. We also need to imagine we will complete our actions, then we're more likely to achieve them. Appendix A has an exercise that can help you work out your underlying beliefs.

Kira is from Russia, spent time in Israel and now lives in Canada. She has faith in herself. "I know that things will be fine... I just don't know when. It might take time to get to a better point, but I know that everything will be fine, for the better." She says this "has never failed me." Not believing in ourselves has the opposite effect, like dragging a sack of potatoes around. It slows us down, tires us out and encourages us to give up.

Chris is 64 and has had a long and illustrious career in branding. He created logos and brands for many well-known products and organisations yet struggles with believing in himself. "Lack of self-worth has been a very dominant factor in my life." Chris talked about this with his wife who said, "Look at yourself. You don't have to prove anything to the world." But he wasn't so sure. "I was thinking, yes I do, I've got to prove to the world and the world's got to acknowledge it." Chris went on to say, "I wouldn't want approval from my father because he's a really unpleasant piece of work, but having completely denigrated me, he has removed any sense of worth that I may have had in myself."

❝ ❝ When I look at myself and I picture how I was back then compared to now, I just don't feel like I'm that same person. I guess my confidence has gone down. — Hannah (interviewee)

Hope is important in any change process. Snyder's *Hope Theory* says we need to: 1) create goals, 2) put in place ways to reach those goals and 3) sustain our motivation to do steps 1) and 2). We'll talk more about goals, along with how to stay motivated.

Hope can increase our tolerance for pain and discomfort, both necessary in a shift process. In 2008, health psychologists Carla Berg, Rick Snyder, and Nancy Hamilton ran an experiment[30]. They dunked the participants' hands in freezing water and found that the *high-hope* participants tolerated pain twice as long as the *low-hope* participants were able to do. So, having hope that you'll achieve your end goal means you're more likely to keep going through the painful parts of your project.

Optimism is a related trait. Optimists are often more persistent, resilient and have better work and health outcomes than pessimists. Career coaches Hambly and Bomford[31] write, "Optimists are more likely to deal positively with setbacks and persist for longer in the face of difficulties. They are less likely to blame themselves when things go wrong, and therefore, have higher self-esteem." For example, when things *do* go wrong a pessimist will see the issue as permanent, whereas an optimist will see it as a temporary setback. However, don't be despondent if you're a pessimist! The good news is that you can teach yourself to become more optimistic. There will be more about this and ways you can help yourself.

ACTUALLY, AS I LOOK
AROUND, THIS IS A
WONDERFUL HOLE... OH!
AND LOOK, THERE'S A
LADDER!

Research has also shown that self-confidence is also key, driving better health and relationships. It improves our performance, increases our energy and motivation, and reduces anxiety. Equally our confidence in ourselves increases if we know we can learn and adapt. One of the posts I wrote in my blog was called *Old Dog New Tricks*. It was about *neuroplasticity*, the brain's ability to adapt and learn. *Neuro* means the brain and *plasticity* is the ability to change.

Scientists used to think we had a finite number of cells and became less good at adapting as we aged. But now we know better. We carry on creating new cells and connections throughout life. Patricia Riddell is a British psychologist who teaches and researches neuroscience. She says this area of study provides real evidence that whatever our age, we can change our behaviour. Not only that, but it's key to how our brain functions. Since these processes last a lifetime, it removes our excuse that we can't teach an old dog new tricks. It gives us confidence that change is more than possible, it's bound to happen.

If our brains are so well adapted for change, then why do we find shifting so difficult? It's because we don't *believe* we can change, we have a fixed mindset[32] that we can't develop, there's no point trying, because we'll only fail. Scans of the brain[33] have shown that people who think their intelligence is fixed have more activity in the frontal cortex when they get negative feedback. This suggests that they might feel a little stupid, which in turn impacts how much they can learn.

On the other hand, having a growth mindset, means knowing our brains are designed for change. There's a lot of research[34] on this that shows if we believe we can change then we'll be more motivated to learn and won't fear failure so much[35]. Believing this means we're onto a winner. So, let's just kick *Self-Fulfilling Prophecy* into the can by having faith and belief in ourselves!

At 65, Malcolm is one of the oldest of the participants in my project, and rather than retiring, he has just become an entrepreneur. Trying new things increases our levels of neuroplasticity, which Malcom is clearly doing. He isn't predicting he'll fail. He's just having fun. "I already have an embryonic web-building business" developing websites for clients. "The business I started last week is an e-commerce website selling T-shirts with my own designs."

So, why isn't Malcolm off playing golf? "I enjoy doing it. It's not work, it's fun. I've been watching videos on how to make money in the T-shirt business, which is very, very competitive. There's an opportunity to develop passive income streams, but it's being creative too. So, I love it." In her book *Hardwired to Learn*[36], Teri Hart says that older brains are actually better at pulling disparate information together and solving challenging problems; Malcolm is re-wiring his brain through creativity, which is proven to work. In a research project[37] participants took art classes for 10 weeks and when they used hand and brain skills together, this increased their brain connectivity, improved their memory, attention, focus and empathy... all in just one week.

Exercise 7: Building neuroplasticity

If you'd like to stop telling yourself you won't achieve your goals, then one way is to build up your neuroplasticity. You'll encourage more learning and adaptation, and this will help you feel more confident. Why not ask yourself:

- What new topic, skill, idea, thought, route to work, etc. have I learned today, this week, last month?
- When was the last time I worked on solving a problem, be it a crossword, Sudoku, word searches, or even getting the TV remote control working.
- When did I last use hand-brain skills, such as painting, drawing, putting up shelves, assembling flat packed furniture, or cooking a new and complicated meal?

If you've answered "not much" to all the above, you can encourage neuroplasticity, by reading, building vocabulary, learning a language, memory training, puzzles or *neurobics*, which is doing things differently to keep your brain on its toes. It's like fitness exercises for your mind. These can be as simple as brushing your teeth or stirring your tea with your non-dominant hand. It can be taking a different route when you drive or catching a different bus.

3) Acceptance and Values

Gestalt psychotherapists talk about the *Paradox of Change* which means the more we try to change, the more we stay stuck… unless we accept ourselves as we are. It sounds counter-intuitive, but it means that if we accept our failings and flaws, we'll have a firmer footing from which to swim, jump or fly through change. In his book *Happiness by Design*, Paul Dolan[38] writes that we need to accept much more about ourselves, since effective behaviour change only happens if we do. Buddhists also believe that much of our unhappiness is down to the gap between how our lives really are and how we believe they should be.

British writer Douglas Adams also wrote about acceptance in *The Book of Joy*[39]. He says that acceptance isn't about resignation or defeat, it's the opposite. Adams mentions that Archbishop Desmond Tutu and the Dalai Lama were both tireless in their quest to create a better world and their actions came from a deep acceptance of the state of the world, of what is. Desmond Tutu, for example, didn't accept apartheid was inevitable, but he did accept it was real.

I like the work of Dr Barry Scott Kaufman too. He is developing a coaching approach based on self-actualisation and you can read more about it in his book *Transcend*[40]. He says one of the principles in this type of coaching is to accept your whole self, not just your best self. Accepting isn't the same as liking. We can accept ourselves by being clear about who we are: strengths, weaknesses and the values we hold.

Values were so important to the participants in my research that they appeared in most of the interviews. The third most frequent theme was 'Aligning with our Values.' In the research it came up 208 times, and appeared as these topics: 'fitting in with work culture and behaviours', a loss of 'fit with work' over time, 'integrity and doing the right thing'. Others were 'our values being threatened,' or 'losing touch with our values', plus 'the choices we make about the future based on our values.'

Here is an example about values from some of the participants. Firstly, Cecilia said "I'd never really considered values much before. I suddenly thought, good Lord, I work in a job which will never really lend itself to ever getting that environment around me." She just felt she wasn't able to be authentic. This is another example from Alma. "Everything about the life I was living was totally against my values. And once I started making decisions based on those values, things got a whole lot better. Listening to my gut, listening to my values was the best sounding board ever. And the more that I've done that, the better it's got." There are more stories about values on the *Swim, Jump, Fly* website.

Authenticity was an example of those values that often came up in the research. In fact, it was sixth out of the top 18 themes, appearing 187 times. It arrived via these topics: 'honesty/authenticity,' 'being open in how we communicate with others,' 'being vulnerable.' It also appeared as its opposite – 'putting on an act,' 'wearing a mask,' 'not being true to ourselves,' 'not being able to talk to family,' 'choosing who we shared our true feelings with.' Participants found they could be more authentic when they heard what others were going through. It normalised the changes and helped them be their true selves. It was also about being heard, about how talking was cathartic, both through professional support like therapy or coaching, but also in the conversations I had arranged.

This is Matt from Texas, who is 46 and works in advertising. "If you want to be cynical, I kind of lie or exaggerate for a living, right?" But this doesn't align with his values. "I want to work for things that I believe in and help people find things that are great. I guess we're getting to honesty, authenticity. I want to always be telling the truth. I want to believe that what I'm doing is right and true."

Values work best when they're in tandem with our goals. Goals are motivating in terms of achievement, but once we've hit them, we're onto the next thing. Values, on the other hand, are what we value most in life. They are with us for the long-haul. You can't deliver a value in the way you can a goal. Values are simply there, sitting patiently waiting for you to notice them. They are hoping you'll realise unhappiness is often a mismatch between your values and the goals you've been chasing for years. The great thing about values is that you can live them in each moment, whereas a goal takes a while to reach. Join the two together and it can become your very own superpower.

Some coaches use an approach called *Acceptance and Commitment Coaching*. This can help you move towards goals that are more meaningful in your life. It's particularly helpful if you are feeling stuck. Perhaps you have a rigid way of looking at things, or have certain experiences you're avoiding that stop you from taking action? Self-doubt and a fear of failure are good examples, especially if you've attached a lot of meaning or self-worth to your goals. An Acceptance and Commitment (AC) coach might help you think through which of your behaviours are helping you and which are holding you back.

A key area that an AC coach might help you on is identifying your values. Dr Tim Anstiss[41] says that so often people aren't sure what their values are or what is important in their lives. Even if they did know at some point, their lives and context changes, and so do their values. AC coaches also help their clients work on acceptance. Dr Anstiss describes acceptance as the process of sitting with difficult, painful sensations and feelings, and embracing them, rather than pushing them away. This means being fully present in life, connecting with all of our experiences, good and bad.

Here's a final thought about acceptance that comes via meditation. Part of the challenge of change is our mindset and the lenses through which we see our lives. How do we judge ourselves? Do we see a big long list of things that need to be fixed? A quicker way of tackling those things, making that list shorter, is by being more compassionate about who we are. We can reduce the volume of change by shifting our relationship with our own judgements, desiring less perfection, being more balanced in our expectations.

Exercise 8: Building Acceptance

If you want to accept yourself, why not try this exercise:
1) Write down five–ten unexpected successes from the last two years. They don't need to be Oscar winning performances or a Nobel Prize. You might like to add the excellent trifle you made your family last week. They can be small, since the point of this exercise is to remember how things often turn out better than we expect.

2) Now write down your strengths. These are the things you're normally good at doing. They don't need to be world-beating. They could be making people laugh, reverse parking, or whistling in tune. The aim is to get you better at focusing on what you do well. Don't worry if you find this hard, you're not alone, as many of us find it difficult to focus on our strengths.

Positive Psychologists talk about character strengths. They say we all have them, but to varying degrees. Many coaches and psychologists use the 24 strengths developed by Professors Martin Seligman and Christopher Peterson[42]. You can find out your top strengths for free by using the *Values In Action (VIA)* survey on the viacharacter.org website. This takes around 15 minutes to complete. You also get personalised results, including tips on how you can use your strengths to find greater well-being.

There is evidence that identifying our top *signature* strengths will help us lead a happier life, feel more confident and have higher self-esteem. Dr Nick Baylis[43] is a psychotherapist, psychologist and coach, and describes signature strengths as the six or so skills that we like using, that make us feel energised, and we are able to learn quickly. Knowing our signature strengths means we're able to align them with our values, so why not check out the website and find out your strengths now?

3) Next draw up a list of your weaknesses. These ones don't need to be massive, even small things are useful to note down. We find it easier to identify the things we do less well, so you might already have a long list in your head. Try to keep this list short as we don't want you in tears. The point is the *Paradox of Change* – accepting who you are, with all your failings and faults. If you accept yourself then the paradox is that you're more likely to be able to change.

4) Next, spend some time focusing on your values. Here are a few examples: autonomy, integrity, adventure, bravery, friendship, learning, spirituality, wisdom, success… there are hundreds more. Just search for value lists on the internet. Write down the ones that are important for you. Check if your life facilitates you living those values. If not, then it's time to make a change.

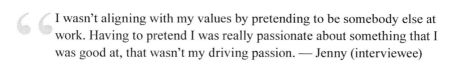 I wasn't aligning with my values by pretending to be somebody else at work. Having to pretend I was really passionate about something that I was good at, that wasn't my driving passion. — Jenny (interviewee)

I help my coaching clients focus on their values and often use the *Liminal Muse Conversation Cards* I mentioned in chapter three. You can try other methods too. For example, find lists of values on the internet and pick out five–ten that resonate. Then put them in order from the most important to the least. Think about your life and where you're able to freely live those values. If you have gaps, then it's time to work on aligning your life to fit your values. If you find it hard to identify your values, ask friends or family to highlight which they think fit you best. Another exercise you can do is to think of a perfect day. What are you doing, who is with you, where are you, what are the most important aspects of the day? Then think through what does that say about your values?

5) Let's focus on self-affirmations. Many of my clients are British and we laugh about our inherent disadvantage, feeling nauseous if we're asked to praise ourselves. I sometimes provide a sick bag… just in case. Self-affirmations are positive statements like "I'm proud of myself" or "I'm doing really well." You can also make them statements of intent. How you'd like to be in the future, even if you're not there yet: "I am eating more healthily" or "I'm better at first

dates." The point is to repeat them often, so you can start living your new life. If you'd like to find out more about self-affirmations, see Appendix A.

4) Thinking errors

Here's a mind experiment: imagine you wear dark glasses all the time. You've worn them all your life and are so devoted to them that you wear them in the bath. They have dark lenses, so the sun often appears to be behind thick black clouds. You often think it's about to rain. If you took off your glasses, you'd be surprised that, more often than not, the sun is actually shining. Repeatedly telling ourselves we're not very good has the same effect on our lives. It can dull our mood, encourage us to give up and make life a bit bleak. What's the point in trying if I'm going to fail anyway?

Bruce Hood is Professor of Developmental Psychology, Bristol University[44]. He says our brains create our consciousness; they aren't always telling us the truth, because they evolved to make sense of information as efficiently as possible. He likens it to an operating system on a computer, comparing information to all the data we've stored in our memory and experiences. Our brains use shortcuts and assumptions, which sometimes give us the incorrect information. He calls these *mind bugs*, software glitches that create biases and distortions and affect our emotions.

Cognitive Behavioural Coaching (CBC) stems from *Cognitive Behavioural Therapy* (CBT) and both of these approaches focus on our thoughts, feelings, physical sensations and actions and how they are all interconnected. Our feelings and behaviour are often driven by what we believe. It can be difficult to change emotions directly, but we can create emotional change by shifting our thought patterns and behaviour.

Both CBC and CBT generally deal with current problems and look at practical ways we can improve our state of mind every day. One area they often focus on is negative thoughts and feelings that can trap us in a vicious cycle. These are called *Thinking Errors* or *Thinking Traps*, which were initially proposed by Aaron Beck[45]. They are faulty patterns of thinking that make us feel bad about ourselves. We sometimes succumb to these types of errors when we don't have enough information to make a judgement... and yet we leap to a conclusion that might make us feel anxious.

> ❝ People are not troubled by things, but by their judgments about things.
> — Epictetus (Greek philosopher 135 AD)

It's important to distinguish between what is inside and outside our heads. Psychologist Susan David[46] says that it's part of our human nature to confuse emotions and feelings with facts and data. Recognising the difference between I'm an angry person and I have angry thoughts creates a space where we can choose how we act. Why not try out the *Thinking Errors* exercise to see if you think this way yourself. It's in Appendix A.

The mental health charity MIND wrote this in a CBT help guide in 2021[47]: *Negative thinking patterns can start from childhood onwards. For example, if you didn't receive much attention or praise from your parents or teachers at school, you might've thought, 'I'm useless, I'm not good enough'. Over time you might come to believe these assumptions, until as an adult these negative thoughts become automatic.*

Our thoughts often don't match reality and we all know people who are intelligent, funny, experienced, creative, successful. People who tell themselves that however much they produce/create/succeed, they are rather useless. Sometimes those people are us.

We can turn down the volume on intrusive or negative thoughts, by focusing on PITs (Performance Interfering Thoughts) and PETs[48] (Performance Enhancing Thoughts). Knowing the difference between these helps when shifting our lives. Let's say I'm going to make a presentation tomorrow. By the way, when I was a consultant, I hated giving presentations, so this is a real example. Here are some thoughts that would drag me into a PIT of despair:

Performance Interfering Thoughts (PITS)
• It's going to go badly.
• I'm terrible at making presentations.
• I won't be able to recall certain words and they'll laugh at me.
• The audience will become bored.
• I'll get embarrassed and my face will flush red.

This is how to PET yourself on the back instead (I know, my jokes aren't fit for Christmas crackers):

Performance Enhancing Thoughts (PETS)
• The presentation will be OK.
• I'm good at other things. I can't be good at everything.
• Generally, past presentations they are fine.
• If I make a mistake or two, people will forget those and remember the rest of the presentation.
• How do I know it will be terrible? I haven't given it yet!

Exercise 9: Getting out of the PIT

Imagine you're about to try something new and scary. How you talk to yourself could be a matter of life and death. You think about it for a moment and then mutter under your breath, "I'm no good. I can't do it, or I'll look stupid." Insert other negative comments here. Now step out onto the high wire and see if you fall off.

1) Perhaps this is a better alternative? Ask yourself what other, more positive, thoughts could I have? What might give me more confidence to start? What would be more supportive? What encouraging words would I say to a friend in the same situation?

2) Think back to previous times when you started projects; new hobbies, sports, finding love, or setting up in a different town or city. List some of these projects that turned out well. Please note *well* is not the same as *perfect*.

3) If you're feeling overwhelmed, break down large shifts into smaller and more manageable parts. This will help increase your forward motion. Ellen is another interviewee, and she agrees: "I think the only way to get action is through momentum." Reward yourself for small wins.

4) Ask whose voice am I listening to? Elliott was an interviewee who said, "after my father died, I realised that my career had been aimed at pleasing him." Other participants had similar views. Hannah advises us to "stay strong to who you are. Don't let other people cloud your judgement." Natalie says don't focus on "what you feel you should do, or society thinks you should do. Instead think 'is this genuinely going to make me happy?' We don't listen to that internal instinct, that inner voice enough. I've ended up down a path I wouldn't choose if I was back in my early 20s again."

Lastly, this is from another interviewee, Pia: "In the past, it was never really about me. It was about twisting myself into a pretzel to fit other people's expectations. I think if I'd had more access to knowing what brings me joy and pursued those avenues... maybe I would be feeling more fulfilled."

Sometimes the voices are from a parent or teacher in the past. Others are more general *shoulds*, things we think society expects us to do. Next time you hear a voice, check if it's how you really feel, or whether it's an echo from the past. Is it a supportive voice, or an inner critic? To explore where these come from, try out the exercise on the *Swim, Jump, Fly* website. You can also hear all about *shoulds* in my podcast *Tyranny of the Shoulds,* where I chat with guests about *shoulds* in their lives. You'll find a link to the podcast on the website too.

 I wake up every single day thinking, 'what do I want to do today?' I try and embrace that instead of 'what should I be doing?'
— Zee (interviewee)

Finally, let's do a quick reflection. Why not review any notes you've made from this chapter and ask yourself: what did I know already? What was surprising or new? What am I enjoying in this book? What do I dislike? Don't worry, I won't be offended. Also ask yourself: what am I confident about in this change process? What makes me nervous? Answering these will help build insight for your change project.

———

There's more on mindsets in the next chapter, but for now, let's summarise what we discussed:

- Mindsets can colour what information we take in, what we filter out and how successful we think our change process will be.
- We covered why we resist change in the first place, predicting our success levels and how believing in ourselves is important. So is accepting who we are right now, not who we would like to be.
- It's key to know our strengths and our values, which both come in handy later in the book. It's also useful to know where we have weak points too, as this is part of the *Paradox of Change*.
- *Cognitive Behavioural Therapy/Coaching* are useful approaches that can help if we have a lot of negative thoughts about ourselves.
- We covered *Thinking Errors* and the voices in our heads – the ones which shape our behaviours, but often come from others.

Chapter 9

This is the second chapter on mindset. You may be thinking two chapters on mindset feels like overkill. But if you get your mindset right, you'll be on the road to success. Here are three more areas I'd like you to reflect on:

1) Thinking outside the box

As an ex-Management Consultant I can't help but use jargon like *blue-sky thinking, boiling the ocean, deep dives, close the loop, low hanging fruit*. I know… it's an affliction. I had to use a filter (my husband) to edit *Swim, Jump, Fly* so he could remove the worst offenders. I'm sure a few words of jargon escaped his red pencil and are lurking in dark corners.

If you like, you can create your own jargon using a website called *Corporate BS Generator*. It creates random phrases that are just like the real thing. These were the first two it generated for me: *Conveniently negotiate error-free intellectual capital* and *collaboratively coordinate out-of-the-box interfaces*. The second is a lovely connector into the next mindset topic: *thinking outside the box*. It's likely the phrase came into being via the *Nine-Dot Problem*. If you've never tried this puzzle, then now is your chance.

Exercise 10: The Nine-Dot Problem and the Equation

Draw nine dots in three rows of three, like the diagram below. Connect the dots by drawing a continuous straight line through them all. Why not have a try now?

How did you get on? If you're struggling, then I can give you a hint. If you want to solve it yourself then look away now: you can go outside the square created by the nine dots.

Why not try again now? Still no joy? The answer is at the end of this chapter.

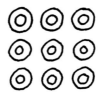

Diagram 13: The Nine-Dot Problem.

Here is another example. Make the numbers on the left of the equation add up to the number on the right. Do this by drawing one line. It can be anywhere in the equation, but it must be just one line. It's an incorrect solution if the numbers on the left **don't** add up to the one on the right: $5 + 5 + 5 = 550$

I saw a video of a family working on this equation. There was a young boy drawing in the background, ignoring his mother's attempts to solve it. She struggled for a while, then brought in other family members, but they weren't successful either. The son glanced over and said, "That's easy," and solved it in a second because he was less fixed in his thinking.

So, how did you get on? Did you work it out? If not, the answer is at the end of this chapter. The point of including both puzzles is to show you how our expectations and previous experience reduces our ability to see all the options.

Much of our thinking occurs instinctively, some say up to 95%. We learn to see problems in a certain way. This prevents us from finding different and creative solutions. Our patterns of thinking (or schemas[49]) are based on repetition and short-cuts, so we don't have to process all the information each time. This saves us brain power. Tying up shoelaces is an everyday example.

But these schemas are automatic and prevent us from seeing all that's present. It's hard to challenge the assumptions we're using because we don't even know we're making them in the first place. That can stop us developing new ways of seeing, understanding and solving problems. This can be particularly difficult for experts. They find it hard to start questioning the knowledge they've built up over many years.

It's the same with any shift that we might want to go through ourselves. If we rush at the challenge using our normal methods of problem solving, then we're likely to get stuck. Particularly if we've be working for a long time in a particular way. Now we need to see things differently. One way to work through a change is to stand back from it and view it from a distance. It can help us see the challenge in a different light. Edward O'Neill has created an interesting video on YouTube that demonstrates how re-framing can help and in his voiceover he says: "The solution comes when we see things from a new perspective or new angle." That is definitely one way to help ourselves get through change. Why not watch his video[50] if you'd like to find out more? The reference to it is at the back of the book.

Another way to work through change is to combine actions that weren't successful before. When we put them together, they create a solution that does work. For example, we might have been trying to bring in more money but failed to stem the flow of money going out. If we focus on income and spending at the same time, we're more likely to sort our finances out. If we also work on our mindset, checking what we really need to be happy in life, then that will create faster change. So, combining all three is even better.

> ❝ Problems that remain persistently insoluble should always be suspected as questions asked in the wrong way. — Alan Watts[51] (British philosopher and writer)

The best approach is to be flexible, to tackle a problem from different angles. One of my blog posts was called *The Big Idea* and it started like this: "The first rule of The Big Idea is there is no such thing as The Big Idea." I wrote that we need to flex and move and be creative, since doing things one way doesn't cut it. I went on to write: "If you only have one tool in your kitbag, a hammer for example, then every problem looks like a nail. So why do we cling to this notion of The Big Idea?"

When thinking about this topic, you might also want to consider diet. I know people who call themselves *flexitarians*, who eat some meat but are usually vegetarian. They adapt to whatever is offered on their plate. It makes feeding them much easier and it makes their lives more flexible. In fact, this is how we used to eat thousands of years ago before the advent of farming. It's likely that our diets were similar to chimpanzees, who are omnivores. They eat whatever is available; fruit, nuts, seeds, blossom, leaves, insects, honey, occasional meat, eggs and an occasional drink too, like palm wine[52]. We all need to be more *flexitarian* in how we problem solve.

One final area to focus on is how stress can impact our problem-solving abilities. Why not try this? Put your hands either side of your ears and look straight ahead. Move your hands slowly towards the back of your head until you can just see them in your peripheral vision. This is your normal field of vision. Now we'll pretend we're under stress. Move your hands forward until they are on your cheeks, with your palms facing each other. Your hands should be much further forward now. The area between your hands is what you might see if you are stressed. This is called *tunnel vision*. Just think what it can do to our problem solving! I like this from Susan Wojcicki[53], CEO of YouTube: "Rarely are opportunities presented to you in a perfect way, in a nice little box with a yellow bow on top... Opportunities, the good ones, they're messy and confusing, and hard to recognize. They're risky. They challenge you."

Over to you now. How can you problem-solve in a way that helps your change process? How can you *Think Outside The Box*? Why not try these ideas:

- Breathe! It'll calm your system down and reduces stress. You'll see the bigger picture.
- Metaphorically walk away from your change process by taking time out. Have a break, your brain will process the problem whilst you're focused on other things.
- Physically walk away by moving to a different location. It will give you a wider view and better perspective.
- Changing the colour of the walls can shift our thinking. Trees and greenery really help, so get outside if you can. The colour blue is also very good. Even looking at photos of nature can be helpful. Find out more about this in Appendix B.
- Share the problem with someone else. We all have unique mindsets and experience, meaning we see challenges in different ways.
- Reframe things. If you're a visual type of person you might try this:

- Imagine walking up a steep climb on a mountain. You reach a roadblock where rocks have fallen and shut off the path.
- Picture yourself stepping off the path, perhaps walking through bushes or trees, taking a different way to get around the blockage.
- By taking this unusual route, new scenery will open up. You'll create a different view.
- Return to this place in your mind from time to time. Your brain will start imagining new ways of tackling your challenge.
- Actively seek out different or opposing viewpoints to the ones you currently hold. It will feel uncomfortable and you may disagree with these new ideas. However, this will help you consider creative solutions or actions you hadn't considered before.
- Alternatively, imagine someone might disagree with you and think about what they would say. It could even be a future version of yourself!
- Teri Hart in *Hardwired to Learn*[54] says that what prevents our potential to learn is mindset. My advice is to take my advice... and work on your mindset. Why not check you've completed all the exercises in the two mindset chapters?

2) Patience (is a virtue, virtue is a grace, grace is a little girl who never washed her face)

Apologies if you don't know this British nursery rhyme, but it was sung to me many times over the years. As my family will tell you, I'm not a patient person. I often feel life is too short to sit around and wait. Over the last half century this mindset has got me into trouble. Just ask my colleagues in my old consulting firm. Often, I would start things too early and fail to put the right foundations or scaffolding in place. I expected to see change too quickly and became despondent when I didn't get results. I'm a slow learner, only working on patience in my 50s. I'm sure you'll be quicker on the uptake than me. In fact, I wrote a blog post called *The Art of Patience*[55], just to remind myself what I needed to do. Being so impatient, as I am, can you imagine what it was like for me to write this book?

Here is an example of impatience from one of my coaching clients. I have been working with a Mexican woman who was experienced in her field and rose to a high level in her organisation. She was a hard worker, someone who just kept going, delivering, doing everything the organisation needed. Then one day she decided life was too stressful and wanted to try her hand at something else. She's now a year into a new career and is feeling impatient. She can't work out why she's not making more progress. Her expectations are high, which might throw her off course.

It's easy to understand why patience is a challenge as we're hard wired for forward motion. Here are some views on patience from my interviewees: Zee is 30 and talked about "a desperate urge to act" in life. "I just think take action, be proactive, build that yourself. And don't wait for the opportunity to come for you." Nick hates to wait too. "I always want stuff to progress right away. I want to take action. I want to roll my sleeves up and make things happen. If you say, 'well it will eventually in its own sweet time,' then I'm gritting my teeth and saying, 'yes but what can I do?'" He's trying to work on this by telling himself, "Time is an important factor in figuring these things out. If I can just relax and let it happen, it will."

In an earlier chapter we talked about potential mismatches between our personality/style and our context, the change we want to make. In these situations, it's likely we'll feel frustrated as we want to move quicker than our normal pace allows. It's important that we give ourselves a break. Change doesn't happen overnight, especially if we're trying to adapt our behaviours and the way that we tackle things. It's a bit like flying a plane whilst also trying to change the wheels. A bit of self-care and tolerance will be needed instead.

The art of patience goes hand in hand with acceptance, acknowledging our situation, realising things will take longer than we had planned. It can be liberating to let go of all of this struggle. David is another interviewee and he agrees: "I've learned the cathartic experience of 'F**k it.' It doesn't really matter. Something good might come of it. Follow the dreams. Follow the stars." When we let go, our lives can start to take off.

———

3) Assuming we're in control/fearing we're not (or the best laid plans of mice and men)

Alain de Botton is a Swiss born British philosopher and I was listening to him on a podcast[56] when he said we have inbuilt impulses for control because we like to manage life around us. Science, literature and politics are all ways we try to order the chaos. Building cities is the way we try to tame nature and its unpredictability. The problem is that control is a false friend. We assume that once we have a plan, everything will go to plan. De Botton says we should be conscious of how much this costs us and how impossible it can sometimes be. We try so hard to line everything up, but it will never fully work and we need to prepare ourselves for that eventuality.

Sometimes not being in control can be an opportunity, allowing us to open up to new ideas and ways of working. Being over-confident can bring a fixed way of thinking and a static way of relating to the world. Letting go a little can enable discovery, uncovering, unearthing new things. Much of this book is about working out what we want and then planning how and when to put it into action. There is a need to work on planning... and at the same time to know and accept that we are rarely in control. I'll explain this conundrum in a moment, but first we need to talk about fear. Below you can read what some of my interviewees had to say on the subject.

So much change is clothed in fear. It can stop us from starting anything new. It's what can make us give up when we're not sure things are shifting. In fact, the word *fear* came up 40 times in my interviews. Have a look at the swimjumpfly. com website to find out more. One of my interviewees, Claire, said this about fear: "For me, it was one of the biggest mindset things to overcome and was mostly subconscious, so it needed to be unpicked. Fear of change, fear of uncertainty, fear of unknown, fear of instability." Or Teresa, who said this about fear: "The more years that went by the more scared I was to even try to do any art. Maybe I wouldn't be good after so long."

Julie is 46 and lives in Australia. She needed to move to the other side of the country for better paid work. She prevaricated for ages, thinking about all the pros and the cons, meanwhile not moving on at all. "I'm fearful of staying. I'm fearful of going. I suppose it's a case of FOMO – fear of missing out." She worries the relationship with her partner will break down. "I'll be single again. I'll be like 'What the hell am I doing this for? I'm down here furiously doing this job to earn money. What for? You don't have a relationship. You don't have a house. You don't have any ambitions? What's your driver in life then?' That's probably the real corker. 'You've got all this money, Julie. What's the purpose?'" Work and relationship are pulling her in different directions. She fears if she has one, she will lose the other.

Many of the other participants talked about fear too. Cecilia said: "Whatever your situation, I do think taking the courageous choice is often the right one.

It's about learning to listen to your intuition and hear it. Being able to identify when it's fear talking. Who's talking when you hear these things that are going through your head?" I agree with Cecilia. It is useful to learn what drives our internal voices. She says, "When I realise it's fear driven, then it does make me stop and think and it does make me question – is that fear?" Sometimes we're frightened for a reason because it will keep us safe. But often it's not based on anything other than the fear of the unknown.

Right, now we're back to plans and planning. To offset all this fear, we feel we must create a detailed plan, grip it tightly, clutch it to our hearts. We believe we can control the outcome by creating spreadsheets. It's what often happened when I was working in consulting. Endless project plans and stakeholder maps and weekly status report meetings – scrupulously attending to the detail so we could control the project. But the problem was that life got in the way. Harold Macmillan (British Prime Minister 1957-1963) was once asked about the most troubling part of his position. He responded, "Events, my dear boy, events."

I often found the same in consulting. Whilst we were managing multi-million-pound projects, things, particularly people, didn't behave as we predicted they would. Activities that were supposed to be easy were hard. Things that we thought would be difficult turned out to be easy. It was an endless round of shifting plans to align to reality. We were *postcasting* not forecasting. I don't want to dismiss all the project work we did. Much of it was very good and made a huge difference to our clients. But my general sense was that we often gripped too tightly onto a plan in the hope it would make the problems go away.

I still believe plans are useful. We've all heard this saying, if we fail to plan, we plan to fail. Plus, the quote (inaccurately) attributed to Abraham Lincoln: "Give me six hours to chop down a tree and I will spend the first four sharpening the axe." Or what about this, by the author Antoine de Saint-Exupéry[57], "A goal without a plan is just a wish."

The challenge is that these have a presumption that we can bend life to our will, that as long as we plan for something, so it shall be. I think we're moving on from that way of thinking, coming to the realisation that complexity can't be accounted for by a few lines on a project plan. Instead, I want to move our attention away from plans and shift it towards planning. This may sound pedantic, but there is a useful distinction between the two. This is what Scottish poet Robert Burns said about plans: "The best-laid schemes o'mice an' men[58]." And this quote has been attributed to a number of people, including Winston Churchill: "Plans are of little importance, but planning is essential."

The process of *planning*, rather than having cast-iron plans, is that it helps us to discover what is important. It enables us to gain clarity over what we want to achieve. It can help us think through what might go wrong. The challenge comes when we hold too rigidly to our plans, because then we'll be disappointed. Life will always get in the way.

Emma is an interviewee who has a personal philosophy about this. "If you're happy, do more of it. And if you're not happy, change it." When she moved to Germany people asked her how long for. She said, "I don't really work like that because I can't tell what I'm going to be doing in five years. I don't know what's going to make me happy in five years." So, instead she said, "I'm going to stay in Germany as long as I'm happy. And when I'm not, I'm going to do something about it."

Control was one of the more frequent themes in the *Thematic Analysis* research, appearing 116 times. Control showed itself via these topics: 'letting go of how we think things *should* be,' 'being clear about the ideal versus the reality of the change,' 'letting go of our idealised version of life.' It was being 'open to opportunities,' 'being a perfectionist,' and a 'control freak,' or trying to avoid both of those things. It was about 'planning versus plans,' 'focusing on freedom and agency.'

These all fit nicely with a thought from writer Seth Godin[59]. He uses the Italian phrase *Salto Mortale,* a dangerous leap into the abyss. The idea that we can throw ourselves off the cliff and trust that we'll grow wings as we fall. He says that at these times we'll be most alive.

Whilst I was writing *Swim, Jump, Fly* I asked a number of people to review the book. One of them said this part of the chapter about plans vs. planning connected well with something she was reading, called *Wilding.* It's a book written by the aptly named Isabella Tree[60], and is about a wilding project taking place at Knepp Castle in the UK. My reviewer said of the book: "It talks about creating a rich and varied, and resilient ecosystem, by letting go a bit and just seeing what happens without having a planned endpoint. Taking small steps and seeing what nature does. Getting rid of the usual boundaries created by trying to put order into nature."

I wrote a blog post about this called *Why our strength comes from letting go.* It covered a few topics, one of which was how much stronger bamboo is than steel. This is because it flexes. I won't go into the detail about bamboo here, but you can read more on the *Swim, Jump, Fly* website.

One way to think about this is resilience and Hambly and Bomford[61] describe it like this: "Resilience is the ability to handle setbacks and manage uncertainty. In making a transition [you] need the skills to handle the inevitable uncertainties that accompany change." It's being able to bounce back and recover from challenges. It's being supple, just like the bamboo, moving with the wind. I've heard others describe it as "bend, bounce back and grow."

We also need to adapt our goals and our planning process when things change. Flexing means we can take advantage of the unexpected. It enables us to be robust enough to deal with roadblocks and disappointments, open to serendipity. We need to have intention and clarity about what we want to achieve, and at the same time we need to be ready to let go, surrender to what comes up (good and bad). Then we'll be ready for anything.

Adeola is 55 and from Nigeria. She used to be in a rush. "I've become a lot more patient... if you met me even a few years ago, I had a plan. I had a plan which had a date on it. And I was driven." Adeola has changed, she is moving on from rigid plans, widening her approach. Nowadays she bases her goals around a vision. Any plans she does have are "more light touch. There's a destination and the route between where I am and where I'm going." It's more about putting "one foot in front of the other today and then noticing what's around me. What opportunities pop up? There is certainly a focus on less hurry and more noticing. In noticing what is popping up, you discover all these surprises."

Exercise 11: Spans of control (mark II)

I suggest you go back to the first exercise you completed in chapter one. I'm sure you will have learned more about yourself since then, so it'll be interesting to see what has shifted. Why not and ask yourself these questions, to see what has changed:

- What do I notice about my list of items from chapter one?
- Are there any new items in the *Outside my control/influence* space?
- How much time do I spend worrying about these things? Has this changed since chapter one?
- What about the *I can influence* space? What am I doing about these now? Am I taking any more action than then?
- Who do I need to help me with the *I can influence* category? Have I got people on board yet?
- What actions do I need to stop? Has this shifted since chapter one?
- What actions do I need to work on because I have influence or control?

———

That's the end of this chapter. There is more about other types of resources in the next one. But first, what have we covered in this one? Here is a quick summary:

- We can get stuck in old habits about how we problem solve. This won't be so helpful if we're trying to make shifts in our lives.
- We covered a number of ways to see challenges differently, to stand back from them and view them in a different light.
- It's also important to be patient with ourselves and the changes we're going through. They won't happen overnight.
- We covered the topic of fear and how it can stop us from trying to change our lives and heard from many participants about how they are afraid of change.
- We also looked at the assumptions we have about being in control – that these aren't so helpful. It's better to flex with what comes up.
- It's also good to focus on planning, rather than plans. Holding rigidly to our plans means we're likely to be disappointed when they don't work out. As they say, life is what happens when we're making plans.

Answers to exercise 10: The Nine-Dot Problem and the Equation

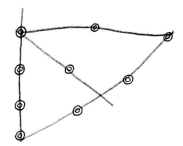

There are plenty of additional solutions if we really throw out the rule book. By the way there is no *rule book* as such. There's just the one we use to constrict ourselves.

How can you solve this equation by drawing one line: $5 + 5 + 5 = 550$. Easy, just draw a line on the first + sign to turn it into a number four.

$$545 + 5 = 500$$

Chapter 10

I wrote a blog for *The Rebel Business School*[62] and one post was called *Pacing Yourself (it's a Marathon not a Sprint)*. It was aimed at entrepreneurs, but it applies to everyone else too. Pacing for the long haul is something we all need to do.

My grandfather, Leslie, was an able runner, selected to represent Great Britain in the 1920 Summer Olympics. No podium finish for him, but to his credit he was also a good short distance runner, often winning 1600 and 5000 metre races as well as long distance. Competing at both ends of the spectrum is no mean feat. My Great Uncle Fred (my grandfather's older brother) was a good athlete too, representing England at hurdles and long jump. Later he coached world class hurdlers and wrote books on the subject.

With this athletic heritage my parents were hopeful. Would it run in the genes? My challenge was short legs and an appetite for chocolate; neither makes for a fast start. I remember one school sports day where pacing first reared its head for me. I was eleven and my parents had expectations I'd do well in a race. The whistle blew and I set off at a good speed. Soon I was at the front, keen to prove my parents right. My mother was picturing ribbons, so I pushed myself harder. The gap got wider and I was further ahead. The cheers went up from the crowd; just a handful of parents, but it felt like a stadium roar to me.

But within moments I ran out of steam. I couldn't breathe, couldn't run, my legs were jelly and the roar was in my chest. Minutes in and I'd given up. My parents' hopes were dashed. I won't beat myself up though, it was the 1970s and there was no training. I wore tennis shoes for running, drank fizzy pop to rehydrate, and no-one told me about pace. I didn't understand stamina, I just thought I had to go fast. Hare and the tortoise. It's something I'm still working on today.

And she's got off to a **spectacular** start! If she can keep this pace up for — Oh, no, she's stopped...

Sean used to be a police officer and, like me, found it difficult to pace himself. He'd go for a month with "pedal to metal, absolutely full on" and then he would be "absolutely wiped out and struggling to get momentum because I was feeling hopeless." He said his "behaviour was quite manic... I'm very ambitious and I'll go at it 100%. Like phosphorus I'm completely committed, burn into it straightaway." But that leads to burnout. Sean said that he'd be "very excited about things and then very bored very quickly."

If you rush headlong into life you'll eventually run out of air. It may be months or years, but you will need to stop at some point. One way to smooth out the highs and lows is to focus on your health. Making sure you're eating well, sleeping well and properly hydrated will carry you much of the way.

1) Exercise and sport:

We learned about neuroplasticity in an earlier chapter and it has an interesting relationship with exercise. Synapses are the connectors between our neurons (our brain cells). Every time we learn something new, or we change our behaviour, new synapses in our brain are created. In fact, it has been estimated that as many as twenty percent[63] of our synapses can change in a 24-hour period! On the flip side, if connections between neurons are inactive for some time, then they will be removed, which leads to the phrase *use it or lose it*.

So, what has any of this got to do with exercise or sport? Not only do we create new synapses (the connectors between the brain cells), but we also create new neurons, the brain cells themselves. In different contexts we make higher or lower numbers, for example when we're depressed or anxious, we create fewer new neurons. When we exercise or are in interesting environments, we create more[64]. In fact, more neurons are created when we exercise than are lost through anxiety or depression. The lesson in all of this? If we want to learn, grow and change, then exercise is really key. Now over to some stories from the participants of my research.

Many of the interviewees found exercise was a way to get *match-fit* and ready for change, even though they didn't know about the neuroscience. Phil has a background in farming but is shifting gear and building a water sports experience business. "If I can get out windsurfing, that's brilliant. Because when you're out windsurfing, all you're thinking about is the wind, the water, the board and the sail. And that's it. Nothing else."

Ruby is a participant who lives in California: "It's definitely something that helps me get through change. Going for hikes, being out in nature, yoga, dance. I was taking dance classes all the time and I even performed a couple of times and that brought me a lot of joy." Likewise, Tim is in Switzerland – "Yoga gives me a break from stressing out about everything. It's all about being present on the mat. The physical element of being flexible and stronger and the mental element of finding peace of mind."

Another interviewee, Chris, left his role under difficult circumstances. "I was in absolute shock because leaving them was like leaving your family." He needed to let his mind freewheel. "It goes somewhere where it's not being forced to think of anything at all. That's definitely been through walking or gardening." He said, "All I did every weekend, I just dug. It was fairly mindless and I was just digging, growing vegetables. It did allow my mind to freewheel. No stress in it at all."

This is from Kathryn: "I've always been a very active person but once I had a son, I found it really hard to fit in exercise." She used to "go out on big hikes, big walks. I loved it, loved it. But we've not really been out since having my son." Now Kathryn's son is old enough they're "going out for walks as a family... That makes a massive difference to me. Being in nature and just being where there aren't loads of cars and noise. Just out in the fresh air and exercise in that combination is just brilliant."

Simon used to work in the Navy but switched careers to change management, helping organisations go through change. "I'm never as fit as I want to be frankly and I'm always carrying more weight than I want." He says, "I am way more confident when I am healthier. The healthier, I am, the more resilient I am, unequivocally. And the better I feel about myself. It makes me feel more confident to be a more effective change agent because I feel I'm more credible because I can manage myself."

Smita is an Indian engineer who now lives in the USA. "Before my daughter was born, I used to exercise three to four times a week and I used to do group exercises outside of work." But things changed after giving birth to her daughter. "I was already taking half an hour off to go and pump. To save time, I would do one of the sessions during lunchtime. So, I even missed out on lunch." But now she's worked out a routine. "I would try to squeeze in a workout, a dance workout, or just to go on a walk with my daughter in a stroller."

James is 44 and for him "it's really important to have that physical outlet." Football was his focus in that past. "That was my real release, my way of getting my frustrations out." But now he's "taken up Jujitsu… and that's been a really amazing outlet for me. Because it's part physical, but part mental. I feel like I'm growing when I'm there. It's that kind of sense of achievement of learning."

Steven is Scottish and played golf when he was growing up, but a round of golf is quite long. "I didn't have the time and space. Who has time to do that?" So, instead he switched to tennis. "I really got to know people that I wouldn't have known otherwise and they're good friends and I also got to exercise as well."

Whatever your level of fitness there will be some exercise you'll be able do. The main aim is to make it sustainable, so you'll keep doing it. If you're not very fit at the moment, then anything from chair exercises to short walks will help. If you'd like to get into jogging or running, then there are plenty of apps like Couch to 5K which can help you improve. You might like to try other apps like Daily Workouts Fitness Trainer, MyFitness Pal, Sworkit, The 7 Minute Workout and Zones for Training. If you're looking for something more vigorous, here is one way to avoid hours in the gym: *High Intensity Interval training* (HIIT). These are short sessions (5–15 minutes) where you repeat vigorous exercise in bursts of a few seconds each. They can be exhausting, but very rewarding and you can see improvements quite quickly.

Resistance training is a good way to build or maintain muscle strength, keeping our metabolic rates high during the day. You can use cans of beans in the place of weights or the furniture in your house. No need for expensive gym membership. Good muscle tone helps balance and co-ordination and keeps our bones, ligaments and tendons in better shape.

> My Mum had ovarian cancer and died at 55. I don't want to live to be 95 necessarily. But I'd quite like to not have a stroke when I'm in my 50s, because there's more to life. — Claire (interviewee)

Pilates can be good for core strength and yoga for strength, flexibility and breathing. Any exercise is useful, just aim for more than you are doing already, even if it's just a walk around the block. Speaking of which, the more time you spend outside the better. People who walk outdoors return in a better mood, feeling more replenished than those who walk inside. Have a look in Appendix B for more on this. Plus, do talk to a health professional if you are out of practice or have been unwell, to see what they advise.

Why not pause a moment and ask yourself these questions: what sport and exercise do I enjoy? How do I feel when I've exercised? What could I do more of? What is holding me back? Could I find an accountability buddy, someone who would like to exercise with me? What changes are sustainable over the longer term?

2) Food and hydration:

There are different types of challenges with eating. For example, one is emotional eating. This is not a conscious food choice. It's more about emotion management, where our mood affects our food choices. There are other situations where food affects our mood and our performance.

Many participants found their eating was impacted by stress. Katerina is 34 and from Greece. She noticed a pattern in what she ate: "When I'm really unhappy I eat nothing and I mean really, really deeply unhappy. If I'm a bit down I eat everything. It seems to always come out in food for me." There were times she was really stressed at work when she could go for days without eating at all. "I realised I was hungry, feeling very weak, very tired, very cold. Then I ate something tiny and felt like I wanted to throw up because my stomach had got used to not eating anything."

Madelana is from Portugal/South Africa and says, "Food has always been an issue. I think for many people it's something you can control to a point. But sometimes it controls you." When she was stressed she, "Always wanted something highly calorific and I'd go for something sugary, which I knew I shouldn't. This is one of the reasons I took up more exercise just to counteract the effects of the eating."

Kristine is 31, Norwegian, and travelled a lot for work. "It was really hard because I didn't have a car, so I'd take the train and a taxi to the only hotel, which was isolated." There was only one restaurant and "everything was unhealthy, fast food, nothing felt really fresh. When I had to eat there four days a week for six weeks or eight weeks, I felt very restricted. I had to eat the food they had, and it wasn't very nice."

Kristine described another occasion. "It was a 2.5-hour train ride to get to the client. I would leave Monday morning and return back Thursday night." She was organising her wedding and honeymoon and "felt very stressed that I couldn't control where I could go or what I could eat. It was a remote location and we had to live at this strange airport hotel, so it was really hard to go outside." She couldn't go for a run "because it was right next to the airstrip. I just felt imprisoned in this consultant lifestyle. I couldn't do the things I wanted to do and I was away from my partner." Kristine said this was the last straw. "That's when I knew I had to get out of consulting. That was a pivotal time."

Another interviewee, Tim, wasn't eating healthily. "I started this intermittent fasting thing. I thought, well, I need to reverse things a bit." Over a few months he lost five kilos/11 pounds. "None of my clothes fitted anymore. And when I went home everyone was like, 'What's happened to you?' I felt great." The difference was stark. "The other day I had to put on a suit and my trousers were ridiculous. I thought, 'This is nuts! Was I that fat? This is crazy!' I couldn't wear them. That positive change happened and that was great."

Diet can impact our health and wellbeing, even affecting memory and problem-solving abilities. The gastrointestinal tract is home to 100 trillion microbes; 1000 species weighing around 2 kilograms, which is heavier than a brain, and they have 200 times more genetic material than we have as humans. Plus, every one of us has a completely unique microbiome inside our gut.

In October 2021 I watched a conversation between Professor Spector and Dr Will Bulsiewicz[65], both experts in the gut microbiome. It included how we can encourage a healthy microbiome – their advice was eat more plants, aiming for 30 different ones a week (including nuts, seeds, herbs and spices); focusing on coloured foods (full of polyphenols), like berries, dark chocolate, coffee, and red wine; and eating fermented foods every day and avoiding processed food. Spector said this will give us a healthy microbiome that will help us survive any environment. You might like to read Tim Spector's book, *Spoon-Fed*[66] or Will Bulsiewicz's book *The Fiber Fueled Cookbook*[67].

Professor Christopher Gardner[68] is a nutrition researcher and Director of Nutrition Studies at the *Stanford Prevention Research Center*. He says the best diet is the one we can sustain, so try to find a diet or way of eating that you can live with. No point in just eating cabbage for two weeks and then giving up. This is how Adriana looks after herself. She is from 44, Venezuelan and has worked hard for years to eat the right food: "When I cut out sugar and simple type of carbs, I do notice a difference as well in my mental health and how I feel. When I have more veggies and fruit and those type of things my mind feels clear and less sluggish."

———

Staying hydrated is vital for our health, happiness and concentration and a way to pace ourselves. Water makes up 60% of our body weight (73% of our brains). Losing just 2% of water in our bodies can impair cognitive performance, attentiveness, short-term memory and affects decision-making abilities. Collectively these are often called *brain fog*.

Sophie Medlin[69] is a dietician and has written about the amount of water our bodies need. She says we are constantly flushing out toxins and our cells can't work effectively without water; yet it's easy to become dehydrated, because we regularly lose water through breathing, sweating and urination.

The challenge is that symptoms of dehydration (fatigue, headache, concentration difficulties) feel like hunger, so medical studies show only two percent of participants drink when they're dehydrated, most just eat more instead. The quickest way to check if you're dehydrated is the colour of your pee. This should be pale yellow.

Dr Michael Mosley[70] is a BBC medical/health journalist. He says when we do drink enough water it can improve our mood, help us to remain calm, enhance our skin and even help us lose weight. One way to consume enough is to eat foods that contain water; melons, lettuce and cooked squash are 90-99% water and yoghurt, apples, oranges, broccoli, and carrots are 80-89% water. We need to watch out for food like pizza, cake, and biscuits, which contain very little water and salty foods like sausages, cheese and crisps which can actually dehydrate us.

Why not try this: monitor your liquid intake for a few days and see how you get on. Ask yourself, am I drinking enough liquid/drinking often enough? What kind of food am I consuming? Do they have enough water content? Do I eat food that has too much salt?

I'd suggest pausing for a moment and asking yourself: what have I learned in this part of the chapter? What was new? What did I already know? If I made one change in my diet or hydration this week, what would it be? Who can I involve who can help me make these changes?

3) Rest:

If you play sport, work out in the gym, or train in other ways, you'll probably know that recovery periods, the days in between working out, are as important as the training days themselves. It's a chance for our bodies to repair and grow stronger. Even if we know this about physical fitness, it's funny how we don't apply this to the rest of our lives!

The more tired we get, the harder we find it to function properly. We have difficulties regulating our emotions. We focus on the short term and become more reactive. Without time to rest we can be overwhelmed. All of this impacts our ability to work through a change project. On the other hand, when we're resting our brains process information more easily, find connections and make decisions. So, hands up who would like some time off to rest?

I stumbled across medic Dr Saundra Dalton-Smith's *TED Talk,* called *The real reason we're tired and what you can do about it*[71]. According to Dalton-Smith, there are different types of rest, including *passive physical rest*, such as sleep, but also *active rest* which is restorative, such as stretching, yoga and massage that help with blood circulation. A quick and easy rest from your work is to stand up for sixty-seconds, shake your arms and legs, stretch your muscles, rotate your core, then sit back down.

There is *mental rest* too, giving ourselves short breaks during the day. If you have whirling thoughts last thing at night, jot them down in a notepad beside your bed. Many interviewees said they liked to write as a way of processing their feelings. Pia said, "I find that writing is just a form of therapy."

Sensory rest is often left out of the equation. We spend much of our lives with bright lights, noise and technology, all leading to overwhelm. I wrote a blog called *Shhh!*[72] about the impact of these, especially in open plan offices. One way to address sensory overload is to put on headphones during the day. At night it means turning off phones and laptops long before we go to bed.

Another type is *creative rest*. Work environments can be soulless places; white walls, functional desks and hard chairs. It's more difficult to problem solve or be creative when there's no life in the place. So, it's important to have breaks to look at colourful art, or to seek out nature/go for walks outside, or to surround ourselves with beautiful things.

A further type is *emotional rest*, being free to express our feelings, which can take courage if we're a people pleaser. There's *social rest* too – differentiating between people who revive us from those that exhaust us – aiming to surround ourselves with positive and supportive people. Finally, there's *spiritual rest* – feeling a deep sense of belonging, love, acceptance and purpose. Dalton-Smith suggests we engage in something greater than ourselves, through prayer, meditation or community involvement.

On *The School of Life* website there's a post called *Why We All Need Quiet Days*[73]. They write that for the last two hundred years there has been a rapid spread of a cult, with millions of followers from every country, including the world's most successful people. This cult is devoted to just one thing, busyness. We've haven't understood that to be productive, we also need regular amounts of rest.

In 2019 Daniel Pink wrote *When: The Scientific Secrets of Perfect Timing*[74]. In it he describes how high performers work for 50 or so minutes, then take a break. Studies show that walking breaks boost energy levels and sharpen focus and Pink says breaks create better mood and reduce fatigue in the afternoon. He suggests making a list of the breaks you're going to take each day. Start with three a day, identifying times and lengths of the breaks, and what you're going to do in each one.

Why not check the types of rest you have over a short period of time, let's say a week, or two weeks. How often are you getting physical rest, not just sleep, but other ways to rest your body like yoga, stretching or massages? Do you manage much mental or sensory rest? What about creative, emotional, or social rest? And finally, one thing that is missing for some is a sense of belonging and purpose. How much spiritual rest do you have in your life?

To improve on your rest, think about which you currently enjoy. Then what you don't get/would like more of. Also ask yourself how you might plan these into your day/week? Who could help support you to increase all types of rest in your life? There's more about rest in Appendix A.

4) Sleep:

Many people find they are chronically under sleeping, or not sleeping well; according to some reports over 35% of us struggle to get the recommended amount of sleep each night. The impact of sleep deprivation has been studied across the world. Even a lack of sleep over 48 hours can be detrimental to our health and wellbeing. Most people need between seven and eight hours a night, but in studies where participants have been forced to sleep less, it affected their mood, increased anxiety, tension, and fatigue, along with impacting memory. Other detrimental effects can include weight gain, type 2 diabetes, and even heart failure.

FALLING ASLEEP IN FRONT OF THE TELLY IS LESS 'WIND-DOWN', MORE 'WIND-UP'...
SNORE

Many participants in my research found that they were in *chicken and egg* situations. Increases in their anxiety impacted their sleep and less sleep also increased their anxiety. Julie from Australia gets stressed and then internalises her feelings. "I don't ring my family and I get caught up in my head, I can't sleep. I am awake all hours of the night tossing and turning. I lose self-esteem and isolate myself, so my friends don't hear from me as much."

This is from Morgan: "When I drank all this wine, I'd get what I called night terrors. I would wake up at three in the morning with this horrible insomnia and I couldn't sleep." Ana Marta is Portuguese and worked with autistic children in a special needs school. She said, "It could be quite mentally and physically challenging when they fought you... even though you knew it wasn't personal and it wasn't really directed at you. You were being the receptacle of that violence. It did take a toll." The stress increased anxiety and "it was having a big impact on my sleep. I had real, real, real insomnia. It was really bad. I had to take proper sleeping pills, prescription ones. And I had to take them about four days in a week." She tried counselling as well and that helped.

Steve is 52 and used to have issues with sleeping. "I got to the point where I dealt with broken sleep for two or three stints of four or five months at a time. Definitely a period of about six months of tears in the car park at least once a month." Jacqui is 45, Australian and lives in Switzerland. She was stressed and not sleeping well. "I'd sit in meetings and almost didn't hear what people were saying because I was so tired." Breathing was an issue too. "Then my heart would get a palpitation or a flutter and that started to really worry me. I thought, 'Oh, God, am I headed for a heart attack or something?'"

Sleep experts say the best way to get a good night's sleep is:

- Have a fixed wake up time (week and weekend).
- Get daylight exposure (helps our circadian rhythms) and be physically active during the day.
- Avoid smoking, as nicotine stimulates the body. Cut down on alcohol and caffeine.
- Eat early as a big, heavy, or spicy meal means you're still digesting when it's time for bed.
- Optimise your bedroom (cool, comfortable bedding, block out light, use earplugs, calming scents).
- Avoid bright lights. They impact melatonin, the hormone that helps the body sleep.
- Switch off distractions like the TV, a computer or your mobile/cell phone. Try not to use any of these in your bedroom, which should be just a place for sleep and rest.
- Have a bedtime routine (PJs, teeth, book etc.), including a 30-minute wind-down before bed.
- If your mind is churning write down what's bothering you.

- Perhaps you struggle to fall asleep? Try relaxing instead (meditation, mindfulness, breathing).
- Give it 20 minutes if you toss and turn, then get up, stretch, read (in low light) then try again.

Now ask yourself how your sleep is at the moment. Which of these methods do you use, which could you try? What else can you do to improve your sleep?

5) Stress/mental health

 When I panic, I can't breathe, I get hysterical and start trembling. There's absolute fear. I will cry and have to calm myself down and go, 'it's going to be alright.' — Ellen (interviewee)

The World Health Organization, United for Global Mental Health and the World Federation for Mental Health created a joint press release in August 2020[75]: "Close to 1 billion people are living with a mental disorder, 3 million people die every year from the harmful use of alcohol and one person dies every 40 seconds by suicide. And now, billions of people around the world have been affected by the COVID-19 pandemic, which is having a further impact on people's mental health."

I mention stress in many of the chapters of *Swim, Jump, Fly*. Stress was also theme that came up 106 times the *Thematic Analysis* research. Gunther had terrible chest pains. "I went through an awful, awful physical time just after my Mum was in hospital." It turned out to be stress. Saavi had a period of time when "the anxiety got so bad I just couldn't function. Panic attacks all the time. I was just a complete mess. I couldn't be alone but couldn't be around people either."

"Like a soldier coming back from the front line." That's how Sean's wife described his behaviour one day in the supermarket. She said: "I was having a conversation with you and you just weren't there. You had a thousand-yard stare, just staring into space. That really scared me." Early in Sean's career as a police officer he was the first person to arrive at a murder scene. "I was in complete shock for the next 48 hours… you see horrible things and get involved with some of the worst sides of humanity."

It took years before Sean realised he had PTSD. "I definitely went through periods of time where I felt inexplicably unhappy, just very, very sad." He said that, "Every time the tap drips the sponge gets full. But the sponge looks exactly the same. It gets to the point where it can't take any more water and it starts to overspill. I think there was a drip, drip, drip. A cumulative effect of tough things that I was dealing with." He was offered counselling but declined. It was common practice to provide help, but "there was still an element of stigma attached to not coping. A stigma attached to getting a therapist."

Claire was getting constant pressure at work. She had bouts of shingles on her face. Then "about six months later I had a massive problem with my sinuses. I was denying it was there. I was in pain but working through it." She was taking conference calls in bed whilst feeling like "death warmed up." She didn't connect this with work-based stress. "My body wasn't managing to fight. There were all sorts of physical signs that I wasn't spotting."

It's important to talk about mental health and make it less taboo. As the first black man to be promoted to the board of his British organisation, Rory often gets asked to speak at events. "One of the elements that seems to be the most impactful for people is me talking about mental health and depression." Rory is happy to talk about it. "People have reflected to me that they don't hear people talking about it and certainly don't hear senior people talking about it." When he visited different locations "young black men particularly would seek me out and want to talk. It made me realise that in the black community, particularly of West Indian heritage, we don't talk about this stuff."

Hormones are central to this. There are *Happy* hormones, such as dopamine (the reward chemical), serotonin (the mood stabiliser), oxytocin (the love hormone) and endorphin (the pain killer). These can help regulate moods and sleep better, give pain relief and make us feel good. You can find out more about hormones in Appendix A. However, when we feel in danger cortisol increases our heart rate and blood pressure, which can increase cholesterol levels. Adrenaline is an emergency hormone that helps us think and react quickly. But too much for too long and it leads to insomnia, weight gain, headaches, anxiety, heart attack and stroke.

> Being able to go to the gym, go to exercise classes, that was my massive release. I could switch my brain off and just kind of get in the zone, especially trying to get those endorphins that you get after you've done exercise. — Teresa (interviewee)

So, how can you keep your stress levels low whilst you're going through change? There are many ways including mindfulness[76] and meditation[77], which can be as simple as focusing on your breathing and observing mind wandering. There is growing evidence that these help with anxiety and depression, plus improve general mental wellbeing, cognitive flexibility and emotional reactivity.

German spiritual teacher Eckhart Tolle wrote a whole book about mindfulness and focusing on the present. In the *Power of Now*[78] he writes that focusing too much on the past or the future can be unhelpful. Focusing on painful memories of the past or worrying about the future won't make us happy. If we can spend more time in the present, then we're more likely to free ourselves from anxiety and attachment to past concerns or future worries.

If you'd like to find other ways to remain calmer, then turn to Appendix A. Before we finish, I suggest one final pause to ask: in this chapter overall, what was useful/what was new that you'll take on board? What did you know already, but are not putting into practice? What is stopping you from making that change? How can you work on your wellbeing? What will you do differently today/next week?

———

We're at the end of the chapter, so here is a summary of what we covered:

- We covered many different topics about how we can build resilience to help ourselves through change.
- These included pacing, along with exercise and sport and how they help us to stay well and healthy for the longer term.
- We talked about food and hydration and how these are key to long term change.
- Rest and sleep are important too. Quality is as important as quantity.
- We met people who have been stressed, how it impacted their health and that it's important to recognise the signs early on and address it in different ways.
- There was practical advice on exercising, eating, sleeping and dealing with stress. Just take a look at Appendix A for more on stress.

Now we'll move onto the next chapter and *scaffolding*.

Chapter 11

In the last chapter we focused on getting physically *match-fit* for change. This chapter deals with *Scaffolding* and is all about the structure that holds us up when we're making a shift, being robust enough to withstand the knocks and bumps. I use scaffolding as an analogy because we see it every day and understand its function. On buildings it gives access to the parts that need work. It provides structure and stability when a wall or a roof needs to come down. Think of yourself as a building going through renovation. You'll need support whilst you shift things around.

We can also think about our own internal scaffolding, which keeps us standing, our skeleton. It is strong and dependable and holds us upright. *Swim, Jump, Fly* offers you a structure via the 5-Step Process, something to grab onto whilst you go through change. But skeletons are jointed, and can flex. They'd be useless if they were rigid and immoveable. The 5-Step Process is just the same. I'm encouraging you to pivot and switch tack when the context shifts around you, so hold the process lightly and switch things up when you need to. By the way, here's an interesting fact: did you know we fully replace our skeletons around every ten years?

In this chapter we'll cover three key areas around scaffolding, the skills you'll need to go through your change project, money and doing a reality check. This means asking yourself whether you really have the time, energy, inclination and money (of course), to do this project real justice. But before all of that we'll dig deeper into some other elements that will bring successful change. Below is a resource from my Change Management days. Whilst it's intended for organisational change, it can work for us too.

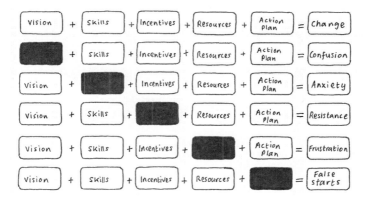

Diagram 14 (previous page): Managing Complex Change

Timothy Knoster used the model shown on page 123 in a TASH conference in 1991 as a framework for thinking about change[79] and the model says:

- We need vision, skills, incentives, resources and action plans to create successful change.
- When we don't have a vision for our change, then we'll be confused.
- Without the right skills, we'll also be anxious.
- If we don't incentivise ourselves, then we'll probably resist making a move.
- We need the right resources, or we'll end up getting frustrated.

Without planning we're unlikely to make sustainable change.

There are a few topics in the *Managing Complex Change* model that we haven't covered yet. These are skills, which we'll discuss in this chapter. Others are incentives and action plans, which we'll cover in the next few chapters.

If you'd like to dive into more detail, there's another model that I've borrowed from to help us in this chapter, which is Sheila Panchal and Stephen Palmer's INSIGHT[80] framework. A few years ago, I took part in training for life transitions coaching, a way of helping people going through life changes, such as moving house, becoming a parent, getting divorced, or retiring at the end of our careers. The INSIGHT framework was one of the tools we used in this training. INSIGHT stands for **I** – increasing self-knowledge, **N** – normalising transitions, **S** – supporting positive coping, **I** – integrating past, present and future, **G** – giving time and space, **H** – highlighting broader context, and **T** – tailoring action. If we successfully transition in one area of our life, then it will help us to transition in other areas too. So, get this one right and you've got a toolkit for all the others.

1) Skills

Let's start with the first *scaffolding* topic, skills. Do you have the right ones to make your shift? If you don't have them all, then you can always outsource some of your actions to other people. We'll talk about who these people might be in the next chapter. Discussing this is part of step 4 – the WHO.

Here are a few examples of skills you might want up your sleeve:

Research: Knowing how to locate what you need, like people, places, resources, and how you can find these via the internet, your network, libraries, or social media. Just being able to search for things is important.

Networking: There will be occasions when your network isn't enough. You will need your network's network. This can take courage if you're not a natural networker or extrovert. The good news is it's a skill you can improve.

Problem solving: Being creative is important if you need to generate and explore options and ideas. But when we're stressed this can be hard to do.

Organisation: Locating the materials you have gathered is important. You don't need to be a member of the Project Management Institute, but you do need to be organised. You can develop a filing system via an online folder, or physical file or box in which to put everything you've accumulated. Otherwise, you'll get lost in the process.

Decision-making and prioritising: Being objective enough to stand back and weigh up the options, but also balancing how the options make you feel.

Reflection: Periodically pausing and taking stock to check your direction is still right. This overlaps into mindset, but there's skill to be learned here as well. If you're not good at it, you can get better with practice.

Evaluation/measurement: Creating a table (physical or digital), setting up a spreadsheet or developing a leader board on your bedroom wall... all the different ways that I will ask you to identify where you started and how much progress you've made.

Asking for help: As they say (or ought to say) *No Woman is an Island.* And note there's a difference between having people who can help you and being able to ask them for that help.

Pivoting: The final one is letting go of the iron grip of what we expected. Instead, being fleet of foot, switching direction and changing our actions around when new information comes in.

Exercise 12: Skills audit

1) Write a list of the top five–ten skills you think you'll need for your shift. Focus on broad topics like networking or asking for help, rather than highly specific, or technical ones, such as abstract algebra or exponential equations. I can't help you with those, so please don't ask.

Some of you might need to dig deep on this. Not because you don't have skills, but because you don't believe you do. If you've got your hand up for this one, then a way round it is to ask others what they think you're good at.

2) Rate the level of skill you think you'll need for your change project. Go through each skill you listed and allocate a number for each one. From one (low skill level needed) to five (high skill level required).

3) Now rate your own current skills next to the numbers above, from one (low) to five (high) and do this for each one. Try to be honest about your strengths and weaknesses.

4) This is where you'll identify gaps that you may have. Which skills do you need to work on? How will you strengthen those? This might include asking other people to teach you how to do this or outsourcing actions to others when you don't have the skills. You'll need this list to help you work through exercises in the next chapters.

2) Money

The Swedish pop band ABBA sang about money and a rich man's world so let's talk about it now: what you think about money, how you manage it and how stressed money can make you feel. Fear of not having enough can stop us making bolder changes in our lives. We may be a bird at heart, but money worries turn us into a fish. In fact, concerns about money might stop us from making any change at all.

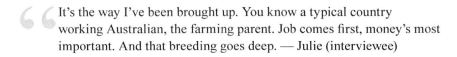

> It's the way I've been brought up. You know a typical country working Australian, the farming parent. Job comes first, money's most important. And that breeding goes deep. — Julie (interviewee)

Money is key if you're reducing your income, going back to study, or taking on extra costs during your shift. It's a big topic so I won't fully do it justice here. A few years ago, I ran a series of free group coaching sessions called *Make Money Work for You*. If you'd like more comprehensive notes from the sessions, please go to the *Swim, Jump, Fly* website (swimjumpfly.com) and you'll find them there.

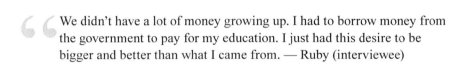

> We didn't have a lot of money growing up. I had to borrow money from the government to pay for my education. I just had this desire to be bigger and better than what I came from. — Ruby (interviewee)

From very early on we're told that being successful will make us happy. We often see success and money as the same thing so we chase the wrong goals. Money doesn't drive our happiness as much as we think it will. Money came up in many of the conversations I had. One person even mentioned it 23 times during their 60 minute conversation with me! Many said it drove their careers and some said it drove their whole lives. Money can act as a sharp edge over which our values can be broken. For some it can mean a complete shift, so they feel more congruent, living a life more in line with their values.

Jake started working for a branch of a finance company in its early days, operating out of a double garage based in the countryside. It was laid back, the people were fun, and he enjoyed the work, but things changed drastically when he transferred to the Dubai head office. "I just realised I was working for a horrible, horrible company. Just a heartless group of people that were just interested in how much money we could make and how quickly. It was a *Wolf of Wall Street* thing."

Jake felt, "If this company didn't exist, the world would still be perfectly happy. It got me thinking about what I wanted to do, what my morals were, what my ethics were." The financial advisors were earning enormous commissions each month. "They would sell somebody a finance plan that they knew the person couldn't afford. None of them had any morals and I really struggled with that. It wasn't necessarily the money they were making, although that was difficult to stomach. It was more of a fact that they just didn't care."

Jake is 30 now and is much happier managing his zero-waste shop. "It just makes me feel like I'm putting something good into the world." He feels that, "Even if I'm not making a lot of money, as long as it ticks along and I can survive off it, then I'm helping a lot of people. I know that I am appreciated, which is nice, because I get told that."

Over the decades Pete worked his way up in advertising until he reached a senior level. "It's a trap when you reach that kind of status and life takes over." He was the main earner in the family, so he felt it was no longer a choice. "Even if you want to change jobs, or lose your job through redundancy, you still have to hit that level. You still have to hit that mark for the next one and achieve even more. Make sure you keep up that level of salary coming in." Pete felt he had to chase the money but, "All I wanted to do is really good work." He says many people in the advertising industry "have burnout, they definitely have that kind of mental anguish. I think it affects more people than they care to admit."

Alexander worked on offshore oil rigs off the coast of Scotland. "I liked the idea of it. I liked the fact that I was earning a lot more money. It seemed to fit with what my social peers expected me to do." Or what he thought they expected him to do. "It turns out your friends don't really care what you do. But at the time, I thought I needed to be earning the same money as them, be able to do the same things."

Slowly Alexander started noticing it wasn't working for him. "I realised I wasn't happy in my work and I split up with a woman I was going out with. I remember the next three or four years being really hard." It wasn't sustainable long term though. "Being offshore for weeks on end and only getting a few days at home and being back offshore for weeks on end, that's a haphazard existence."

When I spoke to Anna she had just gone through a divorce, been made redundant and relocated across the UK, all in quick succession. She said it all started with a feeling years ago. "I reached a point where I felt something needed to change, but I wasn't sure what that was." She said she "wasn't unhappy, but I wasn't entirely happy either."

When Anna came back from a holiday her department announced a re-structure. "It's as if the universe knew what was happening." She grabbed the opportunity for redundancy saying, "I need to do something else. I don't know what that looks like and it's scary as hell. But if I don't do it now, I never will."

Anna had always been cautious with money. Knowing this she worked on her money before she left her role. "For me, the biggest thing was streamlining. It requires a major life overhaul. You move house to reduce your mortgage or rent. You change your spending habits. You basically streamline your life." She focused on outgoings, "Otherwise it's temporary and you just get the financial problem again." She had to do "deep work" to re-evaluate what was important, asking "why do I buy those clothes?" Or "why do I feel the need to have these material things?"

She felt her level of consumption wasn't sustainable because she "needed to earn the money to keep consuming at that rate. I had to really ask 'what am I doing? And why?' That was quite a big mindset shift around what do I really need?" She feels there's a bigger problem too. "We just consume, consume, consume and that's not sustainable for the planet."

Then Anna's change snowballed. Post redundancy she went freelance and found several contracts, then met someone online. Dating was a challenge as they lived 300 miles/482 kms apart. A few months later she decided to rent out her house and move in with her new partner in another part of the country. Then she decided to sell her house. Big changes in just a few months.

It wasn't easy as the house stood for stability in Anna's mind. In fact, after selling it she had "a bit of a meltdown." She describes this as, "Selling my old life because that was all my hard work. All my blood, sweat and tears to achieve that. And now it's got a for sale sign on it. Not just the house, I'm selling all my furniture, everything… it was literally 'Anna's life for sale. One careful owner.'"

———

Let's focus on your own money situation now; how to manage it better, bring more money in and work on your relationship with money. If you feel this isn't an issue for you, then just skip on by and meet us back again at the Reality Check below.

This is how I started the handouts for my *Make Money Work for You* workshops:

Money worries are one of our biggest fears. They can eat away at our confidence. They can be the gremlin on our shoulder stopping us changing our lives. Don't work for money, make money work for you. Getting your money sorted could be the wind beneath your wings.

If money is holding you back from making a change, here are some things you can do. The first part is all about practical steps. It's easy to pick off a few actions each week. The second is harder, your mindset. Don't put if off though, as you do need to tackle it. You won't solve your worries if you don't address your underlying thoughts and feelings about money.

I covered different levels of tackling money, from easiest to hardest:

1) Money housekeeping: Cutting down your unnecessary spending.
2) Income generator: Finding ways to bring in extra cash.
3) Money make-over: A real lifestyle change, like Anna's.
4) Our relationship with money: Our mindset/how we feel about money.

There is a well-known phrase that advertising makes us spend money we don't have on things we don't need to impress people we don't like. I agree. So, this is what I wrote in my workshop hand-outs:

It's hard to re-wire how we see the world, especially if governments and organisations are keen for us to keep buying stuff to prop up their economies. We are surrounded by messages of consumption everywhere. So, this section will take longer. But you have to change your mindset because it's like a piece of elastic. If you don't, you'll just end up back where you started, spending more money than you make. And, in a year, you'll be reading this document again thinking, 'Why don't I have enough money?'

If you're interested in this topic, then you might enjoy a book by British psychologist Oliver James called *Affluenza*[81]. In 2007 he travelled the world to research why so many people want what they haven't got or want to be someone they're not. Yet, when they do eventually achieve their goals to become richer and free from limitations, they find that they are still not very happy. I also like this from social psychologist Daniel Gilbert in his book *Stumbling on Happiness*[82]. He says economies need individuals to thrive because when we work hard and make money, economies are also more successful. It's therefore vital that we (incorrectly) believe that producing and consuming in vast quantities will make us happy.

Exercise 13: Sorting out your money

If money stops you from making change, then this exercise might help. For more detail on how to work on your money see my *Make Money Work for You* handouts on the *Swim, Jump, Fly* website.

1) Money housekeeping: Review your spending. Where could you make savings? For example, gym membership or magazine subscriptions that you don't use. Can you shift utility suppliers (water, gas, electricity etc.), mobile/cell phone, or broadband? Do you have debt you could move to a 0% credit card?

2) Income generator: Find ways to bring in extra cash. How many unused clothes do you have that you could sell? Have your kids grown up? Could you sell their toys or books? (You may want to ask them first!) There are ways to raise capital, increase your mortgage if you own a home, or government loans if you're setting up a new business.

3) Money make-over: This needs a real lifestyle shift. Dropping down a brand in the supermarket, stopping buying things you don't need, being creative with your clothes, such as cutting up dresses and turning them into skirts, letting out clothes that don't fit. You can barter and swap things with neighbours and friends or get free food from apps/websites like *Too Good to Go* or *Olio*. At the extreme it's selling your home and downsizing, although this isn't for the faint-hearted.

4) Money mindset: Spend time thinking about your relationship with money. What messages did you have about money in the past? What did your parents or family say about money when you were growing up? It's also useful to think about your behaviours around money.

Consumption is one way to cope with unpleasant feelings and compulsive buyers often report they have low mood before buying splurges, so when they feel bad they shop[83]. Remember Misha shopped for jewellery in chapter one to tackle her stress? This is called *compensatory spending*, a temporary dopamine rush, so we feel better for a while. It's a temporary distraction and doesn't address the underlying causes. It can sometimes make people feel worse due to debt and family conflicts.

This is how I ended my notes on the workshop: *Run towards the things you love. Stop running from the things you don't. And, if you work on the things you love, the money will follow.*

3) Reality Check

One final area to mention is feedback I had on this book. Early on I asked some colleagues to review certain sections of *Swim, Jump, Fly*. One of them was Annita, who was born in Zambia and moved to Mauritius when she was a young girl. She has a different take on things than me, so I thought it might be useful to add some of her thoughts here.

Annita reflected on the idea that we have "a professional persona, different hats we wear: husband, father, boss, mother, wife, sister, friend and colleague. We get caught up in these roles we play." We often change to meet those expectations. "Sometimes that's good and it's what needs to happen. But sometimes, we lose ourselves in the process. We lose sight of who we are and what we bring."

Annita feels we are impacted by "imagery, information, guidance on what to look like, what to achieve, where to go and what to aspire to. How much are we doing the introspection work?" She says life can be simpler than we make it out to be. "It's just complicated by information overload, the social media phenomenon, by cultural expectations and norms that are changing fast." She says, "We arrive with our own personalities... something within each of us that is unique. Only we can bring that out into the roles we fulfil. If we don't know what our personality is to begin with, then we can't express it."

Annita says that all this means we spend a lot of time aligning to other people's world views. "We need to assess and evaluate whether the expectations that are put on us are things we can actually meet." So, it's important to check stop and reflect on whether the effort we're putting into our change project is going to be bring the right benefits. She thinks it's useful to ask, "Is it realistic? Is it something that's going to add meaning to my life, and therefore do I want to pursue it?"

Prompted by these conversations with Annita, I've created a final section for this *Scaffolding* chapter called *The Reality Check*. This is all about looking at the road ahead and asking yourself, "Do I have the time and energy to do this?" It's fine if you don't. Everything has its moment. Maybe now isn't the time to go through a shift in your life. If you're unsure, then the exercise below will help.

The software I've used to write *Swim, Jump, Fly* gives a total number of words plus the approximate reading time. This is handy because I'm about to tell you how long it'll take you to finish this book. Clearly this depends on a) how quickly you read, b) how often you are interrupted, c) how many sections you skim over and d) how many exercises you do. But here is an approximate view of how long it takes to read the whole book: 6-13 hours. As you're about half way through, this means you have another 3-6 hours still to go.

Be honest. How is it going? Have you been snatching a few minutes here and there? Are you lost in the 5-Step Process because you've picked up the book and put it down so often? Are you trying to read *Swim, Jump, Fly* whilst cooking the kid's dinner? Or is it midnight right now, because you've been working on your tax return? Seriously, do you have this time to read this book and do the exercises? It's possible you're biting off more than you can chew. If you're distracted by all the other things you need to do, then it's unlikely you can focus properly. Then you are likely to find that your project won't get off the ground.

I'm always rushing to get to classes and then thinking about what I'm going to cook for dinner. This is my opportunity to chill for an hour and get that energy back. I'm know I'm wasting this opportunity by looking at the clock. — Sarah (interviewee)

If you don't have much time to do this work, then there are two ways you can address this: 1) Put the book aside and return to it when you have more time and energy, or 2) be less ambitious and break your project down into smaller chunks. Aim to run a shorter distance. Maybe a marathon is too much for you right now? Why not make a half-marathon your goal?

Karen is an example of the Reality Check. Her stepfather and father-in-law were both extremely unwell at the same time. "They were terminally ill with cancer, so I was doing a lot of the caring." Not only was it very emotionally challenging, but she couldn't predict what the future would look like. She couldn't plan anything. "I was too stuck. I couldn't escape that because there was too much uncertainty and difficulty going on. There wasn't the space for me to make a change."

Sadly, both died within a year of each other. "Then I was very lost. I wasn't liking work and I wasn't coming home to look after either of them. They both died at home and they both lived around the corner from us." She felt very uncertain about her future. "It was a bit like waking up and going: 'What do I do now?' That's been our life, not being able to plan, not being able to book holidays. Those things that go with terminal illness." We initially spoke a few years ago but nowadays Karen says, "I'm less focused on planning and more focused on just doing. Covid has taught us all we can't plan that much anyway!"

In the exercise below you can work out whether this change is too much. Find out whether you are trying to squeeze it in, along with everything else. Or perhaps you'll discover it is a priority? It's too important for you to ignore, so you will find a way to carve out time for your health and happiness.

Exercise 14: Reality Check

Ask yourselves these questions to work out if you need to pause or stop this change project:

- What available time do I have to spend on *Swim, Jump, Fly* each week? What is the quality of that time? Are they a few stolen moments whilst waiting for the bus? Or can I devote more focus to the work?
- What energy have I put into doing the exercises so far? Have I been metaphorically pushing them round my plate or eating them with gusto? What percentage have I completed (approximately) and what percentage have I skipped?
- How enthusiastic do I feel about this shift? Did I start off feeling excited, but now my energy is dipping?
- What would my inner voice, my inner critic, say if I decided to press pause? Would it be OK to do this, or do I want to keep going? Am I likely to pick this up again when the time/energy is right?

So, how did you do? Are we still walking down this road of change together? Or is it time to say, *"Au revoir?"* to your change project for a while? There are times for developing and there are times for resting and taking stock. Perhaps you need to pause right now?

———

That's the end of the chapter and we've finished *scaffolding*. Here's what we've covered:

- We spent time working through *The Managing Change framework*, whether we've got all the parts in place.
- We talked about skills that help us through our shift process, plus worked on the skills audit.
- There was a lot of focus on money because worries about it can stop a change project dead in its tracks.
- We heard from quite a few participants as well, in terms of their feelings about money. It was also a chance to work on your own money worries.
- Finally, we've just had a reality check. An opportunity to ask yourself, "Am I really up for this right now?"

The next chapter is the final one on resources and is focused on people and inspirations.

Chapter 12

In the last chapter we focused on *scaffolding* and how it supports our change. This one is about *Other People and Inspirations*. It's our final chapter on resources. I've included two parts to this one, first of all other people and how they can help us through change. The second section is on inspirations, the resources we might find useful in books, quotes, videos or courses.

1) Other People

Our ability to change is boosted by the support of those around us, so having people cheering from the side-lines can be encouraging. Just having someone knowing what we're planning and supporting our endeavour is helpful.

In fact, not getting help from other people can be detrimental to our health! Bruce Hood, Professor of Developmental Psychology, Bristol University[84], says that if we tackle challenges by ourselves, we tend to see them as more stressful. Being stressed impacts our immune system and that makes us more susceptible to infection and disease longer term. Other people are therefore a great resource when we're going through change. We'll explore different people that we might need and the roles they play. They could be those with connections, stress-testers, or critical friends, people who reward us, or commitment buddies who hold us to account. Knowing who fits into which group is important, as we'll find out shortly.

I like to work collaboratively and bounce around ideas, so when I started writing *Swim, Jump, Fly* I created a people resource myself. I invited coaches, therapists, blog readers and consultant colleagues to form a focus group. I wanted them to act as experts, cheerleaders, critical friends and accountability buddies. Each week I asked them to review the topics in each chapter and provide feedback. I'm indebted to them for their ideas, additions and notes, all of which helped me create a better book than I could have done on my own.

Here are some of the people you might need for your own change project.

Cheerleaders: People who understand what you're doing and are keen to celebrate your success. You may need to look outside your network if they don't exist in your family or network right now.

Accountability buddies: These are friends, loved ones, co-workers, or family members, in fact anyone who you can talk to about your actions or SMART goals. When they know the detail of what you're working on, then they can help keep you on track.

Mentors: These are people whose behaviour you admire. They can be real people from your life, or those you don't know at all. They might even be individuals from history, whose behaviour you can model. If you're lucky your mentor/s might get involved in your shift right now.

Expert/networker: These are individuals with experience or knowledge in an area that interests you. An expert in their field who is willing to share what they know or give access to their network.

Critical friend: Is someone who is great at stress-testing things. Avoid involving them at the start as they may bash your new born idea over the head. However, they're excellent at identifying risks and issues, so involve them when your project is a little more mature and can fend for itself.

Professionals: These might be personal trainers, or a nutritionist, for your health or fitness. Or a qualified coach to unravel your behaviours. For deeper emotional issues, a counsellor or therapist might be a good fit for you.

Shoulder to cry on: I know it's obvious, but I feel I need to state this plainly. Your change project won't be sunshine and roses all the time. There'll be times when it isn't going well and you'll want to give up. That's normal. In fact, if you were upbeat 100% of the time, I would worry you were suppressing your emotions... and then we're back to therapists again!

People in the *Shoulder to Cry On* group are no ordinary folk. They don't try to persuade you everything is OK. They sit, listen and let you get it off your chest. They are summed up by an expression I try to use: *Meet someone where they are. Not where you'd like them to be.* I can hear my husband shouting from the other room, "Yes that's all very well for your coaching clients, Charlotte. But what about me?"

The thing is, we love to fix stuff. We find it uncomfortable sitting with someone else's pain. We try to make it go away. We make practical suggestions, we give advice, we often don't really listen to what the other person is truly saying. This creates a blocking motion like karate: we stop someone from expressing what they feel, rather than going with the flow, like judo. Dr Ann Weiser Cornell[85] says the word emotion contains *motion*. That our feelings and emotions are always taking us towards something else. At its worst it can be an obstructing move that turns into *Toxic Positivity*. That can really mess with our heads.

Pushing away difficult emotions or forcing ourselves to feel positive can impact our mental health, wellbeing and our relationships. The problem with being falsely cheerful is that we're suppressing difficult emotions. Fear, sadness and anger are all part of life. But if we try to ignore them, they will pop up somewhere else. It takes energy to keep pushing them down. *Toxic Positivity* is not the same as hope or optimism, which are rooted in reality. *Toxic Positivity* is a denial of the truth. In her book *Emotional Agility*[86], Susan David says that it's a form of gaslighting. The other person is saying your reality is less important than their comfort. I personally believe that positivity is really important, but like salt, too much of it will ruin your food.

I'm therefore a believer in better out than in. It's like asking someone not to pass wind because other people might find it awkward. Imagine not doing so for years, that will feel uncomfortable! It's no different with emotions. Keeping them trapped inside is just the same. To paraphrase the Swiss psychiatrist and psychoanalyst Carl Jung, what we resist not only persists, but gets bigger.

When looking for people to help you in this change project, focus on those who will let you be yourself. Folk who see you for who you are, not who they'd like you to be. Individuals who can sit with the uncomfortable emotions that you might be feeling. Not people who tell you to *cheer up*, or those who want to give you advice, since they won't be much help. Here is what you could say to those types of people:

"I am going through something difficult and I'd like to tell you about it if you have time. But if I do, could I make a request? You will want to be helpful, so you'll probably feel you need to give me advice or cheer me up by pointing out all the things that are going well. Actually, I'd prefer it if you just listened at first, rather than giving me advice or focusing on the positives. Would that be possible?"

If you need help right now and have no shoulder to cry on, a quick action you can take is to ask yourself: what would a good friend say to me right now? How might they help? Imagine them saying those words to you or taking those actions. This may help your emotion lift a little.

Let's look in the opposite direction now. You may know the expression *misery likes company*. Hanging around with people who go the opposite way isn't helpful either. Perhaps they are a stuck record. Maybe they constantly remind you that most things fail. This won't fill you with hope that your change project will be successful. They won't motivate you to keep going through the ups and downs. *Noxious Negativity* is as bad as *Toxic Positivity*.

You may remember Snyder's *Hope Theory*. The following ideas are from a chapter written by Snyder and others, in a book on positive psychology[87]. They say that friends and family relationships can help us increase our hope and that it's useful for us to evaluate our relationships; assessing who gives us energy and who drains us, aiming to spend more time with those who support us in our goals and help us overcome obstacles.

All in all, I'm really just advocating a balance of different types of people when you're going through a change in your life. Pick some who will listen when you want to let off steam, plus others that encourage you a bit further up the hill. Don't look up *Noxious Negativity* by the way. I've just made that one up.

Let's hear how *Other People* helped my research participants work through changes in their lives.

Friends/family:

Alma used to be very ambitious in her career, but when she had her son "everything in my world turned on its head." Things shifted quickly. "I couldn't do things if I wanted to spend time with my son. I was going to have to compromise on those ideas, it just wasn't working." Alma said that she "tried for five years to make that work and I pretty much broke myself. I was absolutely exhausted." But she had lovely shoulders to cry on and this made all the difference. "I had a couple of really good friends at work and would have broken without them. I used to walk with them every lunchtime and would pour my soul out to them. And I'm not that sort of person. They kept me going."

Maeve is from Ireland and her partner supported her through a difficult time: "My boyfriend in particular has been very patient with my rantings, also celebrating the highs, suffering me through the lows." She found accountability buddies useful too. "Have at least one accountability buddy, if not multiples. I think just keeping the momentum going, it really does help."

Iwone is 36, Polish and works in large pharmaceuticals. "I would say that maybe I'm waking up." Iwone now knows that she needs to make a change. "I started to see that very clearly about a year ago. That I should actually go in a different direction." She's working on what's next and making sure she has the right people around her. For example, her boyfriend "is very supportive. I can ask him for help and whenever I take a next step, he supports me. It's the biggest, the most important thing."

Daniel is an interviewee who was a little depressed, but his friends helped him get back on track. "I had a really good network of friends who I spoke to." He went out to lunch with two friends every day. "It seemed a luxury to go out for a lunch with plates and knives and forks. But it was fantastic. That kept everything in check." Andrew is clear about where he finds support. "Primarily it will be other people and at the top of it would be my wife. She's understanding, someone who's always able to listen to my point of view, understanding of the situation. She's a good sounding block."

FEELING FLAT

Rebecca went through a difficult separation from the father of her children. "I know it's a massive cliché, but I'm going to say it because it's very true. When you go through something like that you do find out who your friends are." She had a few surprises: "People that I wasn't particularly close to but who were completely there for me. And then other people who've been in my life for years and years, who let me down."

Sometimes we pull away from friends, the very resources that can help us. Kiron found himself in a downward spiral when he started "looking at myself and not liking myself, or what I was becoming. I didn't think to get out the door and do any exercise. Because I just couldn't. I lost all my motivation." He used to enjoy seeing friends but started finding excuses to cancel meetings. "I'd have a few weeks where I'd be really eager... Then it'd be a couple of weeks where I just couldn't muster the motivation. I'd make excuses not to meet up with people face to face."

Sybille is French and gave up teaching when she suffered anxiety. She had some challenging years. "I found difficulties connecting with others, to make friends. I isolated myself really, I had very few friends. I would cut myself off and I would have these feelings that nobody wanted to talk to me or have anything to do with me. Because I felt I was rejected, then I was rejecting others."

Sometimes we're not good at choosing the right people. Matt is 46, lives in the USA and works in advertising and marketing. When we spoke, he had recently been through a difficult divorce. "Looking back there's just one area of my life that has been kind of a disaster and it's my relationships. I continue to choose destructive dynamics. I don't know how. I'm so blind to it." He says, "I am proud of every person I've ever hired. Proud of every friend I have. I am an excellent judge of character and who's a good fit for me. And yet, here I am not being able to pick a partner." His advice is, "Don't ignore the red flags. Pay more attention to who they really are. Don't think you can fix them later. Don't move forward in a relationship saying, 'Well, it doesn't work today, but it will!'"

Tribes and mentors:
Many of the participants talked about finding a tribe and being surrounded by like-minded folk who understood them. Ellen said, "We're not meant to be living independently, it's just not how we're born as humans. I think there is a deeper need for more of a tribal connection that's not here. So, I have to find it in different ways. I find it in the dancing. I find it gardening. I find it with my friends." When Morgan was in his 20s, he lived and worked in Russia. "I would meet other foreigners who had moved there. People who wanted to have an interesting experience, not just stay at home and have the normal career path. I was really around my tribe. They were on the same wavelength as me."

This is from Adeola: "I joined an organisation called Aspire, created by Sam Collins[88]. And one of the things she talked about was getting yourself a tribe." Adeola has quite a few people who are "there to help me when things get a bit sticky, if I am having a bad day or something has gone wrong. Or I'm confused and need a sounding board. Having a tribe, a group of people who are just there to help me, has been invaluable for me."

There was a time when Jacqui was incredibly stressed and wanted to change her life. But she was finding it hard to make the shift on her own. "I felt like I'd hit a bit of a brick wall without the support network, without the accountability, without the rigour and the discipline of doing things week-to-week. I was just struggling a little bit doing it myself." She joined a programme which came with a ready-made tribe to help her along. "I did find the course was quite good in that regard. Because the network, the support structure, the discipline really kicked me up a level."

Some people mentioned how useful they found mentors. I asked Shaun when he was happiest. "Oh, I would say in my mid 30s. During that time, I was extremely happy. I had a sense of direction. So, I knew where the North Star was. I had a good understanding of what life would be like when I got there, almost a vision of it." Each time he made a shift he saw the next goal in his life. "It was a clear direction." I asked him what gave him that confidence. "I've always remembered being mentored. In my life I've had two really strong mentors."

When I spoke to David he reminisced about a time when he really enjoyed his work. People were friendly and kind to each other. Everyone treated each other on a human level and there was integrity. "My boss and my boss's boss were very much work hard, play hard. They were encouraging mentor type folk. So, I enjoyed that aspect of it as well."

Professionals (such as therapists, counsellors and coaches):

Torsten is 54 and from Germany. He has worked in technology for years. "Knowing what I know now and having changed myself through therapy in the last four or five years, the biggest change I would make is I would get therapy earlier... because I'm aware that I have been an arsehole in a lot of jobs."

Torsten talked about his anger and where it came from: "I had some issues with it from my upbringing. I had a heavy anger or rage problem. So, you could get me into rage mode by pressing a button. If you knew the right thing to say or do, I could rage in a second." He says that on reflection he knows that he could have been a nicer boss. "People could have had more fun. And happy people make happy customers. That's a thing which I would change the most."

Rachel went to see a counsellor and what helped her was "someone just saying very outright and upfront 'you're telling me that you're anxious and that's OK. It's normal and you can manage this. We can talk through it.'"

Liam used to be a Management Consultant. "I just had so many days in a row where I couldn't really tell you what value I added to anyone's life. For me to be happy in work I have to... have a genuine sense that I'm helping humanity and making meaningful connections with other human beings." He has used professionals like counsellors and therapists to help him get through change. From the age of 16 onwards he had insomnia. "I just let it go on for too long. It became my norm." But then he tried "cognitive behavioural therapy for insomnia which really helped."

In the past few years Liam has decided to make another big change. He's now training to be a psychedelic guide and therapist. "I don't know how progressive your book is going be, but I used psychedelics as a therapeutic tool to look into those shadowy parts of myself." He says, "It's mainstream now" mentioning a 2019 article in *The Economist* magazine and another in *The Business Insider FT* "which also did a really glowing report for one of the psychedelic retreats in Holland. It's in *Forbes* too." Liam is going through this training because he feels there's a "building argument over decades. A moral obligation to decriminalise these really useful tools. And that's how I used it, as a tool that really helped."

This is Eli, an American living in Sweden who had therapy in the past. "What I really dug was group therapy in Los Angeles. I was at the end of a bad relationship and I needed some hand holding." Sometimes your friends are not the best people to turn to at this point. "They already hate your partner. They really want you to get it over with. But you're still going through the agonising and they don't want to hear it anymore."

Instead, Eli felt strangers were perfect for him. "It was a group of guys and I assumed that they would all be in the same boat as me, dealing with f*** up relationships." In fact, they had widely different issues, from an elderly man who was coping with a loss of abilities, to someone with anger management issues. "One man was such an introvert, so shy that he couldn't speak a word, even to the cashier at the supermarket. So, it was great to be in that group, because I could offer insight into all of that. They could offer their insights to me. That was great. If I could find that again, I would jump at it."

Interestingly, there is research on sharing personal stories with people we don't know. According to a 2022 study by Michael Kardas[89] and others, participants overestimated how uncomfortable a deep conversation with a stranger might be. They also underestimated how interested strangers might be in their revelations. It was during the deeper conversations that strangers felt more connected.

2) Inspirations

These are resources you turn to for motivation and encouragement. They help you keep going when the going gets tough. What you'll find useful will depend on your personality and style. Inspirations could be articles and books to energise you, TED talks or podcasts, websites, blogs, or inspiring quotes.

Perhaps the ones I've sprinkled throughout *Swim, Jump, Fly* might help?

Other inspirations could be training courses, workshops, creative endeavours like art, pottery, listening to music or playing an instrument, being out in nature with fantastic views, or seeing beautiful artwork in galleries or museums. It could be anything that encourages and motivates you through your change. If you feel inspired riding a unicycle, whilst juggling with fire, then please be my guest.

It's a bit of an iterative process, often a case of trial and error. This is where a good coach or mentor may help you, at least to get started. I've included many potential resources throughout *Swim, Jump, Fly* from articles, books, quotes and groups that are worth joining. I've collated these in one place at the back of this book. So, why not look at Appendix C right now?

———

We're on the home stretch now, as we're nearly finished on resources. The last thing to do is to identify which resources you have now and work out what is still missing.

Exercise 15: Resources quiz

1) Which of the following resources have you found most useful in the past? Building on whatever has worked/is still working for you is a great strategy. You have achieved many things in your life before now so don't throw the baby out with the bathwater; maybe you just need to do more of what is working for you now. From the list below pull out the ones that have worked for you in the past/are still working for you. Write them down and order them, from the most useful at the top, to the least useful at the bottom.

- Friends/family.
- Professionals (coach, counsellor/therapist, personal trainer, nutritionist etc).
- Consistent/quality sleep.
- Relaxation, breathing exercises, meditation, mindfulness and working on your stress levels.
- Eating healthily/staying hydrated.
- Sport/exercise.
- Experts in other areas (e.g. work, science, music, art, or areas that are

part of your change).
- Project plans and structure, such as setting goals.
- Books, TED Talks, websites, quotes, courses, workshops etc.
- Self-affirmations and positive self-talk.
- Staying true to your values.
- Ability to be creative and flex when plans/circumstances change.
- Accountability buddies.
- Focusing on hobbies and creative endeavours outside of work.
- Being outside and in nature.
- Cognitive Behavioural Therapy, other types of therapy or counselling
- Mentors or experts.
- Mindset – understanding what is creating resistance, avoiding self-fulfilling prophecies, having faith in yourself, working on thinking errors, setting reasonable expectations etc.
- Building mental fitness, solving problems and puzzles.
- Project planning, being on top of the detail, setting SMART goals.
- Removing the problem from your environment, such as getting rid of alcohol or unhealthy foods in the house, avoiding cues to behave in a certain way.
- Rewarding yourself in healthy/positive ways.
- Building up your skill levels.
- Staying on top of your finances.
- Pacing yourself.
- You'll have many others to add here.

2) Now I'd like you to look at the list again. Start with the ones that are the most useful that you put at the top of your list. Which of these are you missing that you think might be helpful? Write them on a separate list. Work your way down until you're at the less useful resources, then stop.

3) Next, look at the list above once more and do a final sweep. Are there any resources in this list that you haven't used before? Is this because you didn't have access to them before? Or is it because you haven't considered them as a resource in the past? Would any of these work for you this time around? If the answer is yes, then write those down too.

That's it for the exercise, just put the lists away. We'll come back to them later, when you'll be working out how to fill in the gaps in your resources.

———

That's the end of this chapter and the end of the section on resources. There was a lot to cover! I suggest that now might be a good time to take a solid break, since we've tackled many different topics. Why not come back to the book when you've had time to reflect, digest and generally focus on other areas in your life for a while.

One reminder on all of this – I have covered many resources, which might feel overwhelming: you really don't need to tackle them all at once, just pick one or two and get those sorted before you try any more. After all, this is a marathon, not a sprint! You can always use the resources chapters in the future. Return to them, use them as a reminder of your potential gaps. Dip in and out to jog your memory about the ways you can prepare for change.

Now, before we finish this chapter, let's summarise what we covered:

- We discussed the different types of people that can help us, from cheerleaders, to mentors, professionals and people who will listen to us when we're having a difficult time.
- There were stories from participants about how *Other People* helped them through change.
- We had a short stop-over into inspirations, you can look these up in Appendix C. You can also find out much more on the *Swim, Jump, Fly* website at swimjumpfly.com.
- Finally, we had a resources quiz so you can work out what resources you've got right now and what you might be missing.

The next chapter is all about the WHO and the WHEN – how we can move into action and get our change project to take-off.

Chapter 13

The last few chapters were about getting *match-fit*, ready for your change. Having the right resources is vital to your success and moves us beautifully into my fourth step: WHO and WHEN. As you can see from the diagram, we're out of the first phase, contemplating and insight, and are now diving into preparation and moving to action.

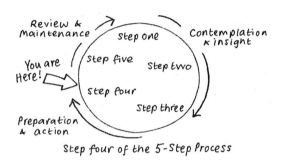

Step four of the 5-Step Process

Diagram 15: Step four of the 5-Step Process

Here are the five steps in the process once more to remind you:

Step one: WHY and WHERE (purpose and destination)
Step two: WHICH (animal, i.e. the distance to travel)
Step three: WHAT and HOW (the type of change)
Step four: WHO and WHEN (planning action/experimentation). We're here!
Step five: HOW MUCH and HOW WELL (reviewing and evaluating progress)

Research from the *transtheoretical model of behaviour change* (TTM) says we need to focus on building insight before we shift, contemplating our behaviours and the impact they have on our lives. Without these, the changes won't last. That's all well and good, but the research also shows that building insight isn't enough. We also need to take action and change our behaviours longer term.

That's why it's time to move into action, step four of the 5-Step Process. I mentioned my coaching/therapist colleague Sarah in chapter six. She says this on the topic of moving to action: "Psychotherapies which focus just on insight may not lead to effective change. That's because they don't move into action-oriented strategies, like SMART goals, habit formation, linking behaviours and cues, etc. Insight alone often isn't enough to facilitate change."

In my research the topic of Moving to Action appeared 120 times across the interviews. It showed up in these topics: 'moving forward,' 'getting out of a hole,' 'failing fast,' 'exit strategies,' 'hitting the groove,' 'being in flow' and 'things starting to shift.' It was about giving enough time to change, that it takes effort and often happens through trial and error. It was sometimes taking steps forward but getting sucked back into old ways of behaviour.

Stepping into action is vital, so what are you waiting for? We're now in the fourth step – WHO and WHEN and we'll start with WHO. You found out about the different types of people resources earlier. For example, friends or family to share your plans/goals with so they can cheer you on. Professionals to keep you on track, a qualified coach, or for deeper emotional issues a counsellor or therapist. Perhaps a nutritionist or a personal trainer is useful to help with your health? Equally, if your change is about learning new skills, discovering different careers, or taking on a new hobby, then you might want to look for an expert in the field, who can share their knowledge with you. Or it might be people with great networks who would introduce you to others.

———

Alma's husband and son helped her through a shift she was going through. "My husband has been really supportive. He never questioned that I should leave." Going through this has "really shown me the people who have my back. The thing that made me do the really difficult stuff and really push me out of my comfort zone was my family – my son and my husband." Together they helped her to move on. "I never want to go back to the place I was in two years ago. I never want to go back."

Steve is 52 and talks about the importance of coaching and how it helps us at different times in our lives. He did a Master's degree in behavioural change whilst running engineering projects and operations. "It was just like therapy, four years of therapy. We had a whole bunch of people learning to be coaches and we practiced through dedicating time to listen to each other's problems." He came to realise everyone has "something going on in their life. None of the participants ever turned up to a workshop without something they wanted to talk about." He believes that, "Coaching isn't just for someone who's got a particular issue to be addressed. Everyone's got something going on in their world they could be talking about. It changed my views. Having problems that are on your mind is normal, not unusual."

Some of my clients think of this step as hiring a Virtual Board of Directors to run their organisation. Creating a board takes a range of people with complimentary skills, often ones you don't have yourself. Other people like to imagine a football team, covering all the positions on the field. If you'd like to check out your own Virtual Board of Directors, you can access the questionnaire on the swimjumpfly.com website.

Ask yourself what motivation does this person/these people have to help you in your change project? What benefits will they get if they do? Sometimes they will support you for purely altruistic reasons, helping someone else often makes us feel good. But for others you might need to think about what help you could offer them in return. Being in a reciprocal friendship is healthy, and more sustainable, than a one-sided relationship. Another thing to ponder is how well you know someone's skills or background. You may overlook those who could be helpful, in favour of someone you're more comfortable with, or know very well.

Exercise 16: WHO to recruit

Why not try this exercise on your own, or invite others to join you too? By now you'll know which works best for you:

1) Firstly, refer to the skills audit exercise in chapter 11, where you identified gaps in the skills you need for your change. Think about people in your network who could help you with this. Why not outsource some of the actions to them? Or could they support by helping you build up the skill level yourself?

2) Now it's time to pick people you want in your team. Take a piece of paper or a notebook. Draw three columns and label them *WHO*, *Finding them*, and *Communicating with them*, like the one below.

WHO

WHO I want/need to support me (+ their role)	Finding them	Communicating with them
1	a	a
	b	b
	c	c
2		
3		
4		

Diagram 16: Working out the WHO

3) In the first column write the types of people you need to connect with, or their names if you have them. Add their role, e.g. a cheerleader, accountability buddy, mentor, shoulder, critical friend, professional support, networker.

4) In the second column write answers to *Finding them*. Skip this if you know them already, but if not, think about ways to find them. Let's say you want to connect with someone in theatre, you might write down friends or colleagues who have contacts there, or names of local theatres. If it's a divorce lawyer, use referrals, adverts on social media groups, or the press.

5) In the third column write up answers to *Communicating with them*. If it's a friend you might write a text or email them, or for your health professional write *call heath centre*, but if it's someone you don't yet know, then work out the best way to contact them.

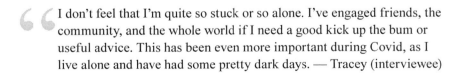

> I don't feel that I'm quite so stuck or so alone. I've engaged friends, the community, and the whole world if I need a good kick up the bum or useful advice. This has been even more important during Covid, as I live alone and have had some pretty dark days. — Tracey (interviewee)

By now you know WHY you're changing, WHERE you want to end up, WHICH type of animal you are, the distance you need to travel, whether it's the WHAT that needs to shift or the HOW. In this last exercise you've written up your WHO. Next you need to plan your actions so you can start experimenting and focusing on WHEN.

Exercise 17: Sorry I wasn't listening. Could you say that again?

This is dedicated to my husband for those times when I've finished speaking and he asks me to repeat everything I've just said. As you're over half-way through *Swim, Jump, Fly* I think it will be useful to repeat yourself… to yourself! Trust me, I haven't gone mad. This will help.

This is the time to pause, turn around and look at how far you've come. That was some climb up the mountain you've made. I'm hoping the landscape is a little clearer for you now that you're further along on the path. This is a good opportunity to summarise what you've learned about yourself.

I'd suggest keeping it high level. Just 20-30 minutes to pick out the main themes:

WHY: Write a few words about why it's important for you to change now. **Purpose**: Being clear about your motivation gives you direction and will support you when the going gets tough.

WHERE: Note where you want to end up and how you'll feel when you've arrived. **Purpose:** Imagining your future means you're more likely to get there.

SMART goals: Summarise how you'll know you've achieved them. **Purpose**: Making a goal Specific, Measurable, Achievable, Realistic and Time-bound gives you a clear goal to pursue.

WHICH: Are you a fish, a grasshopper, or a bird? Do you want to swim, jump, or fly? **Purpose:** Understanding the nature and size of your change means you'll pace yourself effectively. Plus knowing your normal way of working is helpful.

WHAT and HOW: Note down which one is more important, or do you need to shift both? **Purpose:** You'll understand where to focus your efforts and energy.

Resources: Summarise the gaps in your resources. **Purpose**: It'll give you specific actions to take so that you have more tools in your toolbox.

Reminding yourself what you've discovered is important. The action of repeating this information will embed your learning and give you a clearer map of the way ahead. In no time at all you'll be sipping cocktails on the beach, having achieved your goals.

As musicians are keen to remind us, timing is everything. Getting the notes in the right order is quite useful too. This is where planning the detail of your project is important. First, we'll look at how to create a project plan. Depending on your style and personality you'll want to do this in different ways. I've therefore outlined three options below.

1) Simple project plan – create your own spreadsheet or Word document on your laptop or PC. You might include column headings like action, purpose, resources needed, date/s, progress, notes. You'll need to order your list of actions in the right sequence when you create your plan. Having this detail in one place is a way to keep on top of your plan. It'll also help you work out if you're making headway.

2) Software based project plan – if you're technically minded or you like detail, then you might want to use project management planning software. There are plenty of types on the market or you might be using a version for your work. Just use whatever is familiar to you.

3) Creative options – you may like a more free-flowing way of creating your plan. You could use a mind map with lines and key areas highlighted in colours. Or a vision or a mood board might do the trick. Another option is to stick with the project plan but channel music or pictures in the background to keep you stimulated. A coach in my network thinks *Visual Thinking*[90] is a great book to read for this.

The creative options won't be linear like 1) or 2) above. So, you'll need to spend time identifying the sequence of events. We'll work on that in a moment. If you need guidance on mind mapping, there are plenty of resources on the internet and software or online tools that help you to create digital versions. There are many books on the topic too.

Whatever type of project plan you select is fine. The important parts are:
• Use the information you've gathered from all the steps in the 5-Step Process.
• Include them in one place.
• Take a photo of hand-written mind-maps or plans, in case your dog gets hungry.

The Project Management Institute say there are five phases to a project: 1) conception/initiation, 2) planning, 3) execution, 4) performance/monitoring and 5) project close. We've left conception and initiation for dust, so planning is the dish of the day. First you need to work out the order of your actions. No point putting your trousers on before your pants. For our American friends that's putting pants on before your underwear.

Exercise 18: Working out the WHEN

1) First prioritise your actions and identify the order. Let's use an example to bring it alive. Please put these actions in the correct order for a couple buying their first apartment together:

a) The stronger one carries the lighter one over the threshold.
b) Apply for a mortgage.
c) Find a good conveyancing solicitor.
d) Celebrate.
e) Identify location.
f) Argue about the location of the new apartment/make up after argument.
g) Search for apartments on property websites.
h) Review finances and research available mortgages.
i) Put in an offer.
j) Contact estate agents/realtors to book up viewings.
k) Buy the apartment.

l) Move deposit into an easy access bank account.

You get the gist! It's not complicated but it takes a while to a) write out the steps you need to take and b) put them in the right order. As you make your way through this change project new items will come in, or old ones will become redundant. Keep reviewing your project plan over the coming weeks; crossing things out, adding things onto the plan.

2) You may need to break your actions down into smaller chunks. It's important that each action is achievable as not all actions are equal. This is from Tracey who wanted to be a surf chick, but she's 50 now and that didn't work out. "I have a tendency to dream big and research ideas but never take them any further. Now I try to remember to break the big dream down into something more practical and tangible and work out the baby steps needed to move my shift forward."

3) Next identify WHEN you're going to do each action. Remember Daniel Pink's book, *When: The Scientific Secrets of Perfect Timing* [91] from chapter 10? I think it's worth a mention again as it fits beautifully into step four and planning our actions. He talks about our Circadian Rhythms which regulate when we're awake and when we're asleep. There are times when we're alert and other times when we're as useful as a chocolate teapot; for most of us 3.30am is the worst. One way to keep our internal clock on time is to access daylight early in the morning. This was an issue during the pandemic because many of us worked from home. It may be one of the reasons there was a spike in low mood and sleep disturbances (along with all the other challenges going on).

Pink says we need to organise activities to coincide with our peak energy times; working on our actions when our brains are not at their best will impact our levels of success. Bear this in mind when you're planning your activities. You'll know when you're most alert, most willing to take action, and when hiding under a duvet is more inviting.

One final area to think about is brain waves. We have different types: gamma, beta, alpha, theta and delta. Each type has a different purpose, supporting us to behave, think, move, process, and understand the world around us. We spend much of our time during waking hours in beta which helps us with thinking, speaking, problem-solving and decision making. Too much beta and it encourages stress, anxiety and restlessness.

Alpha waves are a connector between conscious thinking (beta) and subconscious (theta) and can help us get into a state of creativity and reduce fears, habits and speed up learning. Gamma waves are associated with bursts of insight and are good for learning, memory and processing. Theta waves are present during deep meditation and light sleep and when we have them in the optimal range, they can be great for creativity and connection to others. Delta waves are the ones we experience in deep and dreamless sleep and are associated with healing and regeneration of our bodies and minds.

We can encourage different brain waves by meditating, breathing and sometimes the simple process of closing our eyes. Take a look at the *Swim, Jump, Fly* website for more information about brain waves and the exercises you can do to increase your levels of alpha and gamma, both helpful for creativity and insight.

———

There are four more areas to cover before we finish: 1) issues and risks, 2) allocating resources to actions, 3) rewarding yourself and 4) keeping your project plan top of mind.

When I ran change management projects for clients, we'd create risks and issues registers. They aren't complicated, and they're useful to have. They are simply a list of current issues you have with the change process and the things you worry might go wrong. There's no need to over engineer this, especially if your change is small. If you plan to increase your family unit by one, let's say buying a goldfish, then your issues might be: I currently have no bowl, fish food or a goldfish. These can be remedied through the actions in your plan.

Your risks might be: the goldfish dies, but don't we all eventually? You tip over the bowl accidentally or you forget to feed the goldfish before going away. You can mitigate these potential risks by creating additional actions. These could be giving your neighbour a key and asking them to feed the goldfish. You could also locate the bowl in a less precarious place, just before you leave.

Exercise 19: Creating Risk and Issues registers

Your task is now to write up a risks and issues register, similar to the one below. Just create one list for risks and one for issues. By thinking these through in advance you'll anticipate problems. It also means you may end up avoiding them all together.

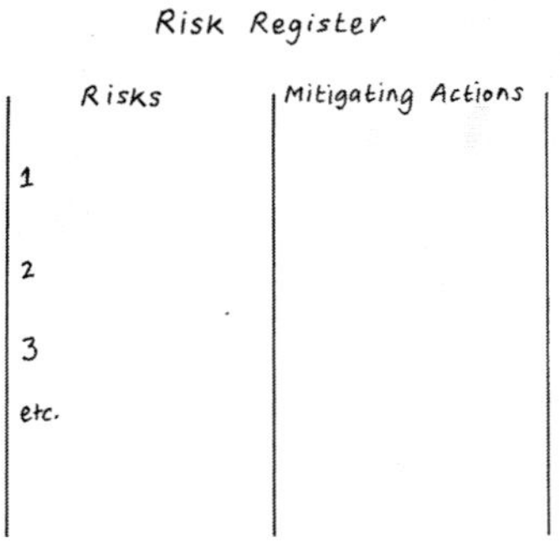

Risk Register

Risks   Mitigating Actions

1

2

3

etc.

Diagram 17 (previous): Risk register

The above exercise can help with a process devised by Peter Gollwitzer, a German professor of psychology who worked at New York University. It's called *If-Then* planning, which neatly builds on the risk and issues registers. It's a simple way to help you successfully implement your goals. You can do any internet search to find the many ways people use *If-Then* planning.

Once you've been through steps one to three, then you'll have your WHY,

WHERE, WHICH, WHAT and HOW. In this chapter we've focused on WHO and WHEN. At this point you should have a specific goal which you can visualise clearly, along with SMART measures. Now review your risk and issues registers to be clear about all the obstacles that might get in your way. It will also help you think through all the actions you might take. If you can't think of many risks or issues you can always bring in a *Critical Friend* who can help you think of more!

Now, spend time thinking about each of the risks or issues. We'll use a couple of examples to bring it alive. I'll use a simple one to begin with. Let's say I'm worried I might feel overwhelmed by all the actions I want to make. The **If** piece of this example is *If I feel overwhelmed.* The **Then** part of the **If-Then** equation could be one of the following: I'll take a break from the work by going for a short work; or call my accountability buddy to share how I'm feeling; or pause for 10 minutes and review how far I've progressed, which will show me how much I have already achieved.

Here is another example of getting back into running. Let's say the risk is that the alarm goes off at 6am. I know I will want to turn it off, roll over and go back to sleep. But I also know I want to get fitter. So, the **Then** part of the *If-Then* equation could be: have another alarm set the other side of the room; or tell my partner I want them to persuade me out of bed; or ask a friend to ring the doorbell at 6.30am etc. **If** I don't want to get up, **Then** I have some solutions to help me. Having already thought through how I might tackle these issues, I'm more likely to get over the challenges.

In fact, planning how we'll tackle issues has been found to really help us. Peter Gollwitzer and Paschal Sheeran[92] ran a meta-analysis, which is simply putting a lot of different studies together to check their overall results. Reviewing over 90 studies showed them that *If-Then* planning works with different types of goals, from exercise, to studying, to changing thoughts. They found that many more people achieved their goals after doing *If-Then* planning.

Exercise 20: Allocating Resources

Allocating resources is like putting together a team at school (soccer, baseball, spelling bee). Of course, you'll want the best resources working with you and you need them in the right place in the field or on the court. So, spend some time going through your project plan and allocating resources to each action. Let's say you want to learn the bassoon. You'll need to buy or rent one, find a teacher, clear your diary an evening a week, find others who play the instrument (if you fancy being in a bassoon quartet), allocate money for lessons and possibly soundproof your house.

Resources might be money, family, carpenter, bassoon shop and teacher. As you progress through your *Bassoon Project* it might lead to additional actions which you'd add to your project plan, e.g., finding a carpenter and buying insulation for the walls, bribing your family so they leave the house one evening each week and locating a group called *Bassooner or Later.*

———

Now we're on the home stretch for WHO and WHEN. Time to schedule in rewards. There are two ways to look at this. One is making the actions pleasurable in themselves. The second is rewarding yourself once you've completed an action. In *Atomic Habits*[93], James Clear says that we're more likely to repeat a behaviour when the experience is satisfying. He talks about feeling satisfied and experiencing good tastes and that we need these incentives, however small. For example, it's more likely we'll wash our hands if the soap smells nice and lathers well. If it feels good, then we're more likely to do it again. Pleasure teaches our brains that this behaviour is worth repeating. So, try to bring in enjoyable parts to your actions.

An additional way is to celebrate your wins as you make progress. This is a *whatever-floats-your boat* moment. It's good to celebrate with people who understand (and agree with) what you are doing. You may need to look for cheerleaders outside your circle. Start by rewarding yourself for the smallest of wins. Look out for the tiniest of signs that you're taking action, that you're moving forward. As you progress, you can reward yourself for bigger wins. But at the start be kind to yourself. You'll create more momentum if you start out rewarding yourself for small steps. This will strengthen your new behaviours. Here is a list of the ways I reward myself: salted pretzels (I'm easily pleased), organising vacations with friends (a slightly more expensive reward than pretzels), buying books, congratulating myself (in my head but sometimes out loud as well), playing music loudly when I'm alone in the house, a bubble bath, then PJs/sitting under blankets on the sofa, watching trashy TV.

OK, that's it, we're done on rewards. You're on your own on this one. Go forth and select whatever makes you happy.

———

Another action to take is keeping your project plan front of mind. You can print it out and put it on a cork board at home or somewhere prominent at work. Or keep it in a digital format and save it somewhere obvious on your PC/laptop, as it is important that you see it every day. Keep checking in with your project plan to see how you're doing and update it when things shift around, which they will.

One note of caution before we bring this to a close. It's entirely possible to *project plan yourself to death*. I have seen it with my very own eyes. Management Consultants strewn around a client's office at 1am, expired through too much project managing. A common phrase is, *perfect is the enemy of the good*. Shakespeare wrote this in his play, *King Lear*: "Striving to better, often we mar what's well" and Chinese philosopher Confucius is said to have written: "Better a diamond with a flaw than a pebble without."

I'd also like to mention time here. It's a topic that came up 28 times in the interviews. People spoke about 'time speeding up as they got older', 'wanting to turn the clock back'. Worries they were 'getting too old to have children', or failing to 'hit their achievements or milestones' in time. One way to increase your stress about the marching of time is to spend time procrastinating.

Waiting for the right time, or until our ideas are just right, is a form of self-sabotage. It can be a way of procrastinating, using planning as a way to put things off. You may be feeling rather pleased with yourself as you re-work your plan for the 18th time with colour co-ordinated boxes and comments sections. But whilst it appears as though you're moving forward... you're not. You're putting off the real work and this action is a delaying tactic. You can't change your life by fiddling around with a spreadsheet and spending so long staring at your screen will just give you tired eyes and a sore head. If this is you, then please shut the laptop and try out one of your actions instead!

Dr Timothy Pychyl works at the Department of Psychology at Carleton University. He also studies procrastination. In conversation with Christian Jarrett on the British Psychological Society's podcast[94], he said that if our goals don't align with our values, or who we feel we are, then we're more likely to procrastinate. Remember the values work we did in chapter eight? Why not go back and check that your goals are aligned with your values, that way you're less likely to put things off.

Procrastination can also be about how much you link your performance with your self-worth. If you're achievement oriented, then there will be times when your fear of failure collides with your desire to perform. Procrastination is a coping strategy for dealing with these competing needs: performance (= our self-worth) vs. fear of failure (= potential to dent our self-worth).

A way to work on procrastination is to be aware of the performance/self-worth relationship that you have. You might like to work on your inner voice and what you tell yourself about needing to succeed. For example, "I will do my very best and it won't be perfect and that's OK." You might also like to try some self-affirmations which we covered in chapter eight and in Appendix A. Finally, try thinking about what you're running away from (fear of failure) versus what you might be running towards (a desire to move forwards and take action or learn new skills etc).

Just before you go, learning theory says that one way to make progress is to reflect on what you've just read. So, thinking about this chapter, why not ask yourself: what did I already know? What was new in this chapter? What did I enjoy reading about? What was less interesting? How will I put all these actions into practice?

—

We're at the end of the chapter, so this is what we covered:

- We started talking about action and then moved on to the WHOs.
- Then the exercise reviewing our WHY, WHERE, SMART goals etc.
- There was a section on the different types of project plans you can set up, plus how to prioritise actions and break bigger ones down into smaller chunks.
- We also looked at *Circadian Rhythms*, not a Jazz band, but the times in the day when it's best to do different types of actions for our project.
- There was a discussion about risks/issues and an exercise to think through your own.
- We also discussed allocating resources to the different parts of our project, plus ways to reward progress and congratulate ourselves on how much we have already achieved.

The next chapter is on experimentation: how to try things out and decide what we like, what works and what is a bit of a damp squib – that's a colloquialism for disappointing, if you're wondering.

Chapter 14

In January 2000 I made a New Year's resolution to spend more time with my parents. I came up with a plan; once a month I would invite one of them to have dinner with me in London. To make it more piquant (it was food after all) I decided to choose a restaurant based on three things: 1) We hadn't been to it before, 2) we'd pick food we wouldn't normally eat and 3) we'd work our way through the alphabet. Back then we all had a lot more time on our hands!

We started with A, aiming for Z, so our trip around food-land was in this order over the months: Austrian, Belgian, Chilean, Danish, Egyptian, Finnish, Greek. This last restaurant was a cheat, as there weren't any Guyanese, Gambian or Guatemalan restaurants in London at the time. Then we tried Hungarian, Indonesian, Jordanian, Korean food... my memory fails at this point. I know we made it to *S* for Swedish though before it all petered out.

It was lovely experimenting with food and broadening our horizons, learning a bit more about each country and exploring different parts of London. It was silly and frivolous which was nice, because life can be a bit too serious at times. Not every meal was a success. There was some that weren't so tasty and others eventful. I learned that I liked Korean food but was a bit more *meh* about raw pickled herring. My memory of Hungarian food is a little hazy, overprinted as it was, by an incident on the night. The chef stormed out with a meat cleaver, shouting at a diner who refused to pay. I can't recall the food. It could have been lovely.

Why am I sharing this story? Well, it's to reinforce the point that we can't be sure we **will** or **won't** like something until we give it a go. You might wonder if Lebanese cuisine is delicious. You could ask around, read a cookbook, or watch a documentary on the country. Will any of these guarantee you will like Lebanese food? Of course not. The only way to **work** that out is to **try** it out. Lebanese food is a definite yes for, me by the way.

It's no different with any change process you're going through. Let's say you want to move to a new city, or swap countries. How will you know if it's sleepless in Seattle or good morning Vietnam unless you've been there? Perhaps you want to meet a romantic partner, but spend all your time swiping left. Without meeting them how will you know? They will just be a fantasy. And the problem with fantasies is they're only loosely connected with reality.

> Trust your intuition… also build a plan and act according to your intuition. And if you are risk averse, then build the plan the way that you can test it out. — Kira (interviewee)

This chapter is about taking a small spoonful of dessert, just to see if it tastes good. It will help the confused, the uncertain, the unsure. Anyone who is thinking, "I'm still not clear about WHERE my destination is, so I need to try some things out." Experimentation is useful for everyone else too, even if you're clear about where you're heading. That's because the path ahead will never be straight. How will you know which actions have the greatest impact, or which have none at all unless… you try?

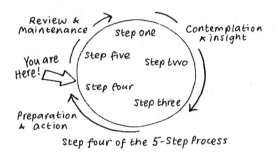

Step four of the 5-Step Process

Diagram 18: Step four of the 5-Step Process

Here are the five steps in the process once more to remind you:

Step one: WHY and WHERE (purpose and destination)
Step two: WHICH (animal, i.e. the distance to travel)
Step three: WHAT and HOW (the type of change)
Step four: WHO and WHEN (planning action/experimentation). We're here!
Step five: HOW MUCH and HOW WELL (reviewing and evaluating progress)

I'll give you another example from my Management Consulting days. Have you heard of Design Thinking (DT)? This is a process that designers follow to improve consumer products. It's been used for years to design products for the world's leading brands like Apple, Google, Samsung and GE. It's gaining in popularity now, so is also used in many other organisations. In fact, you can study it at university as well. We covered being outside the box earlier and DT is often referred to as *outside the box thinking,* because designers use it to develop new ways of problem solving. It's all about experimenting and iterating ideas, and of course, being open to things going wrong.

> ❝ Freedom is not worth having if it does not include the freedom to make mistakes. — Mahatma Gandhi

When designers work with DT they use the results to assess and review their initial assumptions, identify new insights and create alternative solutions. This just means better results come from trying things out, testing what works, stopping what doesn't and re-orientating when necessary; things we can all use when we're going through a change in life.

Escape The City[95] is a global community, a movement of people who write on their website that life is short, so we need to stop doing the things that we don't find meaningful. If your change is around career, then you might want to check them out. *Escape The City* are big on experimentation and iteration. They say that to successfully shift we need to try things out and test them. Next, we'll turn to experimentation stories from some of the interviewees.

———

First, we'll meet Sara who is in her late 30s. When she was younger, she studied event management, but this didn't bring her the career she hoped for. "I ended up in the industry but in hindsight, it didn't really feel like the course provided me with a great career opportunity. I wanted a profession and I ended up working in admin in events." As she put it, she "floated" from role to role and then decided to switch career in her mid 20s. "I did a fashion clothing tech course. I put myself through university again but realised it wasn't really what I wanted to do. What I should have done was tested it whereas I jumped in with my head-first."

Karen is 41 and a play therapist who works with children. She says this about experimentation and how to get unstuck. "I'm on one of my new mentality things and I'm just going to say yes to most things and try it and see." In the past she's been hit by inertia and, "Wasted a lot of years with indecision and not taking action... I'd be in a different place now if I'd done it sooner. And avoided a lot of anguish. You're never stuck, not really. You just think you are."

❝ Nothing will ever be attempted if all possible objections must first be overcome. — Samuel Johnson (poet, playwright, essayist)

This is Mark from Germany, who isn't so good at experimentation. "Before I launch into something, I do quite a lot of research, probably far too much." He knows he needs to "reduce the amount of analysis and just try out things at a faster pace, just test things out." He says that the whole point is to fail fast. "Try things quickly with little faffing so you get an answer: good or bad. Then adjust from there going forward. Lots of little loops."

Mark had injured his foot tripping over the family rabbit. It sounds like a punchline to a joke, but it meant he couldn't ski, do mountaineering or battle re-enactments, all the things he liked to do in his spare time. So, he decided to find something he could do whilst he had a broken foot. He landed on jewellery making. "I was probably wrong on how I approached the whole jewellery making thing." He watched some videos and immediately launched himself in. "I should have tried it in smaller experimental loops. Even though it worked out OK and I enjoy it." His advice to other people? "Try to do these little projects. It's the right way to go about it. All sorts of things whether that's life, hobbies, jobs, it doesn't really matter."

Suzanne was having a difficult time in her life and decided to get away to Scotland with a good friend. "It was one of the best holidays I've ever had because I suddenly realised all my needs were being met in those 10 days in the camper van." She felt a real sense of identity that she hadn't had for ages. "Fooling around with someone you get on with and have a connection with. Someone who laughs at your stupid jokes and who thinks you're funny." Even being confined in a small space wasn't a problem. "You're part of a team. You have to keep that camper van running when there's a problem. The freedom of driving and movement – I found it quite soothing." If Suzanne hadn't tried her holiday on wheels, she wouldn't have known that liberty was such an important focus for her life.

Finally, Misha, who thinks we need a mind-set shift on all of this. "We're always told that you should know everything. Work, how to look after your children, how to build a strong relationship. Sometimes we just don't and I think that's the thing. You make mistakes, but it's how you take those mistakes and learn from them." She prefers it when people are honest about this. "I think, 'oh my God, that's really cool, that you're actually saying that out loud, the fact that you don't know'… I think people don't say often enough. I don't hear often enough that I don't know what the answer is. I just know that I don't want this. I don't know what it is I do want, but I want to go and find out."

Hmn… unexpected step. Useful to know…

John Krumboltz[96] was a professor of education and psychology at Stanford University who developed the *Planned Happenstance Learning Theory*. Happenstance just means something happening due to chance. It says that we need to actively embrace unplanned events and be responsive to the unpredictable twists and turns of life. If you break down the name of the theory it means being **planned**, deciding what to do and putting those actions into place; **happen**, that things occur by chance and are often unpredictable; and **stance**, our attitude to this will really help us, for example, being open to chance and focusing on planning, rather than plans, which we talked about before.

Exercise 21: Building your Happenstance Muscles

Krumboltz outlines five qualities that will help us to deal with happenstance: curiosity, persistence, flexibility, optimism and willingness to take risks. So, how can you make the most of *Planned Happenstance* in your life?

To build your happenstance muscles, why not ask yourself some of these questions?

- What is my normal approach to life? Am I flexible or more rigid?
- When I've come across challenges before, how have I recovered/come out stronger?
- How can I open myself to new ideas and opportunities?
- What can I do to take advantage of events I haven't planned for?
- What would happen if I converted, *"I can't"* into *"can I?"*
- What am I naturally curious about, that can be turned into an experiment?
- Which of my interests can I follow?

- How can I turn unexpected events, chance meetings, phones calls into a further action?
- How can I get involved with activities, learning and developing skills?

———

Another thought from *Escape The City* in their ebook is that we spend too much time researching and naval gazing and not actually moving to action. Reflection is important because it helps us head in the right direction. But at some point, we need to take the first steps, even though we won't be certain of our precise destination. So, how can you boldly engage with the world yourself? What steps can you take to experiment and try things out? Whilst *Escape the City* focuses their attention on career change, the same principles apply to any shift you want to go through. Here are some ideas that I have for you:

- Try to create a series of small projects, rather than pushing for one large change all at once.
- See each project as an experiment. It doesn't matter if it works or not. It's all useful knowledge that you're gathering, that will help you keep your ship heading in the right direction.
- You might find yourself in *flow*[97] whilst you're trying this. You'll know it if you are since you'll be totally immersed in the project and time will go by fast. On the other hand, you may find it hard, dislike the work and you can't wait for it to finish! Neither is good or bad. It's just information that will help you.
- Sometimes we may term it *failing,* but failing isn't failing at all. What we need to do is reframe these situations. See them as a way of gathering information. I'll share other peoples' experiments later, projects that helped them to pivot their change.
- You don't have to be fully prepared before you start. Just try small steps, little things to see how you feel. In fact, over-preparing is just a form of procrastination. This is what Marcia says. "I know I want to change but I don't know what I want to do next. I just overthink things and don't really act. So, my issue now is act."
- Don't invest too much money or time at the start. Only ramp things up when you have more certainty and it feels less of a risk.
- That said, if you have a cast-iron certainty about your WHERE, your end destination, or you're clear how you want to proceed, then ignore this chapter (and me) and move on!

> You're not going to find the perfect solution. Let go of the idea of the right answer. Just play, be messy, make mistakes… the fastest way to learning is failing. The fastest way to learning is making a mistake. — Tim (interviewee)

Finally, let's return to the idea of your WHICH. This is the distance you need to travel and is brought alive by which type of animal you need to be in this shift. Whether you're a fish (small iterations) a grasshopper (willing to take bigger leaps) or a bird (up for all-out change). In an earlier chapter we covered how close your personality fits with the size of the change. If there's a match, it makes things easier, but if you are farther apart, it may take more time.

The main focus is not that this match will stop your change happening. It's about being realistic over how long it will take, or how manageable the project will be. You may remember that I suggested two options if you find yourself in this situation:

1) Stretch out your timeframe

Try to reduce your expectations of what you can achieve in the time. If you like to take smaller steps, then it will take longer. Why not go back to chapter 13 and review your project plan. Are your deadlines achievable? Look at your SMART goals again. Is it possible to get the work done in this time?

If you're someone (like me) who wants to run fast at new projects, then try to be patient and slow things down. You'll need to extend your timeframe, expect this project to take longer. You'll reduce the size of your steps and the pace at which you take them, so of course, your goals will stretch further out.

Think about what is driving your need for speed. Is it something you want to achieve, or are you doing it to prove yourself to others? Maybe try reviewing your WHY and WHERE again. Who are you making this change for? Is it really for you? Try to be kind to yourself. If this shift is going to be sustainable, then you'll need to be patient and be aware it will take longer than you had planned. Then you won't be disappointed.

2) Reduce the size of the change you want to make

Are you biting off more than you can chew? Let's say you're struggling with your finances and you want to turn this around. You want to increase your income, reduce your spending, sort out your relationship with money and generally organise your life. That's a lot to work on all at once!

Could you lower your expectations about what you can tackle? Start with getting your bills in order. Aim to sort those out in a month and reward yourself when you hit that goal. Then, aim to look at your income/salary, spending a few months benchmarking what others make in the same position, preparing for a chat with your manager about a possible pay-rise and then having that conversation. Reward yourself again with something that will make you happy. Only now aim to tackle your relationship with money. And, if you need to, perhaps work with a coach, counsellor or therapist.

If you are someone who works too fast and expects too much, then it will be better to cut your change project into smaller chunks. If you are over-ambitious, taking on too much will mean you're more likely to give up. Like everything in this chapter, it's all about experimentation, so try out smaller steps to see if you can move forward. Momentum can be self-perpetuating – the more progress you make, the more likely you'll want to continue. It's better to aim for a less ambitious project, to achieve a smaller part of your overall goal, than to aim for the moon and miss it.

———

That's us done with this chapter; it's a shorter one than some, as ultimately what and how you experiment is entirely up to you. In the next chapter we'll cover how you can review your change projects to see what's working and what is not: HOW MUCH and HOW WELL. For the moment let's summarise the key ideas that we talked about in this chapter:

- We discussed how there is no substitute for trying things out. How will you know if you don't give it a go?
- We covered *Design Thinking* because this is a way to encourage us to try, test, pivot, iterate actions whilst going through change. It's a great way to check out what's working and what's not so hot.
- There were quite a few quotes and stories from the participants about how they managed to experiment. Plus, those situations where they didn't experiment enough.
- We looked at a number of ways you could experiment and try things out for yourself.
- There was also a discussion about setting expectations if your WHICH is a bit muddled – you want to make a big change, but you're used to taking things slowly.
- We also looked at those who like to run too fast and how it makes sense to take a bit more time to reflect and take things slowly.

The next chapter is on HOW MUCH and HOW WELL – how we can assess our progress and work out how well we're doing.

Chapter 15

Have you ever built a sandcastle on a beach, or in a sandpit? Perhaps you were engrossed in making turrets and digging out the moat. Maybe you forgot to stop and check if the structure was straight, lost in the joy of it, until the sandcastle collapsed under the weight of shells you piled on top.

We can get so involved in our change projects, enjoying the momentum, deep in concentration, that the idea of stopping, stepping back and reflecting can pass us by. This chapter is a reminder to do just that. This is the final step in the 5-Step Process: HOW MUCH and HOW WELL. We're now in the third and last phase of your journey, review and maintenance.

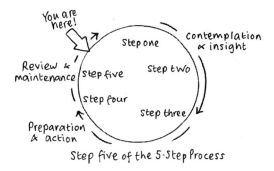

Step five of the 5-Step Process

Diagram 19: Step five of the 5-Step Process

Here are the five steps in the process one more time:

Step one: WHY and WHERE (purpose and destination)
Step two: WHICH (animal, i.e. the distance to travel)
Step three: WHAT and HOW (the type of change)
Step four: WHO and WHEN (planning action and experimentation)
Step five: HOW MUCH and HOW WELL (reviewing and evaluating progress). Hurray we're here!

HOW MUCH and HOW WELL is also about checking what's working (and doing more of it) and checking what isn't (and doing less of that). The Project Management Institute says there are five phases to any project: conception/ initiation, planning, execution, performance and monitoring, then close. This chapter is all about performance and monitoring.

In his book *Changeology*[98], Professor John Norcross writes about actions that will help you start or speed up change. This includes monitoring and logging progress, setting and honouring goals, rewarding yourself and ensuring your environment will support, not impede, your progress. HOW MUCH and HOW WELL is my version of this. I've included two ways to evaluate progress: HOW MUCH, which is the **quantity** of the change and HOW WELL, which is the **quality**. Sometimes you need to switch between the two to assess your progress in a more nuanced way.

———

Like many people I put on weight during the first 18 months of the global pandemic. When the level of the virus reduced in the second autumn my husband and I went on a short break to Scotland. It was exciting, our first time away since Covid-19 had reared its ugly head. We ate, we drank, we drove, we sang, we visited places and we argued... much like any other holiday. The difference was that by the end of the holiday I couldn't look at myself in the mirror. Anyone familiar with a Scottish Breakfast knows that it's a thing of beauty. It's also a plate of cholesterol, calories and (after one every day for a week) serves up another dress size.

When I returned, I realised things needed to change. I'd been putting on weight for a year. I wasn't healthy, I didn't like the way I looked, I puffed when I walked up hills and my zips didn't close on my jeans. It was time to lose weight and get fit. I chose a low carbohydrate and low sugar diet because I'd tried something similar before and people swore by it. This diet involved *Time Restricted Eating* – consuming food over no more than 12 hours a day, as well as reducing calories. It also advised doing exercise, but I was too busy to do that part.

A week in and I paused to check my progress. The expectation was I'd lose 2–3 pounds or 1–1.3kg a week. Using the last step in my 5-Step Process I assessed HOW MUCH I'd lost. Disappointingly I hadn't lost any weight at all. Where was I going wrong?

Firstly, I wasn't following the diet's guidelines, I was eating the same amount each day, but in two meals rather than three. Secondly, I didn't know if I'd lost weight, I just thought I looked about the same. The problem was that I hadn't weighed myself at the beginning because our scales had stopped working. Assessing progress in your change project is the same as standing on scales.

You need to work out where you are before you start.

Tip number 1: Baseline. Know your weight before you begin a weight loss programme (note to self). Know where you are before you start a change project (note to everyone else).

I bought batteries for the scales and started again. But the second week wasn't any better. The scales were working fine, I just wasn't losing weight. My husband suggested I tried on some clothes instead. It was a joyful moment as I could just close the zip on jeans I hadn't worn in months. I wasn't losing weight, but I was losing mass.

Tip number 2: Different ratings. Use multiple tools to measure progress.

I added a measuring tape to my assessment tools so I could check my circumference as well as my weight. Using different measures means we're more likely to pick up smaller steps in our progress. I'm currently working with a coaching client on this very topic.

From then on it was great for six weeks. I began to feel lighter, enjoying hopping up and down the three floors in our house. But then I hit another roadblock and my weight loss ground to a halt. I realised I wasn't following all the guidelines. I wasn't doing any exercise. I started with short HIIT sessions each morning and made sure I walked every day. Find out more about HIIT on the *Swim Jump, Fly*[99] website.

Tip number 3: Bypass roadblocks. If progress stalls find a different route.

As well as HOW MUCH, I also focused on HOW WELL. Weight loss was the HOW MUCH. How I was feeling (physically and mentally) was HOW WELL. Assessing both is important, as this can encourage ourselves, especially if we're making small, but powerful shifts in our change journey. Quality can often be a better scorekeeper than quantity.

Tip number 4: Different lenses. Focus on quality and quantity, for more nuance.

Over time the speed of my weight loss slowed, but my wellbeing continued to increase. On Zoom calls people commented that my skin looked better and I seemed to be more my old self (telling bad jokes). I also slept better and seemed to have a clearer mind. As well as assessing weight and mass, I now included wellbeing. The way I was capturing these measurements was via me and other people. So, here is another tip:

Tip number 5: Internal and external. Measure yourself and ask others what they see.

One final area to focus on is balancing what's going well with what isn't. It's easy to pay attention to what we haven't achieved and to look at the negative. It's a human trait to focus more on what's going wrong, rather than what's going right. It's called *negativity bias* and it means we don't just register negative events more often, we also dwell on them much longer.

This may be down to evolution. It would have paid dividends to focus on dangerous threats, since it would have been a life-or-death situation. If you were focused on danger your descendants would thank you. But if you only looked out for the positives, you'd be lunch for a Sabre-Toothed tiger, so there would be no descendants to pat you on the back.

In my case *negative bias* was when I poked at my belly fat and got despondent, rather than looking at other ways I was making progress. As I became kinder to myself, I tried on clothes I hadn't worn for years and enjoyed the satisfaction of my hard work taking effect.

Tip number 6: The Good, The Bad and The Ugly. Review what is going well as often as what isn't.

"ok, it's risen – what else?"

Remember Alexander who used to work on the oil rigs? He knows all about this. "As soon as something is taken care of I don't congratulate myself about it or think, 'Oh, that's good I've got this, or that's good I've got that.'" Instead, he moves straight back onto what's missing, rather than taking time to celebrate what's going well. "I have my eyes on the horizon, saying, 'Well I want to be happy with this, or want to be better at that. Or I want to have a girlfriend that I love. Or I want to have children, or I want a big house out in the countryside.'"

Alexander beats himself up too: "It's a double whammy as well as looking at the future saying, 'this is what I want.' I spend an awful lot of time looking to the past going, 'Why didn't you do that? This was stupid. You shouldn't have done that. I wish I'd done this earlier. Or I should have chosen a different career 10 years ago.'"

I'll pull out another tool from my Management Consulting/psychology kit bag – *Appreciative Enquiry*. Developed by David Cooperider[100] and Suresh Srivastva in the 1990s, it was developed for organisational change but can be applied to individuals too. It basically goes like this: if we just look for the things that aren't working and problems to be solved, then all we'll come up with is how to fix issues. But if we focus on our core strengths we can build on the areas where we've succeeded and use our skills. This can be helpful when we're planning for the future.

So, focusing on what's going well, is just as important as working out what isn't. It's a useful mindset shift to take if you want to succeed in your change project. Try to beat yourself up less about apparent failures. Instead, see them as opportunities to gather information about your situation and where you might head to next. Also, be aware that we're more likely to focus on incomplete tasks. This is the *Zeigarnik Effect* [101]. It happens when we're interrupted in our work. The theory says that we'll remember these unfinished tasks better than the ones we completed.

Balance your focus on what you haven't achieved with congratulating yourself on what is going well. Reorient from those areas in your life that aren't going right to those you don't even notice anymore, because you take them for granted. Try to use multiple motivation strategies from identifying supporters; people cheering on the side lines, to rewarding yourself with something that makes you happy. You might even like to practice gratitude, which is the positive emotion we feel after receiving something valuable.

People who are grateful feel happier, have a greater sense of connectedness to others, greater life satisfaction and an improved sense of wellbeing. Why not try out the gratitude exercise in Appendix A? Finally, make sure you're using the strengths and values that you gathered earlier on. These will help energise you and support you to push ahead.

it's important to take joy from the little things — particularly if you never ever get any of the big things...

Here is some advice from one of my participants, Steve: "I think people get too focused on their weaknesses and how to address them, rather than being comfortable in their own skin... I worked for 32 years before I realised what I'm really good at. It's better to just focus on strengths, than trying to fit in." He suggests you "understand your strengths, explore your strengths, develop your strengths. It's a much better use of your time and energy than trying to plug the gaps." He also says focus on what you enjoy. "You could be much happier at work... just by working on something that's closer to what motivates you. Something that really uses your strengths."

I emailed Smita, another interviewee, five months after our conversation. I wanted to find out how she was doing, so I sent her a list of questions to help her reflect on her progress. Here are some of her responses:
• "I am more aware of my emotions and trigger points on most days."
• "I make an action plan at the beginning of every week using a list making app and allotting time (pomodoro technique) for every task. This helps me keep in check my urge to boil the ocean for every small task and keep realistic goals."
• "Movement at regular intervals is essential to spark creativity and work with focus. I need to make an intentional effort to stand up and move about before starting on a task. Especially true on the weekends."
• "Keep reaching out to people outside your reality bubble. For me this has been the single most important tool so far."
• In response to my list of questions she said: "It was good to do this exercise, kind of like a mini post-mortem review of the last few months."

Earlier I mentioned that I've been helping a coaching client to measure her progress. Juana (not her real name) has been making a big shift in her life. She grew up in Mexico and her family were focused and hardworking, so she made sure to always do her best always pushing herself. She's a perfectionist and always believes she can do better. Juana is never easy on herself.

Juana made it to the top of the corporate ladder, but now wants to do something more meaningful and less stressful. She has therefore been setting up her own business. Whilst it has only been a short amount of time, she's beating herself up about not doing better. One of the things we're working on is a leader board to measure her progress. In the past she focused on new business and income, but the levels of both of these were low, because the business was still in its infancy. This made Juana feel despondent, since she wasn't making as much progress as she wanted.

Instead, we are widening the number of activities Juana is measuring, which include progress on:
a) The level of effort she put into the work/hours she is working.
b) Setting up foundations for her business (website, email, mailing lists).
c) Networking and building contacts in her new field.
d) Increasing skills in new areas.
e) Growing her awareness of the way she works best etc.

This means she can see real progress in certain areas (and can measure how hard she is working). Even if it hasn't resulted in more sales and income from her new business… yet!

This is what one my interviwees, Walter, said about HOW MUCH and HOW WELL. I asked him how his business was doing. "I'm looking to close the dog business, but not because COVID has closed it." He was shutting it down because he'd started a new business and it was taking off. "I started in February and I swear to God, it's a grand and half a week I'm pulling in since February."

On both counts (HOW MUCH and HOW WELL) Walter was exceeding his expectations. He was making money and enjoying himself. This was particularly encouraging as he'd launched the new business during the pandemic lockdown. "I mean what the hell? It's like a godsend… It's erupted. I just got a friend to build a website now and I can't stop the money coming in. This is not me – these things don't happen to me."

Another participant is Fola who is 45, Nigerian, and works in Human Resources. She is going through a huge shift. Sadly, both her parents died in quick succession and she's trying to re-adjust her life. "One thing has helped and this insight came from a conversation with a doctor friend. They said to look at all the spheres of my life and evaluate how I'm doing on those various spheres." Fola says that it's important not to give too much weight to one aspect of life, such as work, "Not to give it more weight than it deserves. And contemplate or realise what's going on in the other spheres. If your health is at risk, then your work or your career shrinks in proportion to everything else. So, I guess it's appreciating what's going well in my life."

Sometimes HOW MUCH and HOW WELL isn't just a line on a project plan. It can also be connecting with others to share how we're feeling. One of the questions I asked my interviewees was what they thought about our conversation. This is from Christine, who is in her early 40s: "Really interesting. Sometimes you don't always reflect on where you've got to. Sometimes you can feel like you're not actually making any progress. Or sometimes you can think you're making lots of progress and you're not." She doesn't often take time to reflect "and talk about why I've made some of the choices that I have. Or even thought about the support I looked for."

This is what another person said: "It's been really useful for me to get a bit of perspective again. I live in my head a lot and it's a bit of a jungle in there at the moment… It has helped me to articulate things. Cleared out the cobwebs and gave me a bit more clarity, which I've been lacking. It's been really interesting and has given me a bit more positivity. Together with clear guidance on what I do need to keep prioritising, making sure there are things I'm doing every day."

The conversations I was having were semi-structured interviews on the telephone between strangers. So, you can imagine how much more powerful a conversation with a friend could be! Here is some more feedback about the interviews I ran:

- "It's nice to feel heard and someone's interested. Hearing your responses – that my story is not completely different to other people's and that this is something other people struggle with." — Karen
- "It's been really helpful to try and convey exactly what's going on in my head. A lot came out – things that I'd been thinking about that I haven't actually verbalised before." — Steven
- "Like a mini coaching session, allowing me to process some of the stuff that has happened." — John
- "That discussion was like take a step back from the situation and look at this from a little bit of distance." — Iwone
- "It was like a conversation, which I really appreciated... and together we walked around and looked at it from a few different directions... I really appreciated it. It was easy and helpful." — Matt

Brené Brown[102] says that true listening isn't trying to make things better, it's about making a good connection. Thich Nhat Hanh[103] was a Vietnamese Buddhist monk, peace activist, author, poet and teacher who was still writing into his 90s. He said deep listening is relieving the suffering of another person by helping them empty their heart. So why not try to find others who will deeply listen to you? It could really help you make a shift in your life. Now it's over to you to assess your progress. Here is another exercise you can do.

Exercise 22: Checking progress using HOW MUCH and HOW WELL

1) First of all, make sure you benchmark where you are now before you get going. Measuring what you're starting with is key, otherwise it'll be hard to check your progress.

2) Next, create a scoring system from least good to the best you could ever do. You might like to do it in four steps where **1** is not very good, **2** is OK, **3** is quite good and **4** is amazing. Just use whatever words work for you. All you're doing here is creating a way of scoring yourself on how you are improving. For example, perhaps you want to increase the amount of time you socialise. In week one you might give yourself a **1** if you half-heartedly messaged a friend and then didn't follow it up. Maybe you worked harder the next week and contacted quite a few people. You also plucked up the courage to join a dance class and took up an invitation to have dinner with a neighbour. Then you might score yourself a **4**. Each week just keep measuring how you're doing so you can see progress.

3) If you want to show more precise progress then you can create a leader board of different aspects of your project. Let's say on you want to increase your confidence when you're out socialising. If you just focused on a measurement called *confidence*, then it will be:
• Hard to measure.
• Contextually based.
• May take some time to show improvement.

Instead, you could create a number of measures like these:
a) Background research on building confidence.
b) Completing exercises to increase assertiveness levels whilst shopping.
c) External measures e.g. asking friends to rate your improvements over time.
d) Different types of people you talked to last week.
e) The number of times you stretched yourself outside your comfort zone etc.

Try to focus on internal and external measures of success. Include different types of measures and measuring tools, such as time, distance, frequency, quality, quantity etc.

4) Logging progress is important. We'll continue with the example of building your confidence:

Week 1:
a) Your background research was excellent. You read an article, watched a TED talk and looked up a course on public speaking and started reading a book on confidence. You give yourself a **4**.
b-e) You didn't do any further actions so you'll give yourself a **1** for all the other measures.

Week 2:
By now you can see real improvement:
a) You finished reading the book, giving yourself a rating of **4** as you learned some good techniques.
b) You actively sought out a salesperson in a shop when you couldn't find what you were looking for, but in another shop you left quickly because you were nervous. You'll give yourself a **2**.
c) You spoke to a work friend about your confidence levels and how you'd like them to give you feedback on how you are doing. This took courage so you'll give yourself a **4**.
c) The same person introduced you to a group of work colleagues at a networking

event. You spoke to one person so you'll give yourself a **3**. And so on…

5) Don't forget to set up rewards for hitting your targets. These can be little (pretzels) or large (holidays). Ideally set small goals at the start to encourage yourself and offer yourself small rewards when you have hit your goals. As you progress, stretch your targets and increase the size of your rewards in line with these bigger goals. Some people like to do accumulators: hit Y number of goals over X amount of time and get Z size of rewards.

6) The last stage of this phase is maintenance. You may need to give yourself a few weeks to identify whether your project is working out. We used to be told that it takes three weeks to form a habit… actually it's a bit more. According to research by psychologist Dr Phillippa Lally[104] and others it's more like two months, or 66 days if you want to be precise. If your project is going well, just keep doing what you're doing, maintaining your actions, moving closer to completing your goal. Give yourself rewards each time you hit an action, as this will help you continue your actions and behaviours.

7) However, if you review your project and find it isn't working out as you had hoped, then it's time to pause. Now it's helpful to reflect on your WHY and your WHERE again, step one of the 5-Step Process. Ask yourself why you're doing this work and where you'd like to end up. It's very likely you've done a lot of foundational work, so much of the action is already under your belt!

Don't worry if this is you. This stage is all part of the process and is totally normal. These things are all part of a cycle of change. You are just course-correcting a little, rather than starting again from scratch. Perhaps it's time to change things round a bit, or switch things up. If this is the case, then just quickly work your way round the 5-Step Process from stages one to five, checking what's in place, where you have gaps and what you can do to fill them.

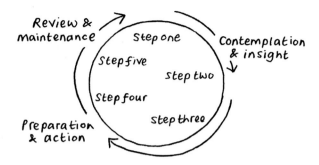

Diagram 20: The 5-Step Process

We're back to where we started – step one!

Step one: WHY and WHERE (purpose and destination)
Step two: WHICH (animal, i.e. the distance to travel)
Step three: WHAT and HOW (the type of change)
Step four: WHO and WHEN (planning action and experimentation)
Step five: HOW MUCH and HOW WELL (reviewing progress)

The arrows on the 5-Step Process are there to demonstrate that this is a cycle. It will go round and round until you're in the maintenance stage. There's a larger focus here too because at some point you'll reach your destination. You'll be happy there for a short time, but then you'll want to head off in a new direction. That's the time to start the process once again at step one. Later you'll read more about how to use the stages to do this longer-term review.

———

Now, for a quick reflection. I'd suggest you review the notes you made and ask yourself: what did I already know? What was surprising or new? What am I confident about? What makes me nervous?

We're now at the end of this chapter, so here is what we looked at:

- Why it's important to stop and reflect on progress, how your change journey is going.
- Six different ways to assess progress, including baselining where you

start, using a number of tools to check forward motion, plus finding ways around the problem if you get stuck.

- We covered measuring quality and quantity. Focusing on quality helps if you have a small number of actions. Measurements can be internal and external – what you see vs. what others see.
- We focused on achieving a balance between reviewing what is going well as well as what is not. We need to encourage ourselves along, rather than beating ourselves up.
- In addition there were stories from participants and how they measured their progress and an opportunity to practice this too.
- We also covered how we can shift into maintenance or go round the process once again.

In the next chapter we'll look at why our profiles change over time, from fish, to grasshopper to bird.

Chapter 16

The last chapter was all about how we measure our progress. Now we'll work out whether that progress is still what we want. If that sounds cryptic, read on. Steven is a sports journalist and he's also a shape shifter. He was the first person whose story highlighted two important things to me. Firstly, a nuance about change and something we often get wrong; that we mix up WHAT we're doing with HOW we're doing it. You'll remember that we covered this earlier.

Secondly, his story made me stop and think about fish, grasshoppers and birds. What I realised is these aren't fixed types; you're not born a fish, live like a fish and die like a fish. Instead we can all be a bit fish, a bit grasshopper or a bit bird at different times. You'll remember in my model WHICH animal you think you might be, is made up of two things. One is your personality, the way you approach life, how you normally behave and your appetite for risk. The other is your context, how big the change is that you want or need, or how far you need to travel. I'll explain this a bit more by telling you about Steven.

On a bitterly cold winter's day at the end of January 2020 Steven and I spoke for quite a while on the phone. Steven had always dreamt of being a sports journalist; in fact, since he was the tender age of ten. Despite achieving his life-long goal of working for a number of prestigious news outlets, by his mid-30's Steven wasn't happy at all. It came to a head one day. To his surprise, he realised that for decades he'd been *"doing the wrong thing entirely."*

Journalism had come naturally to Steven and everything he did was geared up to his work. "It was just dragging me down and down and down and down. Because you're never ever finished. You cannot complete the work." He also felt that he "Just kept hitting the same problem over and over again. It was the realisation that it wasn't a meritocracy. I wasn't going to progress just by working hard." It resulted in a lot of difficult conversations in his organisation and relationships that started breaking down. Over time the stress impacted his mental health and he "literally couldn't switch off from work. It was absolutely consuming me and something had to change."

Steven thought he needed radical change. He was fed up with journalism and its long hours and hard work. The idea, *I'm doing the wrong thing entirely* kept swirling round in his head. He felt stressed that he didn't spend enough time at home with his wife or kids. He felt annoyed that he didn't have the energy left for hobbies, sports, friends, or the other things in his life.

Steven wasn't sure how to fix all this on his own, so he went on a career change[105] course. A piece of advice they gave him was to test out other types of work, by talking to people who were already in those roles. Steven had often wondered what it would be like to be an entrepreneur and thought, "What about creating my own business?" So, he set about finding entrepreneurs to chat with about what they did and whether that might fit him and his life.

But, after quite a few conversations Steven felt he wasn't progressing at all. The problem was that these discussions didn't seem to go anywhere for him. He kept speaking to people but didn't move to action. He started to wonder whether reinvention was actually the way to go. One day he was talking to other career changers on the course and had an epiphany: "They described what they were passionate about and their jobs. These two things were completely different. When I spoke about what I was passionate about as a child, what I'm passionate about now, my job, well... all of them aligned." He said it "wasn't that I was in the **wrong** line of work at all. I was just **doing** it wrong."

Steven was participant number 36 in my reseasrch, and I was still working out what I was hearing from the interviewees at this point. His story opened my eyes to the difference between WHAT we're doing and HOW we're doing it. I realised this was an important step in the change process. It would help us all to focus our effort in the right places.

What did Steven do next? He realised he didn't want 'bird' change at all. In fact, he felt more like a fish out of water that needed to get back into the pond. He closed down the chats with entrepreneurs and stopped trying to find a different WHAT. Instead, he focused on the HOW of being a journalist and what he could change. At the start of our conversation, I described what my research was about and it seemed to make sense to him. "I knew exactly what you meant. It's just these little things that add up to a big thing. And I think it's a really illuminating journey. None of it has been a sudden revelation. All of it has been just a little change here and there."

One of the biggest shifts for Steven was his mindset: "I realised that if I was going to progress my career, it was relationships that mattered. I was less obsessed with getting everything right. I was more concerned about the impact it was making." This is Steven focusing on the HOW and not the WHAT.

Steven summarised these changes in his life like this: "My story is a little bit different in that my journey took me all the way back to exactly where I was. I was just happier. That was not what I expected." He had tried the 'bird' approach, but it wasn't for him, at least not at this point in his life. Steven became a shape shifter instead. He started off thinking that he needed to fly a long distance, like a bird. But really, he just wanted to shimmy, like a fish.

You'll remember we covered experimentation before and as we test out new ideas, we access new information. In turn this can make us pivot and change our minds. We start adapting as we go, reining things in a bit, or trying something more expansive. So, in the future Steven might put on his bird wings again as we all swim, jump or fly at different times.

But I've left Steven's story hanging so I'll bring it to a close because I can you hear you asking "How is he now?" Well, the good news is that he is much happier with his work and his life. "I began to change the way that I spoke with people. I especially began to change the way that I managed the relationships I had at work." He also said that, "Everything just felt more fun."

Don't get me wrong it wasn't all fun and giggles as he had existential moments too. "I began to realise that we're not here for very long. We have to do what we want to be doing, enjoy what we're doing because what's the point otherwise? We're not going to win." He talked about school and the education system and what it produces: "It makes you think this is all about winning. It's all about being the best at things... people who want to clamber over other people to get what they want."

Instead, Steven has changed his views on life. "There is no game here that we win. In the end you just have to build as beautiful a life as you possibly can, for you and the people around you. And you have to be a good person to them and help them build as good a life as possible. That was a great realisation."

I asked how long this shift had taken. "I started the course in February. I'd say by September, I was pretty happy with where I was. I had identified what made me happy and what I wanted to do more. Very quietly I'd stopped doing all the things that I thought weren't important or that I thought I needed to take care of, but I didn't enjoy. I just stopped doing them, and nobody noticed." This is when he realised, "OK, that was the problem. I was trying to be perfect, something that nobody wanted."

So here we are leaving Steven in a much better place: "Once I made peace with that, everything started to roll. Everything started to just work. And I began to allow myself to just enjoy what I was doing at work, rather than worrying about where it was all leading."

Soon after chatting to Steven, I spoke to Yiannis who is Greek and works in sustainability. It took him years to realise that he needed two things to feel fulfilled: "One is to work on something that I believe in. So, there's a purpose around what I do." The second was a role that "aligned with my natural way of working." This is another example of someone working on their HOW.

Yiannis also said that he "originally started working in the environment because I enjoy nature. But that doesn't mean I have to go and write reports about environmental pollution for an oil and gas company." This is precisely what he did for a while, which is why he wasn't happy. Instead, he thought he (or others like him) could be "a forester, a ranger, or a park guide. I think that many people underestimate what their day-to-day work involves. Your purpose is one thing. But sitting in an office in a sterile city corporate environment nine hours a day may not suit you... perhaps you don't want to sit down all the time." This is a lovely rendering of HOW versus WHAT. Thank you, Yiannis.

———

Jo is a 59-year old Australian, who has a background in organising events and conferences. This is how she started our conversation: "My most recent job has made me quit the corporate world altogether and I know that I am never, ever going back." She doesn't want to "play by somebody else's rules" anymore.

Jo used to enjoy her work and her favourite role was for the Sydney Olympics. "I absolutely loved it. It was doing events work that I really enjoyed. Great team of people, common purpose, leading towards the build-up of the games. A lot of prestige in it, it was very hard to get a job there."

But recently it hasn't been so much fun for Jo. "The last few years I've been sick of it... I just reached a point last Christmas where I thought I've had it. This is not me. I'm crazy trying to fit in, I don't want to be here, something's got to give."

Jo had been jumping from role to role, "Feeling dissatisfaction, not fitting in." She'd leave and find another events job, but that would be the same. "It was just a point where I'd done a big conference and thought I'm just doing the same thing over and over and expecting a different outcome." That was rock bottom. "The wake-up call where I just thought I'm done." What kept pulling her back? "A secure job, they pay well, you get a bit of travel and they're interesting. I was seduced by all of that." It took her a while to figure out that, "I'd rather jump into the great unknown than stay with security, because it just wasn't working. That's how we're taught. That's what we're raised with."

She knew it was all over when even the Christmas party became annoying. "I thought it's the same old same old, dress up, fake talk and I just don't want to do that anymore." In the past Jo had counselled people: "As long as you stay in the game, you've got to play by the rules. If you don't want to play by the rules, then get out of the game." This was her situation now, she needed to move.

Jo said that she belonged to "a couple of different groups and they're all women over 40. They've just had enough of playing the game. Usually, rules made by men. I thought I don't want to retire. I quite like working, but I want to be doing what I want to be doing for the last bit of my life." She said when she left school "you could be a nurse or a teacher. That was it, two options. I just give thanks that we're in this exciting time for women where the shackles have come off so much. I think to myself 'stop faffing around. Get out there and do your thing.'"

Jo trained as a hypnotherapist and decided to set up a hypnotherapy business. "I told some good friends that I was going to do my own thing. They were so happy for me and said, 'it's about time, we've been waiting to hear this.'" We spoke in April 2020, just as rates of Covid-19 were climbing steeply, but despite this Jo was in a calm mood. "I'm more relaxed. I'm more trusting that things are going to turn out. I'll get the right people I need. I will find a little something to tide me over if needs be."

Jo says she is "much more chilled and it makes a world of difference. It's changing your thoughts, your mindset because everything else is the same. The uncertainty is still out there. It's trusting in something greater, that this is all meant to happen. It's going to be for the greater good, I just can't see it, yet."

I asked Jo what wisdom she might tell her younger self. "I would say, 'Think outside the box and take some risks. Just start things and see where they go.' I've always been a person who looks down the road, looks at all the obstacles and says, 'no, I can't do it.' This 59-year-old person would say, 'Just start it and see where it takes you.'"

So why have I included Jo's story alongside Steven's? She took the fishes' way and reinvented herself as a hypnotherapy practitioner. Her story is happy ever after, right? Not so fast. I got in touch with her two years after our conversation, when I was finalising my book, as I contacted all the participants to check they were happy with their quotes. But Jo wasn't OK with her quote at all. Her story hadn't ended here. It had a second part.

Jo wrote me a long email explaining what had happened. "It seems my work life has gone full circle. I'm in a completely different place to the person who said these words two years ago. I can see how reactive my words were to my last role back in 2019. It was not a pleasant place to work." But isn't she managing her hypnotherapy practice now? "I did set up a therapy business and saw quite a few clients during the Covid period. However, I found I didn't like working at home and I didn't like working by myself."

This is a great example of the HOW not being a good fit for Jo. She missed being with people and doing interesting, active work. So, two years on what is she doing now? "I felt called back to the events industry, which I mostly enjoyed. I'm now working at a great venue near home. My role is a step back from organising events, but I'm still have my hand in, and I absolutely love it."

Like Steven, Jo really enjoyed her work, the WHAT. It was some of the HOW that she didn't like. "I work with a great team (what a difference that makes) and I enjoy going to work. I also enjoy a regular pay cheque and I don't have to do the continuous marketing/ selling that a small business owner needs to do." She found this side of things particularly draining. "It's funny how self-employment is the usual offer to people unhappy at work. In fact, it's a whole new world that is not suited to many people!"

That's such a useful note to us all. Be clear on our HOWs, as much as our WHATs. For Jo it's being with other people, not having to constantly market herself and also how important it is for her to have a regular income. She didn't get any of these managing her own business. She experimented, it wasn't a good fit and now she has pivoted back to her old line of work, this time avoiding the bits she doesn't like!

———

Here is a final example of a shape shifter. Her name is Charlotte and she's an occupational (organisational) and coaching psychologist. Oh, hang on, that's me. Earlier I said I'd tell you how I shifted from a bird to a fish and then a grasshopper. Clearly, I can't make up my mind.

Here is a story from one of the changes I've been through in my life. I was fed up after years of working in Management Consulting. It was full of long hours, challenging clients and towards the end, a lack of meaning in my work. Sunday nights were the worst. I often had to travel as I was expected in the client's office bright and early Monday morning, whatever the country. I'd pack up a bag on Sunday, unpack again on Friday night, wash clothes and repeat it all again on Sunday. On those long journeys to client sites, I would have flights of fancy. Could I reinvent myself and do something totally different? Something that didn't involve laptops, spreadsheets or curled up sandwiches on the last train to Inverness? Could I be a bird and launch myself into a new career?

I tried random things in my spare time: hours inside sweaty beekeeping outfits, courses in de-cluttering followed by organising people's houses and talking to alpaca owners about breeding as a business. Fairly quickly I realised alpacas were irritable beasts. They were only interested if I had food and ignored me if I didn't. They also spat a lot, which was at odds with their fluffy faces and ringlets of curly hair.

So, where have I ended up? Back where I started, applying all the skills I used before. So why do I skip into my office every day as if everything has changed? Well, it wasn't the **work** I didn't like it was the **way** I did that work. The HOW needed to shift, not the WHAT, which has stayed much the same. Rather than a bird I discovered I was a fish.

Sometimes we overstate the size of change we need to make. This is what I wrote about Anupa back in chapter two: *Anupa wanted something that was less harsh, so she identified an alternative treatment plan, following Ayurvedic principles. She saw an Ayurverdic doctor who gave her herbal medicines and a diet to follow, plus she went on an Ayurvedic retreat and came back 'feeling very healthy and detoxed.'*

Anupa's style is different to how I approach change in life. It's a bit all or nothing for me. For example, when I got in shape for a half-marathon, I created spreadsheets with a daily exercise and eating plan. I acquired two new pairs of identical trainers, so I could swap them between runs. I bought fancy outfits, because it's true, the more kit you buy, the faster you will run. It was therefore no surprise to me that my future career could be a complete reinvention from Management Consultant to alpaca farmer or bee keeper, or even de-cluttering other peoples' homes.

Imagine my confusion a year on when I woke up and found I was back where I started. I was managing a business that was jam-packed full of psychology, coaching and helping people to go through change. Wasn't that what I did before, the thing I didn't want to do anymore? I had overblown the size of the change I needed to make. It was a bit like *Snakes and Ladders*, the game you might have played as a child. I had just landed on the snake's head and slid back to the start again.

Later, I came to realise that whilst my WHAT may have stayed the same, my HOW was entirely different. No more travel on Sundays, as I worked via Zoom and rarely met my coaching clients in person. I still ran consulting projects now and again. But these were done remotely, from my home deep in the countryside. The internet and video conferencing were amazing tools for me, as I facilitated workshops for coaches who arrived on my screen from all around the world.

I reverted to a fish type of change, sticking with what I knew. I was happy as a fish blowing bubbles... for about six months. But then, over time, I gained confidence in my new business ventures. I started to branch out, doing different activities, pushing myself to do much more. I was changing into a grasshopper, jumping into new actions that were more of a stretch. For example, in October 2020, I spoke at a conference about my shift from Management Consultant to writer. There were 1,600 people from 60 countries and we all fitted into Zoom. It was a tight squeeze. In the past I had hated public speaking, managing 50 people at most. But there I was, chatting away to all these folk, like I was someone else.

I created a podcast called *Tyranny of the Shoulds,* helping people to open up about their lives in public, to share with thousands of people on Spotify, Apple and Google Podcasts. I spent a considerable amount of time writing, but not dry client change management reports of yesteryear. Now I was using my own voice about topics I loved, hundreds of blogs, articles for publications where I could be myself (like writing *Swim, Jump, Fly*). Another new area was combining my photography with people development. I turned my photographic images into a way to coach my clients, developing *Liminal Muse Conversation Cards.* I then started to train up other coaches, facilitators and therapists in this approach. It was great fun working with other professionals from around the world to learn how to use them too.

So, that is my story. I shape-shifted quite a bit over a couple of years. I changed from a bird into a fish and then into a grasshopper. The thing is that you may well change like this too.

Shape shifting between animals is also about failing. You might remember that in a previous chapter I wrote: *failing isn't actually failing at all*. When we *fail* it's just a useful way to gather information about what we do, or don't want to do next.

This is Anna on the topic of failing: "Things will go wrong, but it doesn't mean it's wrong. We might say, 'Oh, this hasn't worked out exactly as I had expected. I made the wrong move.' But you probably didn't, it's just your expectations weren't truly realistic." She adds that, "The other thing is you can go back. And I don't mean go back to a previous situation. But you can go back a step and that's OK."

We may envisage a huge change but it doesn't always work out that way. Anna launched herself into a new life and told everybody what she would be doing. But then, she felt embarrassed when it didn't work out the way she had planned. At first, she beat herself up telling herself, "Oh, God, I failed." But over time she realised it wasn't true. "I didn't fail at all. It was just that was what was right for me at that particular moment, because of other things that were happening."

The thing about shape shifting is that you need to experiment. You won't know whether you really want to swim, jump, or fly until you've tried. You may surprise yourself, like Steven and me, both *supersizing* ourselves and then going *Mini-Me*. For Steven the change was smaller than he first thought. For me, I wanted to go big again, once I'd gained some confidence. Trying my hand at other skills like podcasting and writing this book.

Adwoa is 40 and is experimenting with a new area too. She grew up in Ghana and ended up working in technology for decades, despite not enjoying it. "I did computer science for one semester at university and I knew I just didn't like it.

I didn't enjoy programming. I felt it was a cold subject. But here I was working, starting off a career in precisely the area I didn't like. I stuck with it because it paid well."

Adwoa is enjoying other areas of her life. "I'm quite happy with family life. My husband and my two kids and my parents, siblings, etc. I think what gives me the biggest headache or the biggest dissatisfaction on a daily basis is my job." She stayed in her professional services role for years, despite not liking it. "What kept me there was the very generous maternity policy. So, I said to myself, 'I don't like what I do. But I will stick around because someday I know I want to have children. I can take a year off and get paid for it.'"

However, it's never too late to shape-shift and try something completely different. At 40 Adwoa is trying out a very different venture but is still feeling a little low in confidence. "I want to make clothes, but I'm so scared of the unknown. I'm already thinking I'm not going to make enough money. I don't know how to advertise. How am I going to brand myself?" She doesn't believe she's good enough yet and is still taking lessons. "When am I going to get to the point where I think I'm an expert?" Adwoa is trying not to listen to the negative voices in her head. Instead, she is trying to put one step in front of the other. "I think I have to take it slowly. Even if it's one skirt I can do for now and try to start selling that. That's where I'll start."

Before we move on, here are some examples of animals in the natural world. Let's begin with the fish. In general, a middle of the road fish doesn't tend to swim that far, particularly if it's in an enclosed environment, like a pond or a lake. But there are fish that could be part of the Olympic Squad. Salmon, for example, can swim long distances each day and, as you know, they swim upstream. When it comes to human fish, the ones I've been describing in this book, it's perfectly possible to travel long distances too. So, you might be able to equate that to the shifts you make in life; leaping out of the water, changing yourself quite a bit.

Now to the grasshoppers. Certain types can swim, at least when push comes to shove, and many can fly short distances too. Grasshoppers also have an Olympic team, as some can travel long distances, flying as fast as 10 miles/16 kms per hour. So, if you're a grasshopper in your change project, you'll be able to slow down, do less and reflect. And you'll also be able to speed things up, press the accelerator and go further.

Finally, let's end with the birds. Of course, there are the long-distance marathon runners of the bird world, like the Bar-Tailed Godwit. One had a personal best of 6,800 miles/11,000 kms when it flew between Alaska and New Zealand. However, we've all seen tiny birds in our garden or the park, hopping along, rarely bothering to take to their wings. So, if you have a tendency to be more bird-like, whilst you can travel long distances, you can also slow down, you don't always need to fly.

You may remember Annita, who reviewed an early copy of *Swim, Jump, Fly* and gave me feedback. We had some long conversations about the book and one area she was keen to discuss was shape shifting.

During the Covid-19 lockdown she watched natural history documentaries, along with her family. Annita was particularly drawn into learning about chameleons. Whilst she really likes the idea of *Swim, Jump, Fly* and the concept of the fish, the grasshopper and the bird, she thought a chameleon might be a useful addition. Chameleons like "to blend into the background and to not stand out." They adapt to their circumstances, sometimes they don't know what they want to be. It's the same with us. Sometimes we're not sure who we are because we are influenced by the people around us.

Annita wanted to add that, "Chameleons tend to stay quite still." She thought this might be useful as a metaphor for people going through change. It might remind us that sometimes change isn't about changing at all. We might need to pause instead, assess our direction and be still enough for a while, so we can work out where we want to go next.

Finally, I'll bring Yiannis back in again since he agrees with this idea. "Take your time, take it easy… sometimes not doing is doing, you know. Sometimes just letting things be, being idle about things. Something else is growing that you're not aware of. You've just got to let that process be." Yiannis says he would like to be better at this himself. "I don't think I do as well as I could… let things unfold and have trust in the process, as tough as that may be."

———

That's it for this chapter, so here is a summary of what we covered, before we move on:

- We revisited HOW and WHAT via Steven's story, how he had spent years working in his dream role, journalism, only to realise he wasn't happy.
- Steven had an epiphany though, thinking he needed a bird sized change, only to discover what he needed was actually to be more of a fish.
- We heard from Jo who wanted to be more bird, tried it out and realised she really wanted to be more fish. She focused much more on the HOW and less the WHAT.
- I also shared my story about my change. How I too thought I was a bird, but that over time this became a fish and then longer term, I oriented towards a grasshopper.
- We also read stories about Anna, Adwoa, Annita and Yiannis – all who had some wisdom to share with us.
- Finally, we discussed how we need to try on change to work out if it fits. Standing on the side lines isn't enough. We have to throw ourselves in.

Next, we'll be discussing why your change might not be working in the way you would like. It's all about what blocks us from moving forward and how we can tackle those obstacles.

Chapter 17

Have you ever had a dream where you're running as fast as you can, but you're not moving at all? You wake up in a sweat, heart pounding, unsure which way is up. It can be just like this if your change project isn't going well.

As we know, there are things we can't control, from an asteroid hitting the planet, to rain next Thursday afternoon... I'm going to spend no time at all on that topic as it could be a very long list. However, there are many things we **can** control, so the next few chapters will be all about those.

At times, going through change can feel like standing on a wobble board on top of an elephant that's surfing a gigantic wave. What can you hold onto when nothing is firm under foot? My first piece of advice is get off the wobble board. What I mean is, don't make change harder than it needs to be. You can't do much about waves or elephants, but you have the choice to get off the board. Secondly, hold on to the 5-Step Process. It will keep you afloat if you fall off. Think of the process as a safety ring/lifesaver, the kind you get on boats. They're not always comfortable to wear, but they will keep you safe.

> " I am not afraid of storms for I am learning how to sail my ship.
> — Louisa May Alcott[106] (American novelist)

Things we can't control: Here are some events that would knock you sideways, if you were starting a new chapter in your life:
- You get hit by a cyclist on your first run around the block. Breaking your foot before you begin your fitness campaign isn't a good way to start.
- Your divorce comes through and the next day your ex, after years of fruitless lottery tickets, wins a prize. It's ten million pounds/dollars/euros.
- A blazing asteroid hits your home (fortunately you aren't in) and half your house burns down. Luckily, it's also Thursday, so it rains, which puts the rest of the fire out.
- Chicken Licken (a.k.a Henny Penny) is correct. The sky does fall in.

You think I'm being ridiculous, which of course I am. My point is don't waste time scenario-planning everything that might go wrong, especially if you can't influence it. Instead, focus on what you can do something about. Below are some more sensible suggestions about what you can do. By the way, Argentinian organisational psychologist Tomas Chamorro-Premuzic[107] says much of our success is down to luck anyway. He says talent and effort make up about 45%, leaving over half or our success down to luck.

What's in our gift: I'll cover a number of areas that are in our control. I'll spread them across three chapters as there are quite a few. In this first chapter on this topic we'll cover:

1) Own goal
2) Running away or running towards
3) Overly ambitious
4) The stories we tell
5) Fear of…

1) Own goal

If you don't know your football (Soccer) from your football (American), then you may not know the expression *own goal*. It's the moment when a soccer player accidentally kicks the ball into their own net. An own goal in a change project is exactly the same. You'll create one for yourself if you don't set the right objectives at the start. If you find your project isn't going as well as you had hoped, then maybe your initial goal was off.

Perhaps you've had a nagging feeling from the start that your goal wasn't right? Maybe you've been steadfastly ignoring the doubts from the beginning, marching on anyway? From the age of 16, Louisa wanted to work in fashion. "I had my heart set on being a fashion buyer. I'm the type of person when I've got a goal in my head I don't give up until I've reached it." But she was young and didn't think it through. "Once I started in the job, I probably realised that it wasn't 100% for me. But I had this end goal in sight, and I just ignored all those thoughts."

Many of Louisa's friends and family were doing vocational roles. "My sister's a nurse, my mum worked in the NHS, my boyfriend was a special needs teacher.

I always felt I wanted to give back a bit more. I didn't feel very rewarded. I felt I wasn't really contributing anything positive to the world." As her career progressed and she changed organisations, she ended up in a creative role. "I'm not really a naturally creative person. I was good at the business side, but the creative stuff didn't come easily. So, I felt I was… putting a mask on every day, having to be this really creative person."

People often told Louisa that her work seemed fun and cool. "I got to travel, but I never felt proud to talk about it, really… I went through some really hard times when I realised, that actually this isn't what I want to do, but I'd worked my butt off to get there. When I got there, I thought: 'It's not what I want to do anymore. So, what do I do now?'" Sometimes we're stubborn. We persevere with a goal because we told ourselves (or others) we'd do it. We continue down the path, even though it no longer works for us. Is it pride? Is it embarrassment, is it regret? If you're interested in the topic of regret, Daniel Pink's latest book, might be for you: *The Power of Regret, How Looking Backwards Moves us Forwards?*[108]

Or maybe it's the sunk cost effect? *Sunk Cost* is an economics term for when we can't recover costs because they're already spent. Whilst this often refers to financial costs, it can also relate to time and effort. If you're pushing for a goal you don't believe in, try to focus on prospective costs instead. These are future costs that you could avoid if you took action. You've invested money and time in learning to dance Salsa but are not enjoying it at all. You force yourself to continue because of your investment, even though you dread the classes each week. Or perhaps it's *cognitive dissonance*, feeling uncomfortable when there's a discrepancy between what we think and what we do. The theory says we strive for internal consistency and do everything to bring the two into line. So, it's often quicker to bring our attitudes in line with our behaviour, rather than changing our behaviour to fit our beliefs.

Cecilia knew what she needed to do but found it hard to change her behaviour. "I could see the warning signs that things were going downhill for me, and I didn't act fast enough, knowing full well the things that would have made a difference." She was distracted by other things. "I knew exercising was important. I knew reducing alcohol was important. I knew eating well was important and probably going to therapy was important. I did start therapy, but probably a little bit late." Her advice is "catching it early and making those non-negotiable. That's the key takeaway."

One final thought about goals from Professor Bruce Hood[109]. He says we often set ourselves goals because we think they'll make us happy. But many don't bring as much joy as we think they will, especially if they are materialist goals. He's not suggesting we shouldn't aspire and be ambitious, but just avoid thinking once we've achieved the goal, we'll be happy ever after. Perhaps your goals are too materially focused? If so, then you might like to change them, better to pick something that will offer you long term contentment. You can hear more about this topic in my podcast episode called *Milestones that become Millstones*. Why not check it out via the swimjumpfly.com website?

2) Running away or running towards?

I wrote a post about this topic, highlighting the difference between *away* and *towards*. Here is my introduction to it: *From a distance it's hard to know why someone is running. Are they fleeing from or racing to? To the casual observer they look the same. It can be equally baffling to the runner. Some of my interviewees are running to. But many are running from. It takes distance and time to figure out which.*

One of the themes that came up in my research was something I called *Snap Response*. It appeared 85 times in ideas like 'running away' because it had all become too much, rather seeking out something the person really wanted. I saw it in 'sudden quitting' and 'unplanned for change'. Quite a few interviewees used the term *straw on the camel's back* for example. Others talked about 'jumping out of their everyday life' and escaping, needing 'radical change'. Sometimes this worked out, but often it was a false start – they ran away from something they didn't like, but fell into the arms of something just as bad. Occasionally it was even worse.

Let's catch up again with one of my interviewees, Louisa. After deciding she wanted to get out of the fashion industry, she ran headlong into something else. "I made quite a drastic change two years ago. Because I wanted to feel more rewarded." What work is she doing now? She's in procurement and sourcing in the health industry. Louisa says she went through a huge change. "It's not the right way to go about it. Picking a completely different career and just jumping into it without even trying it." She's been working out the difference between 'away' and 'towards.' "Now I'm just on the completely opposite side – I just don't enjoy the public sector at all. It's really slow paced. It's quite a negative environment. And it's not very dynamic."

Louisa ran away from fashion, rather than towards procurement. So at 30 she's now "miserable again, in a different job. But I'm figuring out a lot about myself in the process and what I think I'm good at and what my values and my natural talents are. I still don't 100% know, but I think I've learned a lot along the way."

Psychologists distinguish between *approach goals*, going after something we want in our life, versus *avoidance goals*, moving away from a negative aspect in our life. These types of goals have been studied many times and the research shows it's harder to work on avoidance goals. They are less clear and less motivating. We're much more likely to succeed if we set an approach goal, seeking something better for ourselves, a positive presence in our lives e.g. a focus on being healthier rather than giving up smoking.

Andrew exercises to take his mind off the changes he's trying to work through. This is helpful if we're running towards a healthy way of living or a well-earned break. But it can be an issue if we use it to run away from the task in hand. "I'll do something as a bit of escapism rather than address what the actual problem is. I think part of the problem is too much of that." He uses time off as avoidance, saying to himself, "'Right, that'll help take my mind off something – let's enjoy the weekend.' So, we'll go and do that, or we'll go on holiday and forget about it. But then the problem is still there at the end of the holiday and I've done nothing to address it."

Rob is another participant and he ran away for a long time. "I just continued to run away from it and not face my past. I think I lived most of my life in fear, just probably looking to escape." He was fleeing from himself, particularly difficult childhood memories. "You think that you will sort yourself out tomorrow. But obviously tomorrow never comes. The impact on your future is enormous and the impact on your present as well." A few years of psychotherapy really helped

Rob. "There's no doubt talking about it saved my life. It's literally as black and white as that. Personally, the last three and a half years have just been a voyage of discovery."

In his book, *The Art of Travel*,[110] Alain de Botton recounts a holiday he took to Barbados. Despite the pristine sandy beaches and beautiful palm trees, he wasn't enjoying himself. Over the day he became irritated and grumpy, culminating in an argument with his partner. It suddenly struck him what the problem was, he'd brought himself to the island. And, as Bob Marley and the Wailers famously sang, you can't run away from yourself.

Ellen works in the film industry and runs away from her problems. Once she took a freelance role on a big film. "I remember sitting there and looking at the chaos around the office. Everyone's complaining about the job, they're overworked, too much to do. I was coming on as a trial, and I was thinking, 'what am I doing here?' No-one got on with the director, everyone was being rude to each other."

Ellen went out to search for locations but was feeling unsupported because there just weren't enough people on the team. "I sent an email to say I'm really sorry, I can't do this. I'm going to leave the job. It was very unprofessional... I think I had very relaxed parents that never disciplined me. So, when they called me saying 'what the **** is going on?' I found it difficult to hold myself in that situation." How did she react? "The easiest thing was to switch the phone off and hope it would go away. That's how I deal with things, which isn't dealing with things. I didn't know what to do."

We talked about patterns of avoidance from Emma's upbringing. "That's what my parents do. I've noticed it, they don't ever deal with problems, they just ignore them because it's easier. Or run away. That's what I do permanently." She lives in a house share and there's conflict quite a lot of the time. "It's not a way to deal with stuff. But that's how I used to do it. As a child I used to go and hide... I didn't know how to deal with my feelings, so I used to hide. Or go quiet." Going quiet can also be a form of hiding.

3) Overly ambitious

Be honest, have you bitten off more than you can chew? Is life too hectic to add one more thing into the mix? Is this change project a straw on your camel's back? Remember the *Reality Check* in chapter 11? Ask yourself, "Do I have the time and energy to do this? Am I too busy? Will my life help me or hinder my change?"

Balance was one of the themes in my *Thematic Analysis* research. It appeared 76 times and showed itself in the loss of boundaries between work and home-life, not being able to balance the challenges of motherhood/fatherhood and the rest of their lives. It was about trying to focus on paying the bills but also trying to spend time on the fun things in life. Much of the time my interviewees felt they weren't achieving that balance at all and needed to stop doing so much.

Annita says we sometimes "choose paths that we think are going to work, because they've been done by others, without looking to see whether they're truly feasible for ourselves." The project may be unsuccessful because of, "The immovable puzzle pieces of our own lives. It doesn't fit with the reality of our day-to day." If you decide it's time to put this project on hold, then put a date in your diary for a few months' time. Re-visit it when you have more energy.

Another *Overly Ambitious* topic sits on my own shoulder like an annoying chipmunk, chattering in my ear. I'm a *multipotentialite*[111], which sounds like a grand term, but it simply means I can't make up my mind. I like to have many projects on the go. That's why I'm writing this book, run a coaching psychology practice, train coaches on my *Liminal Muse Conversation Cards*, consult for a number of organisations, run the *Tyranny of the Shoulds* podcast and… try to have a life. It's all fine and dandy when the plates are spinning, but that doesn't happen all the time. I have to work on managing overwhelm and resting enough. I need to de-prioritise some things, so I have time to sleep and eat. If I don't rein things in, I have too much choice.

Psychologist Barry Schwartz wrote a book called *The Paradox of Choice: why more is less*[112]. He says choice is so embedded it doesn't occur to us to question it. But too much choice produces paralysis rather than liberation. The more we have, the easier it is to regret anything that is disappointing about the option we've chosen. So ask yourself – are you making life difficult? Could you cut back on some options? It might give your brain a rest.

Another topic is expectations which we covered earlier. We looked at your WHICH, the type of change you want to make, how far you need to travel and how you normally deal with change. If there is a mismatch between the two, I suggested you lower your expectations on how quickly you could shift. I gave a few options, including stretching your timeframe and taking longer over the change, or reducing the size of the change you want to make.

I have two more suggestions to add here as well: quality and money. Can you lower your benchmark, deliver a result that's good enough, but not perfect? Is it possible to throw more cash at a project to make it happen more quickly? For example, delegating/outsourcing work to other people.

4) The stories we tell (ourselves and everyone else)

> I didn't leave because I was caught in a thought loop of what else would I do? I was a teacher. This is what I'd been doing for 10 years. This was me. I had assigned a lot of value to it and it became my identity. I definitely lost myself. — Emma (interviewee)

I've used storytelling in *Swim, Jump, Fly* because stories bring ideas to life and when we hear other people's stories it helps to normalise what we're going through. This is what one of the participants Jack said about hearing the experiences of others: "The feeling that you're not the only one going through this… at least you're in the same boat as somebody else, instead of stuck out on the ocean on your own." Sometimes we tell ourselves (and others) stories that aren't so helpful. We often think of ourselves in a certain way, with a certain identity, but often that's just a narrative that we've created. And that can change if we can shift our storyline. The story we tell ourselves can shape, limit and define our lives.

Instead, why not ask yourself this: Is there a difference between the stories I'm telling myself and the stories I'm living? It's important to know the difference because we become what we pay attention to or focus on. Or, "Are my stories helping or hindering me?" If you're focusing on a storyline that's not helpful, why not try telling yourself (and others) a different one? Don't let your story get in the way of a meaningful life.

One of the stories we often tell ourselves is that we have to get things right. We can't mess up, we need to do well. This might come from our family, our schooling or the messages we got when we were growing up. Maeve is one of the interviewees and has something to say about this. "Done is better than perfect. I keep reminding myself of that. It keeps coming back to me because I'm a perfectionist. So, lots of reasons that I give for not doing things because I knew they wouldn't be perfect. But it doesn't matter because nobody will be judging it."

This is Torsten from Germany. He has stories of perfection that held him back in the past. "Both of my parents had this problem of needing to be perfect." His mother loves to bake. "She does this cream cake – Black Forest Gateaux and it's really complicated stuff and she does it very well. But obviously it's not always perfect. Sometimes things go wrong. She would do the cake again if it wasn't to her standard. She would throw it away... and then she would bake another one." Torsten's father was the same. "There was always a standard. He could spend 80% of his time on the last 10% to make something perfect. Everybody else said 'you are nuts. Why aren't you just doing this good enough, nobody sees.' So, both of them had this from their childhood... And I had this. Good enough was not good enough. So, I would focus on the last attention to detail."

Lucy is 31 and used to be a lawyer. "It was also my own nature that stood in my way." She has a big perfectionist streak. "I've definitely got a fear of failure. There were a lot of things in my psyche that fed into why it culminated in a breakdown, culminated in me needing to change course. There are parts of that I have definitely worked on and I'm still working on. I think I probably should have gone to see a therapist sooner."

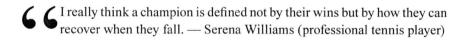

I really think a champion is defined not by their wins but by how they can recover when they fall. — Serena Williams (professional tennis player)

Dr David Drake[113] is the founder of the Center for Narrative Coaching & Design. He says that we have long-held patterns in our storytelling that echo across our lives. We play out the same story over and over, getting caught in the same behavioural responses and roles that we play. Each time we hope that the story will bring us the connection or confidence we've been looking for. It rarely does.

Dr Drake[114] is interested in what we want to achieve by telling these stories. What purpose do we have? What do we want others to pay attention to/what do we hope will happen as a result? A better way is thinking about other perspectives we can take when we're telling our stories, identifying new options, letting go of the old stories so we can welcome in the new ones.

A coaching colleague shared a case study of a client who was in the middle of change and was telling herself stories that kept her stuck. The coach called it *The Postcard of Future Unhappiness*, the way her coaching client predicted that she (the client) wouldn't be very good. "Even before the change my client has what I'd call 'anticipatory dissatisfaction.'" She said it's a deliberate creation of "internal challenges and barriers… What if I get there and don't like it? What's the point? I've never been happy when I get what I want. It's never good enough, I'm better than this." The coach says the client is, "Already writing her own postcard of future unhappiness as a fortune teller's cookie."

So, what strategies has a coach got that could address this difficult task? Together they've been exploring where this behaviour comes from, identifying that it's from a past unresolved place. They are focusing on the likelihood of it surfacing again, what the barriers might be and how the client might guard against them in the future.

You might find yourself having a lot of negative self-talk, blaming yourself, saying you're incompetent. Perhaps you believe other people could deal more easily with this? You might even create a story that's unsolvable. If this is the case, think about your own reservoir of change. Reflect on all the times when you navigated transitions successfully in the past. Remind yourself how you did this. Was it skills, experience, or personality that got you through? You still have those in your toolbox now. If you're beating yourself up, try the *Thinking Errors* exercise in Appendix A. If you can't think of any skills or strengths, ask a friend where they've seen you do this well in the past.

I mentioned the INSIGHT framework which was devised by British coaching psychologists Panchal and Palmer to help people work through transitions in their lives. In a 2020 article Panchal, Palmer and O'Riordan[115] focused on the changes we were facing due to Covid-19. They advised the following actions for two of the steps: N, normalising transitions and H, highlighting broader context.

Normalising transitions:

- Transitions take time. Don't expect too much of yourself and others as you adapt to new circumstances. Recognise small achievements and progress.
- Transitions involve emotions. Accept all the emotions you are feeling – anxiety, fear and sadness. Acknowledge any positive feelings, too, such as gratitude and connection.
- Transitions affect everyone. With Covid-19 transitions in particular, everyone is impacted in the same way, and many will be having similar experiences to you.

Helpful perspectives:

- Ideas connected to the broader context may be useful – 'This is a change that is impacting many people around the world – we are all in this together'; 'We are all required to make changes to help not only ourselves but for the greater good. What we do at this time matters.'
- Check influences. Be mindful of influences from family, friends and colleagues at this time. Make decisions and choices that make sense for you.

What stories are you telling yourself right now? Are they helpful, or are they setting you back? If the narrative you're feeding yourself is negative and unsupportive, then why not go back through the book. Try and pick out some of your favourite stories that might buoy you up.

5) Fear of...

 If you fall… get back on the horse. Otherwise, you're going to be scared of it forever. — Emma (interviewee)

I've mentioned before that fear came up many times in my conversations. The word fear comes from the Old English, *faēr* meaning calamity or danger. Being fearful is a calamity, it's potentially a disaster and a tragedy… that's because it will stop us from living a full life. We often prefer to be unhappy rather than uncertain. Mostly we're not fearful about what *will* happen, we're afraid of what *might* happen. The issue is anticipation. The potential for fear is worse than the fear itself.

This is what incoming US President, Franklin D Roosevelt, said in his inauguration speech in 1933, at the height of the Great Depression: "Let me assert my firm belief that the only thing we have to fear is fear itself—nameless, unreasoning, unjustified terror which paralyzes needed efforts to convert retreat into advance." Delaying action until there's no fear is not an option in your change project. Susan Jeffers wrote a whole book on the topic: *Feel the Fear and Do It Anyway*[116]. New Zealand Prime Minister, Jacinda Arden agrees: "If you sit and wait to feel like you are the most confident person in the room, you are probably going to be left by yourself."

What is important is to be open to all experiences, difficult and easy, good and bad, fulfilling and challenging. Often, we're afraid that things won't work out, they won't give us joy or we take the wrong path. But this mind-set will stop us moving forward. The real art is throwing ourselves in and trying things out. Failing isn't the issue, it's inaction. If we don't explore, we won't move forward. Avoidance won't help us grow.

Zee was one of my interviewees who talked about family relationships. "I didn't really feel I was a good fit in my family." (Zee's mother moved to Britain in the 1980s, having come from economic and social insecurity which drove the way she saw life.) "There were a lot of limitations in conversations with my family… there was no sense of the world and people being an exploration. You just had this fixed set of outcomes that you were trying to achieve."

This way of thinking was so different to Zee's free-thinking and curiosity. The clash in family styles created turbulence whilst growing up. "I am a naturally inquisitive person, and to me every new person is an adventure into the unknown. And that's why I didn't feel like I was a good fit. It was the precise opposite of what they brought me up to believe." Zee understands why this should be. "Unfortunately, my mother grew up scared of the world. The life she painted for us was very much characterised by fear and anxiety." Over time Zee came to realise being yourself "isn't something that you need to try hard at. This is something that you need to accept, that actually you are who you are.

And you need to find a place in the world where you fit."

Another aspect of fear is our hormones. For example, when we have the right level of dopamine (the reward chemical), it makes us feel good, increasing motivation, stimulating creativity and encouraging us to learn new things. But dopamine deficiency brings anxiety and fear. Yet there are simple ways to increase dopamine through exercise, massage, meditation, or stroking a pet. You could try music too, as studies find listening to instrumental songs can increase dopamine levels by nine percent[117]. Try focusing on your diet as well, ensuring you have enough tyrosine, found in almonds, eggs, fish and chicken. Spend more time outside. Increasing your exposure to sunlight can also increase dopamine.

What else can you do to keep calm if all around is uncertain? Here are some thoughts:

1) Know your triggers – acknowledge you're stressed. Remind yourself it's your amygdala's automatic response. Breathe slowly in through your mouth, out through your nose. Watch your belly move. Once you're calmer, reflect on what set you off. Make a note and watch out for the warning signs next time.

2) Make a decision, have clear intentions, set goals – it can be hard to make decisions when we're going through change. But once you decide a goal, it will calm the limbic system down and you'll feel more in control. Focus on a *good enough* decision, don't sweat it out to get to 100%. Perfectionism can overwhelm your brain and tire it out.

3) Money worries – if your fear is about money, go back to chapter 11 and do the money make-over challenge. Or look at the *Swim, Jump, Fly* website. Natalie says, "Money is something that I'm sure lots of people worry about. It stops them from making change, especially those risk averse folk like me!"

4) Subconscious fear – our rational brain knows what we need to do, but subconscious fears can hold us back. Is the story we tell ourselves old news? Is it no longer working for us? If so, then unpick/reframe that story.

5) Get laughing – laughter strengthens our immune system, boosts mood, reduces pain and protects us from stress. Connect with your friends, have fun, watch comedy.

6) Use your hands – touch increases oxytocin levels and reduces the reactivity of our amygdala. Make bread, cook your favourite meal, tend your garden or box of herbs. Make things. Stroke your pet iguana.

———

Instead of summarising this chapter, I'll ask you a number of questions:

- Do your goals need a fresh lick of paint? Do you need to go back and review or change them?
- Is your change project about running away from something you don't like? Or are you running towards something you want?
- Do you have too many options, too many choices to tackle?
- Have you bitten off more than you can chew in terms of the size of your project? Perhaps lower your expectations, reduce your goals, or put the project on ice for a while?
- What stories are you telling yourself that are increasing your fear, reducing your motivation, or stopping yourself in your tracks? Could you tell yourself alternative stories?
- If you're feeling afraid it's totally normal. You're definitely not alone. Have a look at some of my suggestions in this chapter which might lower your feelings of fear.

We have two more chapters on why your change might not be working. Why not take a look at them and see if you're dealing with these other challenges too?

Chapter 18

In this chapter we'll continue the theme of why your change project might not be working. Here are some additional topics you might like to read about:

1) Cheerleaders on strike
2) Normalitis
3) Always stuck in second gear
4) Gripping too tightly

1) Cheerleaders on strike

Having people cheering you on is important, but what if the folk you selected aren't being very supportive? What can you do? Remember critical friends – those talented at stress-testing ideas, perfect when you want to identify issues or potential risks, but not so great when you're uncertain, trying to work out what to do? It's best to keep them out of the room whilst your idea is hatching. Have you got the right people around you? Do you need to review your support network?

Some of the world's greatest inventions would have looked like madness to an inventor's best friends. If people are being downbeat about your plans, remember no-one can predict the future. When Gutenberg launched the printing press most people in Europe were illiterate. Your cheerleaders may not understand your plans because they fear change. Here are some examples I file under *Don't Let Others Underestimate You.*

- "You will never amount to very much." Munich schoolmaster to Albert Einstein, aged 10.
- "You'll never make any money out of children's books." Bloomsbury Publishing, after accepting J. K. Rowling's first book, *Harry Potter and the Philosopher's Stone.*
- "We don't like their sound. Groups of guitars are on the way out." A representative from Decca Recording Company talking about the Beatles in 1962.

I file these under *Don't Drive Looking in the Rear-View Mirror:*

- "There will never be a mass market for motor cars – about 1,000 in Europe – because that is the limit on the number of chauffeurs available!" Spokesman for Daimler Benz.
- "Who the hell wants to hear actors talk?" H.M. Warner from Warner Brothers, 1927.
- "Television won't last. It's a flash in the pan." Mary Somerville, pioneer of radio educational broadcasts, 1948.

Here are participant examples of lack of support. First, from Christine: *"In terms of my family, I don't discuss career plans with them at all. I haven't done for years because I find that deeply unhelpful."* Our experiences can be different from our parents, so it's hard for them to say the right thing. "My mother has never really worked in the corporate world. She doesn't really get it. She's always been very public sector."

Dhaval is 31, from India and went away to study. He had freedom to do what he wanted, so it was challenging coming back home. "It's in our culture. The situation is that parents are deciding for you. The major themes of whom I might marry, what kind of work I should do, choosing a career." This liberty he enjoyed dissipated and he struggled to fit back in. "I still wanted to explore, but because my family insisted that I came back, I had to return."

Sometimes we're brought up in environments with no natural cheerleaders. Here is an example from John, another interviewee. Both John and his wife came from families "that can be cruel... cruelty in the system which was tolerated under the name of 'standing on your own two feet,' being tough and all of that." John is in his late 50s and this still impacts him today. "That mindset is something we both still live with and find ways to deal with... we've definitely had to adopt different behaviours and boundaries, be willing to stand up for what we think is right at times, particularly with our kids."

It's important to choose the right people for cheerleading, people who don't have a vested interest in keeping us where we are. So what advice do participants give the rest of us? Alma says, "You have to be able to take what people say back to you with a pinch of salt. Because other people aren't always right. I always thought that other people knew more than I did."

Tracey advises us to "be careful who you talk to. It's very easy to get sucked back into certain things. I'm learning to trust my gut a lot more, learning that people are concerned for you, but they're also just concerned, generally. So, the advice they're giving is heart-felt, but not necessarily right for you." She isn't advocating we surround ourselves with "yes-people or sycophants." But, equally, don't take on all the views we're given. "Realise it was well meant. It doesn't mean you need to take that advice. It doesn't mean you're completely mad to do the opposite of what they say. You're just on a different wavelength. It's important to realise that."

There are a number of factors that can help us to successfully shift, one of which is ensuring our environment will support our progress; this includes the people around us. So, make sure you have the right cheerleaders and shoulders to cry on to support you. If you find some are too quick to give advice, you might remind them that you're not looking for solutions, that you'd prefer they just listen instead. Why not read my blog post, *Where to go for advice. And it's not your family*, on the *Swim, Jump, Fly* website.

2) Normalitis

We are bombarded with messages from social media, TV, media, advertising and movies, telling us what's normal, how we should behave and what's expected of us. I call this *normalitis*. I use a quote on my website by the author, poet and civil rights activist Maya Angelou: "If you're always trying to be normal you will never know how amazing you can be."

Pressure to conform was one of the themes that came up 72 times in my research. It's a topic that resonates with many who are trying to shift their lives. It appeared in ideas like 'tolerating work' or 'staying because of the money, other people or validation.' It was 'remaining in relationships and situations for the wrong reasons', sometimes out of social expectations, loyalty or because of comparison with others. It's understandable, as it's hard to go against the grain. We evolved in social groups, so we get a lot of support from the people around us and we also are expected to conform. Our emotions are very dependent on feeling accepted by others. In fact when we feel excluded there is increased activity in the area of the brain that feels pain. I also wrote a blog post about this called *Why be Normal?* I've included a shortened version below:

Normal has a lot to answer for. We like to belong and our mantra is: *don't stand out in case you're cast out.* Whilst there are wonderful exceptions, we mostly want to blend in. The worlds of fashion, beauty, technology (and others) would die if we didn't. Look the same, be the same. Just. Be. Normal. It shouldn't surprise us that *normality* constrains us, particularly when we're trying to change ourselves, when we're trying to fly away from the clutches of our friends and family. The word normal comes from the Latin *norma* meaning a rule to regulate behaviour and thought. It's also a Carpenter's Square, a metal tool that measures precise angles. We're encouraged to be normal because our idea of the opposite (abnormal) gets such a bad rap.

Jeanette Winterson's memoir is called *Why be happy when you could be normal*[118]*?* and the problem with striving for another person's version of normal, is that it often makes us deeply unhappy. Cathy is 40 and this is how she described *normalitis* for her. "Two years ago, I couldn't have spoken to you about this. I would have been in floods of tears, my life is over kind of thing." Cathy and her husband always thought they'd have children. They tried for years, including rounds of IVF, but with no success. So, they decided to stop.

With time and distance, Cathy feels differently. "We were just plodding through, doing the expected thing, getting married and having a baby. And actually, I'm questioning, did we really want it? Or was it because we thought we should?" How much was just social pressure and normalitis? "I've spent my whole life so worried about what people think of me... Really, you shouldn't give a damn about what other people think. But it's normal, it's human, isn't it? You want to fit in."

Liam felt the need to conform at a professional services firm. "There was this pressing weight of a reversion to the mean. Outliers, such as myself and others, had to revert to the mean. We had to play the game within this confined set of rules, or struggle, or just move organisation." It's not easy, but we need to look ahead and run our own race.

Madelana is from Portugal and says families create *normalitis* too. "I always feel that I'm so creative, even though I went a different route with my life in order to please my parents. So I think most people do that. They always want to please their parents. They want to be a good daughter."

It's hard to stand inside the precisely drawn square called *normality*. It's stressful when the lines keep moving. Normality isn't a standard measurement like height or temperature. It changes with geography and societies, people and situations. We use *not normal* to exclude and stigmatise, so *normality* makes us anxious. We sand down our oddities until we're fit for public consumption. Asking "Am I being normal enough today?" will stop us making a shift in our life.

Helen said, "I'm different, I'm weird and I'm not your normal interviewee. I'm not sure I'll be useful to you." What made her say this? Because she'd had quite a few roles over the years. John felt called to the Christian faith in his 30s. "There were moments like the first time I took my top off on holiday wearing a crucifix. I can still remember my sister-in-law gasping, 'I didn't realise you were one of them' with genuine concern, in her voice." He felt each time he made a statement there would be a reaction. "The moment before you step into these identities you fear people will ostracise you forever." But over the years he realised, "Quite quickly everybody just gets on with their lives. Who cares? So, John's a Christian, nobody gives a monkey's." In British English this means someone doesn't care, or isn't worried about something.

Steph is in her 30s. "I feel under pressure because I'm a woman of a certain age. Everyone keeps asking, 'When are you going to get married? When are you going to have children? If you don't do it by this stage, you're more likely to have a child with problems. Isn't that selfish of you?'" But Steph isn't so sure, "Part of me thinks I don't know if I ever want to have children. I think I'd rather have a dog at this point."

Jacqui says we limit our ability to shine in the world "because we're worried about the perceptions of others" and the world isn't "the scary judgmental place" that we fear it is. "No one gives two hoots about you. Not in a bad way. It's acknowledging that all these hang-ups we have and all these pressures we place on ourselves are really so futile. Because everyone is so absorbed in their own lives. So, whatever we put out, it's a fleeting moment of brilliance or it's a fleeting moment of failure. But either way it's fleeting."

Comparisonitis stems from *Normalitis* – looking sideways, checking how normal we are in comparison to others. Psychotherapist Alfred Adler said that feelings of inferiority are normal and in the age of social media this is amplified a hundred-fold. Social comparison used to involve around 10-20 close relationships, but in the digital universe there's limitless potential. Our average number of online 'friends' is over 300. We are also rewarded just for comparing. Former Facebook president, Sean Parker[119], described Facebook as a "social validation feedback loop." He admitted the *like* button was deliberately introduced to give "a little dopamine hit" so it would drive continued use.

In fact, our brains are comparing all the time, and this is one of the reasons we can be so dissatisfied. The grass is always greener because when we look at other peoples' lives. It's particularly difficult if we're on social media, because we only see the positive side, which leads us to feeling inadequate about our own lives. Gina is German and wants to stop comparing herself to others. She worries she'll be a failure if she doesn't achieve certain milestones. "I'm having a bit of a life crisis because I turned 30 and think it's too late. But I know that's kind of bullshit I'm telling myself." In our conversation we agreed, this isn't helpful. It's never too late to make a change.

 Don't compare yourself to other people. Stop living your life trying to keep up. You know we're all different. Just be yourself, make yourself happy and realise that all these material things won't actually do it.
— Alexander (interviewee)

Louisa says: "I used to put people I knew and worked with on a pedestal and think they'd got the perfect life." Since she opened up about how she's feeling, many of her friends shared what was going on for them too. Often, they would say, "I have imposter syndrome and I'm not 100% happy at work and I don't know what I want to do." Louisa says, "it just shows that you can't make assumptions about people." None of us has a perfect life, despite what social media may like us to think.

Another *comparisonitis* issue is the prevailing view that we must innately know what our passion is in life. Without it we are empty. This is from Nolan: "I have lost a lot of myself to work. I asked myself what interests do I have? What are my passions? I don't have any. I've become an empty husk of a person." In his book *So Good They Can't Ignore You*[120], Cal Newport says that passion isn't about discovery, it's about cultivation. Passion needs promoting and nurturing, so it's not helpful to think of it as simply buried deep inside, that it just needs surfacing. In her TED talk, Terri Trespicio[121] says we need to stop searching for our passion, instead we just need to live a life of meaning and value, then the passion will follow.

3) Always stuck in second gear (that's right *Friends* aficionados... I am channelling the theme tune):

This is a gearshift from the last two sections, a different challenge, when we just can't drive fast enough. We grind along in second gear, not finding the third gear of momentum. I'll stop the car analogies now. Perhaps you're not dedicating enough time to the work? Were you sold on the goal in the first place? Maybe at a deeper level it's not really what you want to achieve. If this is you I suggest going back to the WHY and WHERE chapters to have a rethink. You might need to adapt, pivot, or change tack or stop the project and work on something else.

Another reason for being stuck could be your personality. Do you tend to get excited at the start, full of ideas and energy, but find the *doing* bit less engaging? Hands up if you want to join me in the *Great-Starter-But-Lousy-Finisher* corner of the room. I'm an ideas factory as I churn them out all the time. But expect me to turn them into something concrete, oh, no, that's not where I'm at. My house and life are littered with unfinished projects from wooden dressers I was going to strip and re-varnish, art materials languishing in the attic for years, to unfinished novels about Neanderthals. My life is a black hole of half-baked projects.

That's why I'm organising frequent rewards to encourage myself to finish writing this book. Why not go back to chapter 15 to remind yourself about motivations and rewards. Another helpful focus is pacing. I received wonderful advice from a journalist a while back. He suggested that rather than starting on a book, I cut my writing teeth on a blog. He was right. Focusing on 1,000 words at a time was much easier to sustain than writing 100,000 words in one sitting. Over two years I wrote 77,000 words of the blog and am using many of the ideas, and some of the copy, here in this book.

 I'm moving on, I'm moving out of where I'm living because I felt this isn't working anymore. I've got to start shifting behaviour patterns. If *it's* not shifting, *you've* got to shift. — Ellen (interviewee)

How can you do the equivalent and change the way you're seeing your project? I remember being disappointed when the journalist suggested a book wasn't the right focus. I had set my heart on creating one and felt a bit despondent at the prospect of blogging. But with hindsight, it was exactly the right thing to do. How can you switch your project around, chunk it up into smaller pieces, so it's easier to manage? Or pivot, change direction? I suggest going back through some of the previous chapters to see where you might have gone off track.

Another option is that you're struggling with decision making. If this is the case, then you're not alone. Julie from Australia finds it difficult too. "It's like a couch-potato having to go out and walk to Antarctica or climb Mount Everest. Like going from zero to 100. My decision-making muscle has been sitting on the couch for the last 20 years." Why not try the decision-making exercise in Appendix A?

 I know I don't want to go backwards. I only want to go forwards. That's always been quite a good source of motivation. So just keep going, things can only get better. — Bill (interviewee)

This is from Saavi, who is keen to get going. "Something is not fitting, my life isn't fitting, my choices aren't fitting. My parents are getting older and time is ticking. I can't piss about anymore. I don't have the time for this nonsense anymore, wasting it on things and people, that quite frankly mean nothing at the end of the day."

What about tackling the voice in your head, dealing with your anxiety? Marcia is from Brazil and she's stuck in second gear. "I'm an Olympic swimmer standing in a bucket of water." That's how she started our conversation, painting a picture of everything she needed to say. This image of her confined in a bucket shouted loud and clear. "This is exactly how I feel. I just feel like I'm ready. I've got the muscles. I've got everything, but I just keep my feet there in the bucket." Marcia believes she can do more. "I know I have the strength and the capability of swimming in the whole ocean. I'm just standing in the bucket and just watching everything around me. And that is very, very frustrating." So, what's holding her back? "The frustration is with myself because at the end of the day, I'm the one who needs to make the move." She wants to change but she's anxious. "I just overthink things and don't really act. My issue now is to act."

Marcia is annoyed with herself. "I'm going to be 40 years old soon and I still have a lot of work to do if I want to get to where I want. To get my own place one day. But for that I need to make more money. I imagined myself being a couple of years further on. I just trapped myself in this small bucket of water."

So, what can Marcia do? She's started working on self-affirmations, encouraging herself into action, even if the way ahead isn't clear yet. "Even if I don't know where I'm going, just walk. Even if I cannot see the steps of the path, I just need to keep walking." Find out more about self-affirmations in Appendix A.

Exercise 23: Creating self-compassion

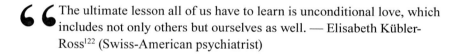 The ultimate lesson all of us have to learn is unconditional love, which includes not only others but ourselves as well. — Elisabeth Kübler-Ross[122] (Swiss-American psychiatrist)

Some of the ways you can create more self-compassion[123] are through:

- **Mindfulness exercises** are all about learning to be more in the moment, to be present, in a non-judgemental and neutral way. The more present we are, the more we understand our own mind. For example: 1) pay attention to your senses. Slow down and notice what you can hear, see, smell, taste; 2) body scan by focusing deliberately on each part of your body. Start with your head and end with your toes. Slowly work your way down, being aware of sensations, emotions, or thoughts you have about each part of your body; 3) You can even do a walking meditation – focusing on the experience of slowly walking, being aware of the sensations in your feet and legs, being present and in the moment.

- **Compassion focused imagery** involves imagining scenarios that help you to develop care and empathy for yourself. Try recalling someone you care about – a family member family, good friend, even an animal. Close your eyes and slow your breathing down. Imagine this person is in front of you and they need your help. Feel a sense of caring towards them, notice your emotions/physical sensations in your body. What would you say to them? What is your tone of voice like? How are you comforting them? Focus on how it's making you feel both emotionally and in your body.

- If you find this hard because you don't have these types of relationships in your life, then you can create a composite of others; an imaginary person or animal that you feel you would feel compassionate towards. It doesn't matter how fanciful this is, it's just to activate your feelings of compassion, so whatever image achieves this will be fine.

- **Relaxation techniques** are important too. Sitting and breathing for just one minute can help. Why not have a look again at Appendix A where you can find more on relaxation and breathing exercises.

- Exploring the roots of your self-critical thoughts and why you believe them, which can include describing how these thoughts make you act and feel. You might need help with this from a professional. You can also learn to change negative thinking patterns. Why not go back to re-read this in earlier chapters? You can also look at the *Thinking Errors* exercise in Appendix A.

- Another way to become more self-compassionate is through setting clear boundaries on what you will say yes to and what you'll say no to. It's too easy to bend to other people's wills and end up being overworked, focusing energy and time on other's needs and not our own. If you'd like to find more about this, then Dr Kristen Neff is a leading expert on self-compassion. You can find a range of useful resources on her website.[124]

4) Gripping too tightly:

Success doesn't happen in straight lines, a direct route from A to B, because life gets in the way. There are unexpected roadblocks, we get distracted, we lose energy, we get bored. Arriving at our goal looks more like this: set off from home to visit a friend, walk for a while then get lost. Discover a new road, get absorbed by the window display in a shop we hadn't seen before. Take a call on our mobile phone. Pop into supermarket to buy milk, wonder what we are doing there. Remind ourselves we were supposed to be heading to our friend's house. Eventually arrive laden with unexpected grocery gifts and milk products.

> " A goal is not always meant to be reached; it often serves simply as something to aim at. — Bruce Lee

Let's revisit the *transtheoretical model of behavior change* (TTM) once more. The different stages are anything but linear. We don't go through the stages in one go. Instead, we go around, get stuck, go back, head off again. Remember my colleague Sarah, the coach and therapist? She says: "The research shows that… people can loop backwards and forwards and it's important to factor in the possibility of setbacks and how you might deal with them." We need to let go of the project delivery date, the expectation we will arrive exactly at 3pm on a Wednesday. We'll only make ourselves disappointed that we've failed again.

Sarah says this of TTM: "Typically people cycle through the process at least three times before a change sticks. Knowing this can help with motivation." Often people use the idea of a spiral. Most people will relapse and will feel like a failure; embarrassed, ashamed or guilty. They'll become demoralised and resist change, heading back into the pre-contemplation stage, potentially ending up there for some time. Slipping up is a normal part of the process. If you're trying to give up alcohol, for example, there's no point in saying, "I might as well go and get drunk" just because you've had one glass. What's more important is how you deal with this set-back, the disappointment you feel in not hitting your goals. Recovering after a lapse, limiting the damage and getting back on track is key. Some people call this *grit*[125].

What will help you is if you can be a little kinder to yourself. Our culture is focused on achievement, which means we rarely stop to think about how success arrives in fits and starts. Successful people mess up, fail, give up, start again. We just see the end result. Why not go back to your project plan and shift the dates a little? Take out actions, re-organise your to-do list? Align it with where you are, not where you feel you *should* be. You might even try visualisations again.

Gripping tightly means we lose the magic of serendipity, unexpected things that happen to take us down a better path. The new people we accidentally meet, the actions we try, things that weren't in the plan. We're so focused on the finish line that we drive through our project like a bull in a china shop. We're busy running headlong towards the finish line. We need to loosen up a bit.

> Don't monkey grip it, not to grip it so much. Just to let it go and see what evolves… try not to try to control it so much. — Julie (interviewee)

Bill says that in the past, "I've made a decision… and I've said, 'I'm going to stick with it, even if it's not making me happy. I feel like I've got a duty to see it through to the end, no matter what that is. If I stayed with a person or stayed with a job, I was a bit fearful of change." Things are improving though for Bill. "Now I know that it's not healthy for me physically or mentally to do that. It can be painful making the change and it's something I'm probably going to have to go through quite soon." Bill says, "I want to be happy with myself and be comfortable with the way I live my life. So, it's something that I need to do."

Alma is trying to shift her behaviour and let go of her iron grip. She says that she used to be "a massive control freak" and wouldn't do anything unless she "knew what the outcome was going to be." But, she persuaded herself to leave "with nothing to go to. And for somebody like me… to have left with nothing and just to see what happened, just go with the flow. That was huge."

Holding on too tightly to deadlines and project plans can mean focusing on quantity over quality. We're rushing through the steps in order to get to the end. In *Atomic Habits*[126], James Clear says it's easy to convince ourselves that we're making headway when we're in motion. It can make us feel we're being productive, even if the actions aren't good quality. If this is you, why not revisit the evaluation chapter again to remind yourself about measuring progress?

Annita agrees. "We spend our lives chasing the change we're looking for, when actually what we need to do is get away from the chase." Sometimes we need to "reassess and re-evaluate and actually do nothing. Or do very little. Sometimes the change needs to be not so much doing, but more about being. Reassessing our values, reassessing what makes us happy, reassessing who we are and how we show up as people."

Cecilia was another participant who needed to take time out. But she couldn't sit still. "The whole premise was to take a break. Before I had even finished, I agreed to stay on part time and do two days a week remotely." She also signed up for "a breathing course, learning how to do different types of breathing for stress and anxiety." She joined a creative art therapy course, plus "started signing up to do pottery and drawing and all these things. And then my therapist said, 'so when are you actually having a break? Because you've somehow gone from resigning and taking time out to filling your day to the max with all these other things.'"

Cecilia says, "I overload myself with it… I turn it into a project and suddenly this is now my new job, to self-improve, and to do whatever it is to fix myself." She realises "sitting alone and sitting quietly and doing nothing terrifies me. So, I can't do that. I have to fill all my time." When Anna was going through a big change in her life, she also wanted to keep busy. She got "straight into list-making, networking, planning, plotting. I felt I had to be productive and my brain was firing in so many directions. I had quite a lot of sleepless nights, lying awake, with my brain going crazy." Sometimes sitting patiently needs to be the order of the day. You might want to go back and read about patience again in chapter nine.

> ❝❝ You have to learn to live in the present and enjoy the process. Enjoy
> what you've got. Enjoy learning because the end goal isn't the point.
> — Lucy (interviewee)

———

That's it - we're now at the end of this chapter, so here are some questions that will cover the topics we discussed:

- Do you have the right cheerleaders on board? Are they cheering you on? Or do you need a re-think in terms of the types of people resources you have around you?
- Are you suffering from *Normalitis*? Are you worried what people think of you, does it stop you from striding out, doing things differently, making a change?
- What about *Comparisonitis*? How much are you wondering what other people are doing with their lives? Is this preventing you from taking action?
- What about motivation? Are you finding it difficult to get the energy or time to set the wheels in motion? Do you need to change your assumptions, aim a little less far, make a pivot in what you're doing?
- Would the self-compassion exercises help? Why don't you do some of them now?
- Or are you gripping onto your project plan, even though it's no longer right for you? Are you holding onto expectations of how this shift *should* be going?

In the next chapter we'll be looking at the last few areas that might explain why your change project isn't working so well. Then we'll have good news stories from people who've successfully made their way through a shift in their lives.

Chapter 19

This is the final chapter on why your shift may not be working yet. Here are the last five topics that we'll cover:

1) Green shoots
2) Toolbox is empty
3) Mood music
4) Have an app for that
5) The crucible

1) Green shoots:

I wrote a blog post about impatience, called *How the Art of Patience can Turn Your Life Around*. It was about a time when I planted vegetable seeds and was too eager for the green shoots to appear. I wrote this in the piece: *The problem is that in our modern world we've lost the art of patience, we want the upper hand in life. We want to bend things to our needs, to will something into being with the power of our minds.* Are you doing this with your change project? Are you staring at your seedlings, willing them into existence, angry because they're not appearing? Or have the green shoots come up, but they are disappointing, a bit weak and feeble? Are you annoyed they aren't bigger yet?

Sometimes we're impatient for changes, expecting things to look different on the outside, even though we might be shifting our mindset, seeing the world differently. We're re-structuring ourselves deep inside. Whilst this may not feel like progress, believe me, it is. We're impatient because we're measuring the wrong things. We're looking for concrete shifts, physical, observable steps forward, unaware of what's changing under the surface. That seed is working hard when you can't see it. By the time it pokes above the soil, it has already travelled some distance.

When we eventually do have some successes, we might miss them because they're small. We were expecting mighty oaks. A series of tiny wins, laid out side by side, stretch quite far. Added together, your change will be quite large. What seedlings and change projects have in common is they don't grow on demand. You plant a seed and it does nothing for weeks, then, when shoots eventually appear above ground, they don't even grow straight. It's frustrating that willpower alone doesn't control the world.

In an earlier chapter we covered HOW MUCH and HOW WELL. I shared these tips with you: needing to baseline before you start, using different ratings for measurement and bypassing roadblocks (if progress stalls). Trying different evaluation lenses (quality/quantity), internal and external measures of success (yourself/others) and measuring the good, the bad and the ugly (assessing what is going well as often as what isn't).

If your change project appears not to be working, check to see if this is really true. Have you used different types of measurements, as outlined above? Are you discounting green shoots because they're too small? Lucy beats herself when she's not doing well against her goals. We talked about the business she had set up and the specific challenges she had that week, creating a video to sell her services. "I can get very stuck on the next goal, the next achievement. Even these videos, telling myself, 'I've got to send them to the person because I want to get PR.'" She reminds herself to "enjoy the process of learning how to create a video. I didn't know how to do this life skill a day ago."

I like this quote by Fred Lebow, co-founder of the New York Marathon: "In running, it doesn't matter whether you come in first, in the middle of the pack, or last. You can say, 'I have finished.' There is a lot of satisfaction in that." We need to reframe what we mean by progress or success. Some might say just finishing is not enough, but whose voice is that? Why isn't that a worthy goal? Is this you speaking, or a parent, teacher, someone from the past? Here's another quote by Kara Goucher[127], a US Olympic marathon runner and writer: "That's the thing about running: your greatest runs are rarely measured by racing success. They are moments in time when running allows you to see how wonderful your life is."

Sometimes it's not helpful to wrestle with the change we're going through. We're trying too hard, beating it into submission, not dancing with this new life. *Motivational Interviewing* (MI) is a way of working with clients to help them through change. Some MI practitioners (coaches and therapists) use ballroom dancing as a metaphor for their work. Ballroom dancing is best when two people dance in partnership, the therapist and client moving together with the music.

They use a contrasting image of wrestling when the work isn't going so well. One person trying to assert their will over the other. Why not think about your own shift using these two sets of images? If you're fighting too hard then it'll be exhausting for you and your change project! Try to coax your new life into being a little more gently. If you're getting frustrated, then pause and ask yourself "Am I dancing or wrestling with this change?"

Try focusing on the fact that you're still going, that you have tenacity, you are applying yourself. So, you haven't hit all your targets, some things haven't gone to plan, never mind, just keep going, don't let that get you down.

2) Toolbox is empty

Did you skip over some of the resources chapters? Did you take one look at the titles and think, "These aren't for me. I've got everything I need already." Perhaps you wanted to save time, who doesn't want that back in their life? If this is you, could I gently persuade you to go back and read them?

Maybe you thought your toolbox was full, but when you opened it, someone had pilfered half your tools. Perhaps you're not sleeping well, or maybe your diet is off? Is it your mindset that isn't helping you, are you doubting yourself? I can assure you the time reading these chapters will be well spent. It's useful to know which resources you need, and which you have, or haven't got.

Perhaps you diligently read those chapters word for word, but you're still no better off. You tried to stock up your toolbox, but it still isn't full. A screwdriver and a wrench aren't sufficient, not enough to create sustainable change. If you haven't resourced yourself fully then why not ask yourself some of these questions?

- Do you have the right skills for this change project? Can you build them up?
- Are you focusing on your strengths, or bashing away at things you're not very good at?
- What about money? Is that something you need to work on? Creating a fund that will support you through this, outsourcing some actions, making you sleep better at night?
- Are you drinking enough? I mean water, rather than alcohol!
- Are you taking time off for sport, exercise and fun hobbies?
- If it's people you're lacking, then go back and re-read Cheerleaders on strike.
- Do you believe in yourself, or rather believe that you'll fail? Is there some work to do on your faith in this project and your ability to achieve it?
- Are you being impatient, trying to push it through too quickly?
- Or perhaps you are too focused on the project plan, not letting serendipity take its course?

Whatever it is, without the right resources you just won't have the tools to do the work. Why not go back to exercise 15, the resources quiz? Then you can fully assess where you are and check for your gaps.

3) Mood music

Any change in life involves a period of mourning, however short. We need to let go of the past to leave space for the future. Elizabeth Kübler-Ross studied death and dying, including people going through bereavement. One message from her work is that you need to say goodbye before you can say hello; you need to let you go before you can welcome something in.

The philosopher Alain de Botton[128] talks about moods and how they can affect us every day. They'll go up and down and when you're in a good mood it might feel as though you have worked life out. But de Botton warns us this will pass and the same will happen in reverse. When we're in a bad mood we might be utterly despairing, feeling that everything will go wrong and we're a complete failure. What we need to do instead is to accept that both good moods and bad ones are just temporary, they are simply states of mind.

Andy Puddicombe is a former Buddhist and founder of meditation app,

Headspace[129]. In one of the app's meditations, he says that sadness and happiness are two sides of the same coin. We spend so much time chasing happiness and scurrying from sadness, but it's impossible to have one without the other. I personally believe happiness and sadness are just two colours in the rainbow of different moods or emotions. Going through difficult emotions can actually help us grow. It doesn't make it fun of course, but that's another issue.

Here is a scientific and hairy example. Dr Michelle Craske[130] at the University of California invited people who were terrified of spiders to handle tarantulas. Who needs a psychologist as a friend? One group distracted themselves with logic, e.g. saying, "It's in a cage. It can't hurt me." A second group were invited to describe their emotions, such as "I'm feeling nervous and scared." The third group were asked to say something irrelevant and the fourth were just shown the spider but asked to say nothing. A week later they had to handle the tarantulas again and were assessed for sweat levels and how distressed they felt. Of all the groups, the second one, those who described how they felt, reduced their emotions the most. So, labelling our emotions can calm us down. Lovely, spidery cuddles for everyone.

We can do this exercise (without spiders), by calling out our moods. The switch from "I am lonely" to "I am feeling lonely" creates a gap between our thoughts and feelings, which we covered in an earlier chapter. When we name our emotions, it can give us separation from them. We can observe, "Oh yes I'm feeling a bit lonely." The step is from "I'm always a lonely person" to "I'm a person who sometimes feels alone."

Another way to reflect on our moods is to think of emotions as data. They are neither good nor bad, just indicators of things that are important to us. It's our bodies and minds telling us that we need to take action, that we are missing something in our lives. We heard earlier about *Toxic Positivity* and how this is just a way of pushing down our true feelings; either because we feel they aren't socially acceptable or because the people we know can't handle them. A resource that might be helpful is Susan Cain's latest book, *Bittersweet: How Sorrow and Longing Make us Whole*[131], where she explores the more complicated emotions like sadness and melancholy.

One of our additional challenges is that we are generally poor at estimating how deeply we will feel positive emotions and how long those will last. This means we strive to reach a goal, let's say getting a pay-rise or buying our first guitar but, once we achieve it, the sense of achievement doesn't last that long.

I recorded an episode of my *Tyranny of the Shoulds* podcast called *Milestones that Become Millstones*, where this happened to a number of guests. You can find that on the website. Of course, there is an upside of our poor predictions, we overestimate how long we will have negative emotions, feeling sad or angry about something that isn't working out in our lives.

Related to this challenge is *adaptation*, which means we get used to new ways of living quite quickly. For example, people who win the lottery often go back to their previous levels of happiness just a short time after their big win. Our brains are wired to deal with sudden change but bathing in champagne loses its appeal after a while. Daniel Gilbert[132] says that a cruel truth is that wonderful things are wonderful when we first encounter them but that feeling diminishes with repetition.

Identifying our own emotions is important and it's what psychologists called *labelling*. Sometimes we know we're feeling something, but we're not quite sure what. If you find it hard to understand your emotions, you might like to watch a film called *Alfred and the Shadow - a short story about emotions*[133], created by psychologist and therapist, Anne Hilde Vassbø Hagen and Dr Leslie Greenberg. They explain why trying to suppress or ignore our emotions can lead to more problems. In contrast, listening to our emotions can help us achieve the goals we really want.

Exercise 24: Working with Your Emotions

1) A quick action you can take is to think about how you're feeling about this book and the suggestions I have been making. Ask yourself:

- How am I feeling about Swim, Jump, Fly, what emotions am I feeling?
- Thinking about these feelings, how am I responding (0 is no emotion, 10 is strongest emotion you could feel)?
- Then ask yourself, what level of emotion would be appropriate (0 none, 10 high). This may put your mood or your emotions into perspective.
- You can also ask yourself if this feeling had a voice, what would it encourage me to do?

2) Perhaps you're finding it hard to know what you're feeling right now? This can be quite common. When we're feeling too much emotion, one of our coping mechanisms is to numb ourselves and not engage with our feelings. This can make it harder for us to access them. If you think this might be you, there's an exercise you can try in Appendix A. Or you can use an app called *Universe of Emotions*[134] which helps you track your emotions and start taking steps towards working on them.

3) Let's also talk about the opposite end of the spectrum, being light-hearted, of course, it's not possible to do that all the time. But let's say you're sitting on the emotional fence. Your mood could go one way or the other. If you're there, why not try to let go a little, see the silliness, the funny side of it all. Life can be absurd and comical at times. Rachel's advice is "don't take yourself so seriously." She says one of the things she has struggled with is "just taking myself too seriously all the time, rather than enjoying what I'm doing." This seems to be working for Rachel as she says, "I'm much happier in my personal life because I'm doing projects and getting involved with things that are fun."

4) Have an app for that

Have you heard of *learned helplessness*? It's a psychology term that means we're conditioned to expect suffering or discomfort without being able to escape it. If this suffering happens to us often enough, eventually we will stop trying to avoid the pain or suffering at all. They just give up. We all know other people that fall into this trap and sometimes we do that ourselves.

The challenge is that once it takes hold in part of our life, then it can impact other areas too, starting in a relationship, spreading into our health and then into work. It's linked to loss of motivation, anxiety, depression, burnout, stress, and behaviours that from the outside don't make sense to other people. However, if we can build our levels of optimism, then we're more likely to avoid, or get over, *learned helplessness*. For example, we can't always control negative life events, but we can change the way we think about them.

Here's another psychology idea that may be of interest, *locus of control*. It's a concept developed by Julian B. Rotter in 1954 and is the amount of influence or control we believe we have over our life. If we have a high external locus of control, we might say external factors control our life, but if we are someone with a high internal locus of control, we'll think what happens is controlled by our actions.

I wonder whether there's a trend nowadays. Corporations latch on to our perceived needs, offer us fixes for everything. There's a hack for this, an app for that, a pill to pop, something to outsource to someone (or something) else. All in, it means we want other people to fix our problems. Sometimes I think we've lost the art of agency, knowing we can sort things out ourselves.

In his book *The Power of Now: A Guide to Spiritual Enlightenment*[135], Eckhart Tolle tells a story of a beggar who has been sitting by the side of a road for 30 years. A stranger walks by and the beggar asks if he can spare some change. The stranger says he has nothing to give the beggar, but instead points at the box the beggar is sitting on. He asks if he has ever looked inside, but the beggar shakes his head, there's no point as it's empty. Eventually, when the stranger persuades the beggar to open the box he is completely surprised, as it's filled with gold. In his book Tolle says that he is the stranger with nothing to offer, except a question – that asks you to look inside yourself.

Now back to one of the participants, Steven. We met him earlier in the book when he was talking about his career in journalism. When we caught up for the interview, Steven recounted others on his career changing course and how they were hoping the work would be done for them: "Some of the people I've spoken to in the group expected some sort of moment... they almost expect there to be a test at the end, and you pass the test and suddenly you have a new career. No, that's not how it works, you have to go and build it yourself."

In chapter eight we *covered Cognitive Behavioural Coaching/Therapy*. One of the key aspects of CBC/CBT is to help clients support themselves over time, so they no longer need help from the coach or therapist. The American Psychological Association[136] writes about CBT on its website, explaining that it focuses on helping people to become their own therapists, using exercises inside and homework outside the session. This way the person will develop coping skills that can help them change their thinking, emotion and behaviour, and support them in achieving their longer-term goals.

What I'm saying is that the shift you're going through is down to you. We can all do with a hand-up and support from others. Collaborating will help us achieve our goals. But take this too far and expect other people to do all the hard work isn't the way to go either. If you do, you'll be putting your life in someone else's hands. You'll be outsourcing your desires and hopes to another person and they won't be as passionate about your life as you are.

5) The crucible

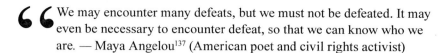
We may encounter many defeats, but we must not be defeated. It may even be necessary to encounter defeat, so that we can know who we are. — Maya Angelou[137] (American poet and civil rights activist)

Kintsugi is a centuries-old Japanese art of fixing cracked pottery. Rather than hide the cracks, the technique involves re-joining the broken pieces with lacquer mixed with powdered gold, silver, or platinum. When put back together, the piece of pottery looks more beautiful than they were it was whole. The pot remembers its broken history, it celebrates its cracks. We're the same, we become better people, stronger, more resilient after a few knocks and bumps. The crucible is just life really, the challenges that we face, the hurdles we have to tackle.

Here's another example from the natural world: fire can be a vital source of growth and some plants need heat for their seeds to germinate. The Lodgepole Pine is one example. It has cones that are sealed with resin and its outer case melts when heated up. Eucalyptus trees are another. They are *re-sprouters* as they have special buds under their bark and when the tree burns the buds emerge to grow into new leaves and branches.

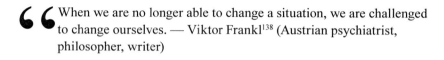
When we are no longer able to change a situation, we are challenged to change ourselves. — Viktor Frankl[138] (Austrian psychiatrist, philosopher, writer)

Post-traumatic growth is a psychological term that suggests it is possible to grow through adversity. Psychologists Richard Tedeschi and Lawrence Calhoun[139] coined the term for those positive changes that can happen after traumatic events. There are times in our lives when we're thrown up into the air and these challenging times can change our assumptions about who we are and the way the world works. It's what some call a psychological seismic earthquake.

During these very difficult events, Tedeschi and Calhoun say that people often find out who their real friends are, seeing the best and the worst in others. They may be disappointed by the actions of their close friends, but surprised by those they know less well, who turn out to be more supportive. At these moments there are opportunities for growth, a change in our priorities and a new-found sense of purpose, meaning and connection with others. Do you feel like you're going through a fire right now in your life? Maybe you need the white-hot challenge of a crucible to rise from the ashes, to use the heat and the smoke to re-calibrate yourself?

In July 2020 journalist Chris Morris[140] wrote about the potential long-term impact of Covid-19 and post-traumatic stress. Not as much was known at that point, but even early in the pandemic doctors could see that some patients were experiencing *post-traumatic growth*; they were emerging from the pandemic with a new outlook, determined to live a good life.

I attended a training session run by psychologist Dr Steve Taylor[141]. For 13 years he's been researching people who experience adversity and transformation. In one project he interviewed people to find out what changes they'd experienced after bereavement. They said they were less materialistic, less afraid of death, more loving, trusting, appreciative or grateful. They were also more open, authentic and compassionate, had changes to their goals (more internal, more altruistic) and had greater appreciation and connection to nature.

In 2020, Scott Barry Kaufman[142] wrote about seven areas of growth that spring from adversity: more appreciation of life, better relationships with close friends and family, more compassion and altruism, discovering new purpose in life, increased knowledge of personal strengths (and then finding ways to use them), creative growth and also spiritual development. In his book *Transcend*[143], he writes that when our foundations are shaken through challenging times we're in the best position to pursue new things. My hope is the last few years of the global pandemic may help many people to see new opportunities in their lives too.

Even if we're not going through a traumatic time, what can we learn from the people who are? Dr Steve Taylor says whatever we experience we need to fully embrace it. "Rather than pushing away our predicaments we need to go towards them." He says we need to explore our reactions and feelings. Reach out and hold them, it will make the negativity shrink. "We need to move into a mode of acceptance and stop resisting. We need to let go and embrace the situation. That will harness the transformational potential."

Did you ever have growing pains when you were a child? The name is accurate. In order to grow, it has to be a bit painful at times. To develop as adults, to see the world with a different perspective, we also have to go through challenges. Whilst it's not much fun, we come out the other end a better person. This is what one of the participants, Helen, said about this topic: "The more you've suffered and the more stuff you've been through, the more playful and light-hearted you can be about life."

For years Walter was trying to push himself into the wrong life. "I was that proverbial square trying to fit into the circle. Trying to force myself in because that's what I felt I should be doing." Over the years it weighed heavily on him, until he had a break-down. "I know it's a cliché to say, but it changed my life. I'm glad I had a break-down, it has formed who I am now. Where I am now. I'm a lot, lot better off." If he hadn't fallen apart, he says, "I wouldn't have given up the alcohol. I may have had a relationship break down. I may have never seen my kids. There are so many other routes it could have taken. I count myself very fortunate that I broke down, I mean, how lucky."

Mel is another participant and she gives us some good advice: "Most things pass, so try not to get too upset about the things that are bothering you here and now, because, with a bit of time and distance, most of them become less important. Try to make sure that you are doing something every day that gives you some kind of fulfilment." I'll end this topic with a final quote from Viktor Frankl, from his book *Man's Search for Meaning*[144]: "In some ways suffering ceases to be suffering at the moment it finds a meaning."

Harvard Professor Robert Kegan[145] developed a theory of adult development that says that we go through five different stages as we mature. He says most of us don't get beyond stage three (what he calls the *socialised mind*) because we're so focused on what other people think. The most important things to us are the ideas, norms and beliefs of the people and systems around us (i.e. family, society, culture etc.). We want validation.

There are fewer people at stage four (*self-authoring mind*) because it's much more focused on defining who we are and not having our lives dictated by others, or our environment. At this stage we become aware of assumptions and unwritten rules, boundaries that we, or others set; sometimes based on passing comments from those around us, that shape our lives for decades. At stage four we start to question expectations and values, re-write how we are living, taking responsibility for our feelings and emotions. We realise we are adapting and changing, we don't need to stay stuck.

However, the transition from stage three to four can be unsettling because many of the things we thought were certain turn out to be flimsy. We may not be resisting change so much as resisting loss. There is an upside too because we start to see the world in different ways and have more choices over the actions we will take. Perhaps you are moving from stage three to four in your life? Perhaps that's why you might be questioning your relationships, work, family, or the society around you and want to change?

One final thought to share. If you're going through a shift in your life things might get a bit worse before they get better. This is often the case in therapy and coaching. When you're picking apart areas of your life that aren't working, it can feel like picking at a wound. What may appear to be lack of progress, or even going backwards, is actually a sign of progress. Feeling bad means you're aware of what needs to shift and are more likely to put in the effort so you can achieve your goals. And don't forget we can only move forwards if we start from where we are.

———

OK, that's the end of this chapter and the section on why things might not be working for you. Again, instead of summarising, I'll ask you the last set of questions:

- Are you missing green shoots of progress because you're expecting something momentous?
- Perhaps you're looking externally for something concrete when the tectonic plates are moving underneath?
- What about your toolbox, has it got enough tools in it to help you move forward? Or do you need to review the resources chapters again, work out what's missing and fill the gaps?
- How about emotions and moods? Have you been feeling up and down over the weeks or months? Can you stand back and see them as swells in the water, which will naturally come and go?
- Are you expecting others to do the work of change for you? Hoping you can outsource all the pain and discomfort to someone else?
- Finally, could you see this challenging time as an opportunity to forge a new version of yourself? Rise from the ashes like a phoenix, become somebody different?

In the next chapter we will focus on good news stories – hearing from all those people who have been through the fire and come out the other side.

Chapter 20

In this chapter we'll focus on good news stories. People who have gone through the mill and come out the other side, happier with life. The reason I use stories is because they are so powerful. Stories motivate and energise, they bring concepts down to earth and ground us in the everyday. They normalise challenges we are going through and make us feel less alone.

Stories are everywhere. On TV, in the movies, in the songs we listen to and in our newsfeeds. The author and lecturer Robert McKee has dedicated 30 years to helping screenwriters, novelists, directors, and playwrights tell better stories. In his book *Story: Substance, Structure, Style, and the Principles of Screenwriting*[146], he says stories help us understand the patterns of living, which can often be a very personal and emotional experience.

> ❝❝There's power in allowing yourself to be known and heard, in owning your unique story, in using your authentic voice. And there's grace in being willing to know and hear others. — Michelle Obama

Storytelling is so prevalent that the word *story* came up 128 times in my interviews. This is from one of the participants, Orla, who told a story about work and how the narrative encouraged her to take a different path. "There were always stories of partners having heart attacks when they weren't expecting it. And people collapsing on the stairs because they'd worked too hard." These were seen as normal stories, not strange at all to the people around her. But she started to think, "This is madness. We're killing ourselves. Why are we doing this?"

Stories were often shared in Walter's Alcoholic Anonymous group. "People's stories – they just resonated with how I was feeling inside. It's that connection. They built a way out of holes a million times worse than mine." These people have gone on to lead successful and happy lives. So, for Walter, it was, "Inspiring if they could do it feeling just like I did inside. I wanted to follow that route."

> ❝❝We realize the importance of our voices only when we are silenced." — Malala Yousafzai[147] (Pakistani activist for female education and Nobel Peace Prize laureate)

Sara used her father's story to guide her decision-making. Her parents were from China and "settled in the UK in the 1970s." They came from a "very difficult background, trying to provide for us and not really speaking the language. When my father passed away it made me think about his story. And how it was completely different to anyone else's story." Sara felt compelled to carry on his legacy of wanting the best for his children, for them to be happy. "I asked myself that question when I had to return to work. 'Am I happy in what I'm doing?' I could continue doing it, but not be happy. And I thought I had to get off the treadmill of just going to work because I felt I should."

Earlier we heard that Rory was the first black man on the Board of a well-known organisation. On one occasion he was invited to present at a diversity event but didn't know what they wanted to hear. He decided just to tell his own story because "I realised that I don't have to do anything. I don't have to create anything, pretend to be anything." So, he talked about the people who had influenced his life. "I told a series of stories that weren't about race or ethnicity. They were about experiences in life and leadership and learning and growth."

At the end of my conversation with Adeola, I asked her how she felt sharing her story with others. "I think it's me offering something out there. Hopefully somebody will learn something from it, take something for their own journey. Because, for me, it's about human connection and telling my story."

Another interviewee, Misha, told me how other peoples' narratives helped her; for example, stories in the books *The Buddhist Boot Camp* by Timber Hawkeye and *The Monk Who Sold His Ferrari* by Robin Sharma. She said, "These are stories about people that were where I am now." I asked what it was like sharing her story with me. "I think just verbalising what I've been thinking actually is quite powerful, I think powerful for myself to hear it, and hopefully, helpful to others. I think it must be really interesting for you to hear people's responses."

When we listen to the accounts of other people, we're often just given the headlines, the big-ticket changes. We don't hear about all the trials and tribulations, we just get hear about the successes. However, behind any change there are a series of small steps, failures, experiments that go wrong and just a lot of hard work. Most of the hard graft is below the waterline because we just don't get to hear about it.

In this chapter I've included good news stories from interviewees. They are made up of changes over time, rather than one or two enormous leaps to success. We met John earlier in chapter 18, so here's a bit more about his story. John was 32 when his life started to unravel. "I sensed that my life was not on a good track. That my ambition and my focus on status and achievement risked taking me over the edge. I was aware of that and I didn't know what the answer to it was."

John went on a course through his work which included in-depth coaching and introspection. "As part of that I got in touch with emotions and memories that were very disturbing, which threw me into a different consciousness. I didn't have a language for it. I didn't have a conceptual framework for it, but I had this experience that I couldn't deny. I knew it had changed me." Because of this, his life has taken a different and more meaningful course over the last 20 or so years.

John describes himself as "a seeker of the truth. I was always digging. I was always curious." Further work revealed something momentous to him, "When I eventually delved sufficiently deeply, I realised there was something that I should know." Unfortunately, it was a tough one to discover. "In reconnecting with that part of me, the child that had gone through that experience, that's where I found the truth to something else. That was the truth of my Faith."

John sees all sorts of changes in this unfolding of himself. "Whilst in one sense, it was a shattering experience it was also very liberating." It took courage to open the door to this world. "You don't know what you're going to find out in there. You're frightened that you will find something you don't want to find."

John's new-found faith became an incredible resource. "Christians talk about being saved. That language of being saved is something I can relate to. When you open that door and face whatever is you need to face, you fear it's going to overwhelm you." But instead of being overwhelmed, his faith increased. "The fact that it doesn't, the fact that you encounter something else in that moment that saves you, I can relate to that. I could quite easily say I was saved in that moment."

John grew up in the 1960s in Yorkshire in the north of England. Back then it was not a place where men were encouraged to readily express all their emotions. "I don't typically use that language, but I can totally relate to that idea, because that's the last thing I expected to happen. I expected to fall, but I didn't. Something broke the fall and lifted me up."

This wasn't the end of John's journey. "The biggest challenge I've had is bringing my faith self into my work self." During his 20s and 30s he worked for a number of organisations in programme management. "I had this very public persona as a business person. Not just a business person, but a very worldly person who had never had a faith. I actually built my whole outlook on life without it."

John kept these changes completely private. "I didn't talk to anybody about it for three years." When he says anybody, this includes his wife. "I was worried that it was like throwing a huge rock in the pond and that everything would just get disturbed. I was very worried about whether it would disturb my relationship with my wife… I thought it might freak her out."

At work John felt, "Very self-conscious about it. I feared ridicule and judgement" and also "when I went to talk about it, there was too much emotion." I asked him how this shifted over time. "It became an evolution rather than revolution. I did change my job eventually and I did find a way to talk to my wife about it eventually. By then I was at a point in the process where it was no longer like an earthquake… Did it change my life? Yes, it did. But it didn't throw everything upside down in 24 hours."

At the age of 56, John now has what he calls a *handshake* between his private and work self. "Over the course of the last 20 years it has been a progressive, building of confidence to just share that with more people and ultimately, to bring it into my business life. And I've put it in the shop window with everything else that I do."

A few days before we spoke John had delivered a talk to 100 people. "It was all about that journey from no faith, to private faith, to public faith, and the milestones along the way. The lessons learned from that whole process. I'm still in the process, but I feel a long, long way down the path to feeling congruent and authentic around those different aspects of my being."

In his speech John referenced the author Ray Bradbury. "He says sometimes you have to jump off cliffs and build your wings on the way down. That's the sort of courage I'm talking about. You jump, that's why it's a leap of faith. You have no idea how you are going to survive the jump, but you do it because you're compelled to do it." John said this is an ongoing need. "Even if it's happened three or four times, which it probably has with me, it doesn't mean I can just do it every day and think nothing of it. It's still a terrifying prospect."

The presentation John gave was clearly important to him. "My dad was in the audience and some friends, as well as a load of people I didn't know. I was talking about something that I would have considered extremely sensitive. But to be able to talk about that publicly to strangers and to friends and family, I just found hugely liberating." He talked about how things have shifted. In the past he was "managing things internally because I was fragmented. All that energy I was using to keep the inner pieces separate. That energy is now available."

As we started to wrap up the conversation, I asked John how he felt about this momentous change in his life. "Real joy and liberation. When different parts of yourself come together and embrace each other." He used the analogy of waiting at the airport for someone to arrive off a plane. "You've been waiting and waiting and waiting, and you wonder when they will ever come. And then you catch their eye and it's that moment of recognition. The embracing of the different parts that fragmented at some point, then bringing them back together. To me that's joyful, it's hugely liberating."

———

Pete collapsed at a railway station in central London. He woke up in A&E. "I looked in the mirror and I had blood all over my face" having bitten off the sides of his tongue whilst having a seizure. He surfaced a second time during a lumbar puncture and then finally woke up in a dark room. "My mum was holding my hand saying, Peter, don't you go before me."

Pete was kept in an isolation ward for a week because initially the doctors thought he had meningitis. But then they began to suspect a possible brain tumour. "I literally just couldn't move. I couldn't talk. I couldn't think." Once he got home, he started having mood swings and wasn't able to go back to work. "Pete before 2008 was fun, creative. Pete after 2008 was moody, serious, changed. I couldn't string a sentence together. I'd lost my sense of identity."

How did things get to this point because on the surface it all looked great? Pete had recently been promoted to his first Executive Creative Director role in advertising. "We had a fantastic 18 months. We were winning awards. We were winning pitches. We were changing the business. It was fantastic." But he'd been suffering from bad headaches for weeks. He'd seen six different GPs, but they just said take painkillers. Then after he'd rushed out of his third client pitch of the week, he collapsed at London Bridge station.

Months later Pete returned to work part-time, but the stress slowly started to ramp back up. "It felt like I was wearing a mask. I was pretending to be someone. I was struggling with confidence, trying to get back to the personality I used to be." Then there was more. "Having to make one person redundant is bad enough, but whole swathes of people in a creative department in Manchester?" Pete also had to let go of more people in London as well. "You don't sign up for that, do you? It had a massive effect on me… It was the worst possible thing I could have done. To have such an impact on peoples' lives."

For years Pete had wanted to focus on other things outside of work, one example was that he'd been harbouring ambitions to write children's books. He recounted an occasion when he'd asked for time off from work; this was some years before he collapsed. He was delighted when his boss said yes.

Pete was determined to do something creative with this time away from work. "I set up in my spare room and I put post-it notes all over the wall about what the plot would be and the backstory of all the characters." But he found it hard to get that story right, so he did a "little creative exercise" instead, writing a poem called *Why are Dinosaurs Naked in a Museum?* This seemed to unlock something interesting for him. "All of a sudden it was an avalanche of creativity. I just couldn't stop. And it led into writing a book, then another book, collaborating with an illustrator."

Over nine months Pete worked on multiple projects with different people. "I was getting excited about it. This really energised me. I found my spark." He even got himself an agent. Someone "who used to manage the pop group Eurythmics." But then "life started to grab hold of me. We'd just had our firstborn." The time off was coming to an end and Pete became nervous. "You run out of savings, then anxiety starts to creep in about 'Oh, no, I've got to get back into a job.'" That's when he returned to dashing around for work, being stressed... eventually resulting in his collapse at London Bridge.

Fast-forward many years again and Pete's life is very different. Whilst we chatted, he reflected on what had changed: "I've learned how to get more out of people, better out of people. When I started off in the ad industry creative directors were quite passionate and emotional... some were even a bit Gordon Ramsay-ish in the kitchen." It doesn't need to be like that. "There's more that you can do to get better things out of people to make them feel as though they're in control."

Nowadays, Pete also creates more time for himself. This is his advice to us: "Work isn't everything. Don't pour so much into work. Alter the balance with home. And don't have this pressure of always driving for a senior position and putting yourself in scenarios where you have to fake-like the stuff you hate." He believes we need to accept changes in our lives and move on. After his accident he said, "I'd become someone else, very weirdly. But I was still trying to pretend that I was the same person."

We had our conversation in May 2020 and Pete had just become a freelancer. "I left my job on the 28th of February, went freelance, registered my company and then next minute, Covid-19 hit. So it was the best possible time ever." Of course, Pete is being sarcastic about the timing. Why did he make this shift to being self-employed? "I wanted to do just enough to get some balance back in my life. You know that's the whole inspiration for it."

How is Pete's new business now, bearing in mind the challenging timing? He says it's going very well, he couldn't be happier. "It's amazing, I count my blessings for it. It's brilliant." He has clients he enjoys working for and he feels he's in the driving seat. "I can re-evaluate because I'm in control. I know I can say no to work… and just get back to more emphasis on my health, on my weight, on my mental wellbeing." Pete says he's now able to look "after myself and ultimately getting back those creative projects I put to bed over 10 years ago."

You may also be wondering about Pete's health. Fortunately, he's absolutely fine. Since his collapse he's had nine MRI scans and has the all-clear. But what about the diagnosis? "Oh, they think it was simply a brain infection." It's lovely to hear how much happier Pete is, having shimmied a little, focusing less on WHAT and more on HOW he does his work.

———

This final example isn't the story of one person, it's a discussion between two. I ran interviews with William and Anne individually, and then thought it might be fun to bring them together. That's because they happened to be the oldest and the youngest participants in my research group. I was intrigued to see what 40 years difference in age and experience would bring to a conversation. When we came together William was 68 and Anne was 28. Coincidentally, I was exactly halfway between the two, at 48. Here is how their conversation started:

William: "I suppose you get to a stage, a time of your life, where you tend to get in a bit of a rut. When you're in that rut you're less likely to notice it yourself, whereas others might. So, I'd be happy for any honest feedback."

Anne: "I think when you're very junior you don't really dare to say anything to someone very senior because you think, 'Oh, this person is so experienced. You know so much and I'm just a very inexperienced person.' I don't know if I have enough experience to share."

William: "Don't worry, because as you get older, you start to lose your faculties. So whatever experience I might have had, the chances are that I've probably forgotten a lot."

———

Let's wind back and have a little background on Anne and William. Anne grew up in France but wanted to live in another country. So, at a young age she took herself off to live in Ireland to study a law degree that was taught in English, her second language. It was a bold move, especially for her. She said "that was really a decision I took for myself. I used to be a very good people pleaser. Do as my parents told me and my grandparents told me." Anne even chose her degree in line with her grandfather's advice. "He said 'oh you are very good at school. You should go to law school.'"

Whilst she was at school Anne worked hard to get top grades. "I was always doing everything to please everyone. But moving away was something I did for myself and it truly helped me for my self-esteem. I think I wouldn't be how I am now. I wouldn't be on in this path now if I hadn't moved." She decided to tell her family at the last minute "because I knew they would be a bit negative. So, I told them when I didn't have any other choice but to tell them." But what started well for Anne, didn't progress as she had hoped. She ended up working for a professional services firm in Ireland, because she wasn't "thinking about a career. I just needed to find something to pay my bills. I left after two years because it was really metric driven and really stressful. We had to be online all the time. I was very unhappy."

Anne decided to join another organisation as a company secretary. "But after a few months, I realised that was not for me at all." She realised that "studying law and being in a law career was not really for me." Her parents had wanted her to get a prestigious degree that would also pay well. But what she wanted was to "write because that's what I really like. Maybe to work in the arts sector. So, my plan now is to move to London."

How is Anne aiming to do this? She'll swim like a fish, shimmying a bit, making small moves. "I'm trying to do that via my current company. I think just moving with my suitcase would be a bit risky with the current situation, the pandemic and Brexit." She's aiming to move internally in her current organisation and stay there for a few years. "At the moment I have an interview for a project management role which would be quite interesting." She thinks this will enable her to gain great skills for the future, "Even if I want to go freelance or write more, because those project management skills would be useful."

———

Now to William, although it's harder to summarise the decades of his career. "It was actually exactly fifty years ago that I decided to embark on my profession... I was pretty clear that I wanted to enter psychology." William said his "mission has always been within psychology. I could never imagine myself doing anything else." His particular interest was "working with children with very complex needs. Children with severe multiple disabilities. Since retirement I have stayed on as a voluntary director of a multi-academy trust, which consists of special schools in the area." In fact, he's been working in the same field for forty years.

William told us how his career progressed working in Children's Services. "Every so often public services tried to create the illusion of progress by re-organising." It was during one of those re-organisation phases that he "came a cropper. I actually suffered what I would call a stress-induced breakdown, which lasted for about six months." More about this in a moment.

In terms of his career William went on to become head of service and ultimately landed what he considered to be "a very plum job" staying for 12 years until he retired. "It was during a period when there was a lot happening to affect the communities I served. We were able to successfully fulfil a pivotal role in providing support."

William has a strong interest in post-traumatic growth and "the way in which people gain strength from having had a really difficult period of adversity and what they learn from it. It's an interest that is also based on my own personal experience." This came in useful when William had his own personal challenges. "The difficulty is that you don't know at the time if you're going to come out. You don't know if there's going to be a happy ending. My doctor said, 'one day you'll look back at all of this and it will be all over and done with, and you will have sorted it.'" But at that point William felt that getting better was "a million miles away."

Despite this, William feels this period in his life enabled him to become stronger and to find out more about himself. "That's one of the learning experiences of coming through a fairly major mental emotional problem. It was a very valuable learning process for me." He realised there was no point in "blaming those responsible for my predicament, or dwelling on a sense of injustice, as it only made me feel worse."

William also became aware of how much of his self-respect had become dependent on recognition and approval from others; he overcommitted to cope with his workload and got himself into a rut. He also knew from his psychology training that a positive resolution needed "active participation in driving my recovery." But still, it was a long and difficult journey that lasted many months.

William went on to talk about the psychotherapist, *Vicktor Frankl*[148]. "He has a well quoted phrase which says that *between stimulus and response there's a space. And in that space rests your freedom and your future happiness*[149]." What this means it that how we react to situations is up to us. We can make choices, much in the same way that Anne did when she decided to move to Ireland to study. "Making that choice is a first step towards seeing that you can change course if you want. You can alter your direction and transform the process in which you work." William says that you don't have to be driven by your reaction to events, "you can be pro-active and determine for yourself how you are going to respond."

At this point in the conversation Anne started to interview William. I just sat back and listened. "So, you think it is important when you're facing a challenge that you know you have a choice." You can choose between thinking the world is against you, "Just being completely depressed and everything. Or choose to think, 'OK, this is a challenge. But maybe I can tackle it. Try to find the resources to go through?'"

William responded, "Yes and I suppose experience has taught me that one should never underestimate how difficult that is. The first time we find ourselves overwhelmed emotionally by a really difficult situation, it is really hard to feel that we have a choice, especially when you're in that hole and you're trying to find your way out." Having succeeded once it gives you an "enormous amount of strength and resolve because you realise you can do it."

William believes he was able to face harder situations after that. "I managed to take them in my stride simply because I knew I could deal with them... one of the benefits of getting older is that you have had to face difficult situations and if you've managed to overcome them, you know you can cope." He contrasted this with experiences of younger people, like Anne. "Starting out, you might anticipate that things could happen that would worry you; that you're not sure if, or how, you would manage. But you do and you find a way."

William was also keen to discuss our desire for an ideal life, and our expectations for fairness. "This idea one has a claim for an ideal life. There is no ideal life. You have to take the rough with the smooth. There is no point dwelling on feelings of unfairness, ultimately you have to engage with the hand you've got." He says you need to "face the obstacles with a resourceful frame of mind and seek out the possibilities."

The conversation then switched as William asked Anne a question. "What kind of qualities do you feel helped you on your path?" Anne said she was very determined. "When I want something, I work for it and I get it. It's funny because sometimes I think 'Oh, yeah I can never do that'. But then when I look back, I can say each time I want to do something and I put the energy to do something, it happens." She says she is also "more independent now. I don't really care about what people think... I don't really mind if they don't understand."

I concluded the conversation by asking Anne what she might have done differently if she looked back over this time. "I don't really tend to have regrets because I think that everything happened for a reason. If I chose to do something at some point that's because that was my life then." I asked her what wisdom she might share with her younger self. "Just do what you want, instead of doing what your parents, or everyone is telling you to do. I think that would be the only thing." Anne finished by saying "if I hadn't studied law I wouldn't be in Ireland. I like the way I am now. All the decisions I took before led me to this decision, to this situation."

Despite having 40 years difference in age, Anne and William ended up saying many of the same things: worry less about what other people think; plough your own furrow and find your own path; believe in yourself; accept the life you've been given; know you have more choice than you realise and keep an open mind to possibility.

If you'd like to hear some more good news stories, why not take a look at the *Swim, Jump, Fly* website at swimjumpfly.com.

I'm going to suggest you reflect in a different way this time. Try to channel Victor Frankl and think about choice. How can you choose to react to the challenges that are happening in your life? *In that space rests your freedom and your future happiness.* This is an opportunity to work on your narrative, the stories that you tell yourself. Rather than one of problems and challenges, why not re-write your story to cover the amazing things you've done so far? Why not do the exercise below?

Exercise 25: Creating your Future Happiness

1) Think back over a difficult period in your life. How could you re-tell your story in a more positive way? Think about how you reacted, using the best resources you had at the time. What did you do well? What did you achieve, despite all the challenges you were going through? Bear in mind you didn't have the hindsight you have now. Why not write this story down, record yourself talking it through, or chat about it with another person?

2) Now reflect on that story with its different narrative and ending. Ask yourself some of these questions: what strengths do I see in myself? What values was I showing at that time? How have I developed since then?

3) Finally, how might this be useful for the change process you're going through now? You might ask yourself: what possibilities do these things give me for my future life? What positive ways can this support my next steps? What was surprising or new to me? What did I already know, but needed reminding about?

———

We're at the end of this chapter now, so here is a quick summary of what we looked at:

- The chapter started with a conversation about stories. Why they are so prevalent through history and why we still use them today. I shared participant examples about how they have used storytelling to make sense of their lives, and to learn and grow.
- We also heard stories from John, Pete, Anne and William about how they turned challenging situations in to opportunities for positive change.

- It was lovely to hear how John became a bird and flew into a new way of life.
- It was also great to find out that Pete is now well and has shimmied his way into a different way of working.
- We sat in on William and Anne's conversation, experiences separated by 40 years of life, yet showing many similarities.
- Anne flew away from France to land in Ireland. She's much more independent now and happier following her own path. She'll be flying over to the UK soon.
- William learned so much over the years and found a difficult patch made him stronger. Like salmon swimming upstream, he has followed his own direction and never wavered.

The next chapter is all about how you can keep steering your boat through the turbulent seas of life.

Chapter 21

As you're coming to the end of the book why not stand back from your change project for a moment? A time to pause and reflect on what you've learned. To think about the future and how you will sustain momentum. You'll experience ups and downs as you're working on your shift and will need motivation and energy to keep going. This is especially hard when the end isn't in sight.

Another theme for reflection is your destination. When you're going through a change in your life, you'll be focusing on reaching your goal. You might be thinking, "I'll be happy once I've bought my apartment, been promoted, got fit, lost weight, had my first child, got married, got divorced." If this is the case don't forget to enjoy the journey as you travel, otherwise you'll just be holding your breath. You'll be in the *Happy When* loop, not fully here, waiting until you're fully there.

A third topic to ponder is whether you see your goal as the final destination, or not. Of course, achieving this goal will make you feel good... for a while. But, before too long your mind will start to wander and you'll turn to thinking about your next change project. In this chapter I'm going to use the analogy of a sailing boat. It's a handy metaphor for change because it covers different aspects of the journey. If you keep a sailboat in mind as you travel, you'll remember the stages in the process and the underlying themes.

- Let's start with plotting a direction of travel to a group of tropical islands. Having read this book you will know that you're likely to get blown off course. This isn't down to bad planning, just storms and currents.
- Planning means filling the boat with food, water, equipment, no different from the resources in this book. Being prepared means setting sail feeling calm and ready for the journey.
- This sailing boat metaphor may also remind you about the tools you will need for different conditions on the trip, just as sails work with different types of wind.
- There will be uneventful days, where not much happens, nothing to look at but the wide blue ocean. Sometimes your boat will stop moving completely, motionless on a flat sea. You'll become frustrated and worried that you will be late.
- Then after many weeks you'll arrive, excited to finally be there. As you

> pull into the harbour, houses, palm trees and people will grow larger.
> You'll tie up the boat and go on shore to celebrate, an opportunity to
> relax and enjoy yourself.
> • But, soon enough, you will become restless. The island is a small place
>   after all. Then, you'll unhitch your boat from the dock, and head off to
>   new and interesting lands.

All these stages will apply to any change project you might be going through. You may end up circling back at times, which can be frustrating, but you will always be moving forwards in time. Every day you will be learning something new, even if it's just about yourself, even if your destination is still far away.

I'm going to make one final point here too. It's useful to think of your destination, the tropical island, as a stopping off point on a longer journey. It's easy to get complacent and think, "I've arrived. What else is there to do?" when in fact, this is a life-long practice. It's the way to grow and develop throughout your life. You will need to continue checking where you are going, changing course at times. You will find new islands to explore as you navigate the high seas.

Anna was one of the participants in my research and I caught up with her six months after our first conversation. This is what she said when I asked her how her change project was going. "Am I happier? Yes. Is it still hard? Of course. Am I reinventing again? Yes. Will I reinvent again later… probably." She says that she is still a work in progress. "I know that I will continue to work on this for the rest of my life. I know myself well enough now that I will want to do something else again."

Nothing stays the same for long. Your context will alter, people will change, work will become boring or stressful and what was once fun will become a chore. As you grow older you also change as your goals and desires shift, so you'll need to keep course correcting. Whilst you can manage yourself, to an extent, the world is outside your control. There will be storms that are so strong they will completely blow your boat off course. Then you may find yourself arriving at an entirely new groups of islands. This might seem frustrating but waking up to a different way of living can be a great joy in life. This is exactly what one of the interviewees, Chris, found when he reflected on difficult times: "Things that looked really terrible for me actually had huge benefits that I only saw a couple of years down the line."

As we're on the topic of boats, here is an idea from *Acceptive and Commitment Therapy (ACT)*: *Demons on the Boat*. This is a story that ACT professionals sometimes use. It can be a way of helping us realise that if we take action towards something important in our lives, then we need to accept the challenges we'll experience along the way. Find out more about this on the website, at swimjumpfly.com. Now, here is another thought from Daniel Pink[150], who says good endings don't make us happy, they create something much better: Insight. Leaving behind something we thought we wanted enables us to get something we actually need.

With all of this in mind I suggest you review the 5-Step Process every three to six months. Start at step one, checking your WHY and your WHERE. Are they still fit for purpose? Do you want to change course? If they are still working for you then great, shut the book and get on with your life. But if you find yourself longing for another destination, then work your way through the five steps again. That's why I've drawn the 5-Step Process as an ongoing cycle. Once you've spent time in review and maintenance, you may need to pivot your project and change things around. Or you might want to start contemplating a new project, a different destination.

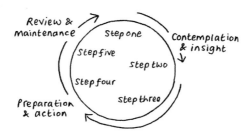

Diagram 21: The 5-Step Process

Step one: WHY and WHERE (purpose and destination)
Step two: WHICH (animal, i.e. the distance to travel)
Step three: WHAT and HOW (the type of change)
Step four: WHO and WHEN (planning action and experimentation)
Step five: HOW MUCH and HOW WELL (reviewing and evaluating progress)

It's good to keep stretching yourself throughout life. The best way to keep your brain on its toes is to learn new skills. You will naturally find that as you travel through your change project, you will stretch yourself a little further each time... until you find you are sailing much further afield. These new goals could well be destinations you never think you might reach when you were at the start of your journey.

Standing back and creating some distance from your life can also be useful. If you can, try to watch the highs and the lows with interest, with a slight detachment and as a compassionate observer. Your separation from *being in the middle of it*, to *watching yourself go through it*, can smooth out your feelings, lower your anxiety and help you stay grounded. If you expect that things won't always go smoothly, then you will also be less surprised. Changing your mindset on *failure* can help you a lot too. Realising that mistakes, dead-ends and getting lost may be the making of you.

I'm sure you get my point on all this, so I'll stop the poetic embrace now. In summary, the 5-Step Process is just a framework for you to use each time you want to make a shift. The rest of the book is just a guide to help you navigate your way. Feel free to rip out, or ignore, the sections you don't find useful, or take a highlighter to the parts that fit you best. Make it your own, do with it what you will. It's yours to adapt to your needs.

How can we make our way through life as happy and fulfilled as possible? Psychologist Dr Martin Seligman is a pioneer of Positive Psychology and wrote about this in 2002 in his book *Authentic Happiness*[151]. Another good book by him is *Flourish*[152] which you might like to read. Seligman says that to be happy we need to appreciate the basic pleasures, discover our unique strengths and craft a meaningful life, by using those strengths for a greater purpose than ourselves. What can you do to bring these three things into your life? Why don't you go back to chapter three and look at your WHY, your purpose again? Or perhaps go back to chapter eight and find out more about your values? You might even like to review the resources sections (chapters 8-12) and the piece about gratitude (chapter 15).

The rest of this chapter is focused on some final insights from the participants; how they are continuing to steer their boats, whatever the weather. So, here are the last few stories on creating long-term sustainable change.

Suzanne has some helpful ideas and I think this is a good place to start, how you treat yourself: "Be a bit kinder to yourself and not so scared of everything. There are always options, nothing is black and white. Every decision isn't necessarily the end of the world. OK, there's not always choice in life, but more often than not, there is." Or at least there's "a different way of doing it, another way round." Why beat yourself up? Why not be kind? Loosen your grip and just enjoy the ride.

Morgan and Tim are focused on being present. This is from Morgan: "Enjoy the moment more and use your time more. It's all about embracing the moment. Stop waiting for tomorrow." And this from Tim: "Be in the present, be in the moment. Enjoy the sunrise, enjoy your swim in the lake. These things, they are still happening every day... appreciate them while you can."

Mel and Dominic advise us to be patient when times are tough. Mel: "Most things pass, so try not to get too upset about the things that are bothering you here and now. Because, with a bit of time and distance, most of them become less important. I would also say try make sure that you are doing something every day that gives you some kind of fulfilment." Dominic says this: "Accepting that it will pass, as everything does... Any challenge you're going through in life will pass. Time passes, situations change, people change. And what you think one day is absolutely awful and there for eternity is gone in 24 hours or a week's time."

It might be hard to steer your boat if you're looking enviously at your neighbour's larger ship. Try to focus on your own goal, not what others achieve. Gina is 30 and from Germany and wanted to be creative. But her parents persuaded her not to pursue a creative career, suggesting she worked in large organisations instead, which she dutifully did. *"I get sucked into this whole rat race of wanting to always keep getting pay raises. Always wanting a promotion and wanting a specific job title because I assumed it means I'm worth something."*

Gina spent so much time believing a senior role meant she was *"a good person and good at things."* She got blown off course. *"When everyone around you is chasing that, you start chasing it too. When there wasn't any monetary worth attached to my skills, that's when I enjoyed being creative and working on projects."*

Teresa agrees with this — that we need focus on our own direction. *"People aren't as interested in me as I think they are. I had that sense of, I can't do this because what would someone else think? Or I've got to be looking like this because that's what everyone else does. But actually, everyone else is so in their own heads and own worlds that it doesn't matter. It's better to stay focused on what feels right for me."*

We met Yiannis earlier, who is Greek and works in sustainability. On our call he'd been animated and chatty, but at the end he went a little quiet. *"I'm looking outside my window now. There's a lady pushing a stroller with a baby. We're expecting our first baby, me and my wife."* I congratulated him on this big change in his life. *"You know, the important things in life are not only work. There are other things. We tend to forget that."* He corrects himself. *"I tend to forget that. I tend to connect my self-worth or self-appraisal to work, I have that tendency. There are other things that are much, much, much more important that we're here for... So maybe I'll leave you with that."*

———

Now to the group of people I reconnected with months later. I spoke to Cecilia eight months after our first conversation and was keen to hear her progress and the insights she'd learned. She says this: *"What you put out, you get back. This is an interesting concept for me. I think balance has been a theme for me. Feeling so totally out of balance for a lot of my life, the balance was the thing I wanted to recreate."*

Cecilia advises us to be more courageous too. A lot of the changes "have been accidental, a happy coincidence to some degree. It's also taking a few risks. Taking a few gambles and actually amazing things come out of that." She says, "That has probably been the biggest lesson since last October. How much happens when you actually just invite in things."

Cecilia wanted to share one more nugget with us. Listen to your body "because you feel everything in your body first." She says, "Your own body sits there telling you really what is going on," so just let any emotion "flow through you and then you get released from it. Sometimes that's what you need. It's like a superpower if you can home in on that. It's quite remarkable."

Remember Rob whose life was turned upside down? He went through some dark times when he separated from his partner and had to leave the family home. He was suicidal and at one point was, in his words, "really close to checking out". Nine months after speaking, Rob and I had an email exchange about his progress. These are some of the points he wrote: "I feel more motivated and I like that feeling. I have been more creative. I am painting. I am writing prose." He has also decided to get fit. "I have cycled, I have been spinning, I have done weights (first time in over a decade) and walked and walked and walked. I have started open water swimming in a lake – the euphoria of cold water has helped my depression. Overall, it has helped me immeasurably in an emotional and psychological way. I feel fitter. My mind feels fitter. It's the best I have felt since I was 20." It was great to hear.

What advice would Rob give us? "Do it. Make the change. The risks are the same as not changing. This Coronavirus has amplified how precious life is. Why keep doing something you dislike. Life is too short. Most resistance to change is driven by money and the associated lifestyle. But you can be rich in wealth and poor in health, wellbeing and life. As Beckett said in *Worstward Ho*: 'Ever Tried. Ever Failed. No Matter. Try Again. Fail Again. Fail Better.'" To sum up what Rob is saying, focus on your body, get fit and be bold, make that change. You don't have anything to lose.

I emailed Yasmeen in Canada eight months after we'd had the interview. I was also interested to hear how she was progressing. She has got herself into a better place financially, finding work that enables her "to focus on exploring without having to worry about money. The job isn't in my field, but the people are nice, the work isn't stressful, and the pay is decent. This allows me to pour energy into exploring avenues that I am interested in."

Yasmeen has also shifted her mindset and approach. "I am taking my time. Getting steady work is allowing me not to worry about other things and not rushing the career change process. This is pressure I have been putting on myself for as long as I can remember. I'm paying a lot more attention to what is resonating for me in the world of work." She's making sure "not to rush things. I always want an answer really quickly, which can work against me. This pause has allowed me to slow down and discern whether something jumps me into action because it resonates, or because I am fearful."

Yasmeen's advice to us is: "Be patient. Trial and error are part of the process and are probably the most frustrating parts, but you learn a lot about yourself. The only way out is through – no shortcuts. Also, take more risks. You never know where your micro-decisions take you!" At the end of the email to me she wrote: "I'm glad you sent those follow up questions because it got me to step back and monitor my progress, which has been difficult to do in these trying times." So, in summary Yasmeen is saying give yourself breathing space by sorting out your money. Then change will be less stressful. She's also saying take your time.

Micro-advice from some of the other participants:
"Be brave." — James
"Worry less about the things that will happen... you will find your way." — Katerina
"You are only here once. Make sure what you do between 9-5 puts a smile on your face." — Andy
"Have more fun. Take life a little less seriously." — Lucy
"Listen to how you feel more than what you think." — Jinhai

I spoke to Jacqui 367 days after our first conversation. She had shifted a huge amount in that time. "I've always been a perfectionist, and to some degree, I always will be. But it's knowing where there are healthy behaviours and where there are unhealthy behaviours associated with that." She says, "It's the awareness that's so critical. Once you're aware of unhealthy behaviours in particular, it's knowing that you have the choice to respond, or to react differently to that behaviour."

She's been working on letting go. "I've really been challenging myself to acknowledge the behaviours of the past, how they impacted me. And to go completely the opposite way now." I asked how that feels. "Really quite liberating to just give myself permission to be that way. It was a very deliberate and conscious move on my part to sit with imperfection. To sit with what's not perfect and just be fine with it."

Her advice to us is: "just relax into the moment, find acceptance in the confusion and the uncertainty and be OK with that." She also agrees with Suzanne – be kinder to yourself. "There are going to be so many moments of indecision and uncertainty and confusion and chaos really. And judgement about ourselves – our progress and where we're at. And there doesn't need to be. You're not competing with anyone in this process, it's all just you. So, whatever you impose on yourself is what you're up against. So why not be softer in those moments?" To sum it up Jacqui is saying drop your perfectionism and be kinder to yourself.

Finally, let's hear from Tracey, who I contacted 10 months after we first spoke. She emailed back a beautiful set of bullet points. Thank you, Tracey:

- Break the bigger picture down into bite size chunks – I dream big, and research ideas but never take them further. Break the big dream down into something more practical and tangible. Work out the manageable steps needed to move your shift forward.
- Take action – rather than researching/hypothesising – get out of your head and get into action – meeting up, keeping in touch, trying new things and new people.
- Talk more openly about your shift – I was amazed by the responses from the people I contacted. I also invited others into the conversation and that has made me more accountable for making progress.
- Take the time to repay others for their interest/help/encouragement along the way. 'A stranger is a friend that you do not know.' Gotta love Jim Reeves!
- Look at every encounter as an opportunity to learn (good or bad). Even if something turns out not to be right, at least you've tried it on for size.
- Ask for what you want. Also believe in the power of community. Ask for help.
- Invest in yourself. If you are serious about making a shift, then invest in making it happen. Stump up the cash, put in the hours and seek expert advice.

- Be patient – probably the biggest thing I've learned. Tracey says, Good things take time to come to fruition. Enjoy where you are now and be present for the journey. You learn so much along the way.

Let's do one final reflection on this chapter now. Think about which stories resonated the most for you. What was it about them that rang true? How will you follow their advice? What's the first action you'll take tomorrow?

That's it for this chapter, so here is one last summary before you move on to the final chapter and the end of *Swim, Jump, Fly*:

- We used a metaphor of a sailing boat as it can be helpful when thinking about a shift project - planning the route, getting your resources sorted, expecting slow days with no progress, getting blown off course.
- We also used it to think about longer term change – the idea that goals may not be the final destination. That you will get itchy feet and want to move onto the next goal.
- We discussed reviewing your goals every three-six months using the 5-Step Process, plus stretching yourself by learning new skills and taking on fresh endeavours.
- We included the idea that creating some mental distance from the highs and the lows will smooth out your emotions and keep you grounded.
- Then we heard from 18 interviewees, sharing how they keep momentum through their change projects and stay motivated through the difficult days.

So, having heard from all the participants, what can you do to maintain your energy levels? How can you build up your resources to maintain momentum? Finally, what actions can you take to stay motivated over the coming weeks and months?

Right, we're nearly there. Just one more chapter to go and then we're at the end of the book.

Chapter 22

I'm sorry to say this, but it's time for goodbye. I won't make this a long, drawn-out affair. There's nothing worse than closing down a conversation, seeing the other person a few minutes later, and then awkwardly nodding and smiling with nothing left to say. Better to give them a great send off and then walk away.

In *Swim, Jump, Fly* I have offered a variety of ideas that might help you through change, big or small. The 5-Step Process is there for you to hold onto when the weather gets stormy. Think of it as a life-raft. It's great when you're being tossed around on the open seas. But don't grip on too tightly when the weather is calm. It's a useful floatation device that you can ditch if you don't need help anymore. But keep it close at hand, in case the sea gets rough again.

Some people dislike a process. Danielle is someone in my network who told me this in no uncertain terms. Luckily, she loves a good story. The stories I have included are all about sharing experiences, giving examples of transitions, events and changes that may resonate for you. Since we were children we learned about life through stories, so why change now, just because we're grown up? Some stories might have been helpful. Ignore the ones that weren't useful.

I included many exercises because learning theory says practice makes perfect. It's hard to take on board new ways of thinking or behaving without trying them out... and of course repeating them until they feel like they've always been there. I've included extra information in the appendices and on the *Swim, Jump, Fly* website (at swimjumpfly.com), for the times when you would like a deeper dive. Don't forget resources work differently depending on the context we're in, the time in our lives and our moods. So, I suggest you keep going back to the resources list as you might find something useful that didn't grab you last time. Also, don't forget my blog has more stories and information in it too.

Please don't take this book as gospel. It's not a set of rules you must follow. My aim has been a collaboration between us – I'm simply a guide, trekking up the hill beside you, offering a framework that may help you to climb the steepest slopes. I hope that by sharing a range of voices, some will have been useful – psychologists, coaches, therapists, change managers, meditators and mindfulness practitioners, philosophers, poets, writers... and the 108 lovely people who spoke to me.

> Whatever you're going through... it's going to be fine. It may not end the way you think it's going to end. But you will survive it and you'll be stronger for it. You'll be better for it and it's all going to be OK.
> — Drew (interviewee)

I'll leave you with a few thoughts before I say, "*Au revoir.*" Firstly, don't beat yourself up. You're a work in progress, like every one of us. I bet you are really lovely just as you are. As you know, the *Paradox of Change* says you can't shift unless you accept yourself, flaws and all. Like flowers, we unfold our petals in sunny conditions, so be kind to yourself.

Secondly, try not to focus too much on your destination. You may be disappointed when you get there. If you spend the entire journey thinking about when the train is due to arrive, you'll miss all the fabulous views. Instead focus on the amazing landscapes, interesting people and beautiful buildings whizzing by.

Finally, I'd like to say none of this is a contest. There's no prize for arriving first, being the best, or having a badge. Each of us will pick our path and walk at our own pace. I hope what I've offered in *Swim, Jump, Fly* is an invitation to walk that route together.

———

Would you be up for one more reflection? Rather than focusing on yourself, why not reflect on the book itself? Let's say a friend, family member or loved one has seen you reading *Swim, Jump, Fly*. They notice you've nearly finished and ask: "What was it all about? What did you learn?" So, what would you tell them? What have you taken away? How would you sum up what you'll do next? We're now at the end of the chapter and the end of the book. I feel a little sad saying goodbye. If you want to hang around for a bit longer, I've got drinks and snacks to keep you entertained in the form of the appendices at the back of the book. Or you'd be welcome to take a look at the additional information on the website. Otherwise, we're done for now, so thank you for staying the course.

I'll leave you with the words of Maya Angelou: "People will forget what you said, people will forget what you did, but people will never forget how you made them feel." Even if you forget everything I've written in this book, I hope that you felt understood. Whether you swim, jump or fly, I wish you great success in your life. Why not get in touch and let me know how you are doing. If you need support to get through your change, then I'd be delighted to help you through coaching. You can reach me via the website swimjumpfly.com.

Adios, adieu and goodbye.

Acknowledgements

I just want to thank my husband, my friends, my agent... oh, sorry, that's the wrong speech. However, it does feel like one of those Oscar ceremony moments, because I couldn't have written *Swim, Jump, Fly* without the support and kindness of many people. So here goes. I hope to bring it under three minutes, before I get ushered off stage. Scarlett Johansson is on next.

Thank you, Steven, for advising me to write blogs before I wrote a book. Initially I was disappointed, having wanted to write a book for a while. But practicing was what I needed. Steven guided me over the 18 months that I wrote my *Spoon-by-Spoon* blog, slowly taking off the stabilisers over time. I'm not sure I could have written a readable book without doing the blogs first. Learning to write one page at a time created the building blocks to write a book.

I have been lucky to have support from two amazing researchers, Zeenat and Helen. They sweated away for hours on the audio recordings, helping me turn them into useful transcripts. These gave me a quality base from which to build the research. Thank you both for your time and dedication.

I'm so appreciative of my Book Focus Group, made up of people willing to support this endeavour. These were a group of friends, colleagues, coaches, therapists, blog readers and consultants, who gave me feedback on the concepts I'd amassed for *Swim, Jump, Fly*. On occasions it was tough, particularly when they said some ideas weren't very good! It was lovely when they encouraged me to build on what I had and cheered me on until I crossed the finish line. Collectively they helped me write a much better book. Thank you, Sarah, Anouchka, Cath, Martin, Claire, Tracy, Anton, Dani, Emma, Nicola, Sally, Bernadette, Caroline and Emma.

I'm also extremely grateful for Sally, Anton and Annabel's hard graft at wading through pages of copy, trying to get their heads around what I was writing and giving me much better alternatives. Thank you Sarah for introducing me to John Norcross's work and the *transtheoretical model of behavior* plus *Acceptance and Commitment Therapy*. Thanks also to Cath and Claire, for so many helpful coaching ideas and references, Michelle for working with me for the past three years on our creative coaching projects, plus Adriana for helping me adapt the book so it is easier for neurodiverse people to read.

My speech wouldn't be complete without mentioning the excellent cartoonist and illustrator, Simon Pearsall. He suffered endless changes to his diagrams, illustrations and cartoons which beautifully brought my dense copy to life. It also goes without saying that *Swim, Jump, Fly* would be a quarter of the length and rather turgid without the stories from the interviewees. They bravely signed up to having their lives poked and prodded, which became the foundation for the research. They generously allowed me to use their quotes in my blogs, and now this book. Thank you to you all.

Finally, a note to my wonderful husband Donal for just being himself... and the help he's given me on this project. He spent hours cross-checking the Thematic Analysis results for me, along with countless other skills, from removing the worst jokes, to cooking a mean bowl of pasta when I was too tired to think. There are numerous others who I've worked with, or been supported by, over the years. I'd like to thank you too for the inspiration you've given me to write *Swim, Jump, Fly.*

Appendices

APPENDIX A: ADDITIONAL EXERCISES

I've included a number of additional exercises in this appendix. Please feel free to have a rummage around. Open cupboards, have a look inside and decide what interests you.

Chapter 3

These are the exercises I mentioned in chapter three:

1) Am I ready for change quiz (I also refer to this in chapters seven and eight)
2) Working with metaphors
3) Visualisation and guided imagery exercise
4) Letter from the future
5) Working on WHY

Why not take a look at these and see if any of these might be useful to you?

Exercise 3.1: Am I ready for change?

I know it sounds obvious, but to make a shift in your life, you first need to be aware that something needs to change. If you're reading this book, then I assume that you are. Perhaps you're at the contemplation stage of change? You might remember the *transtheoretical model of behavior change (TTM)* which says there are a number of stages in the change process: pre-contemplation, contemplation, preparation, action, maintenance and termination.

Of course, you might be a coach or therapist who is reading *Swim, Jump, Fly* because you want to help your clients. Or perhaps you are reading the book before giving it to a loved one. You're planning to slip it under their pillow in the hope it'll persuade them to change themselves. I'm sorry to say that this last one is unlikely to work. Unless we are willing to change ourselves, it's hard for us to make the right level of commitment. That's why it can be helpful to check if we are ready for change.

We can find out whether we're willing to make a shift, by reviewing these questions:

1) Is this a challenge in my life that needs addressing?
2) Who else is it impacting?
3) What are the pros and cons of changing? For me and for others?
4) What are the pros and cons of not changing? For me and for others?
5) What is stopping me from changing? Do I have mixed feelings about this?
6) How ready do I feel to change, 0 (not at all), to 10 (already made a shift)?
7) When do I intend to make changes? Today, this week, next month, next year?

Here are some examples of answers you might have given if you're at pre-contemplation, contemplation or preparation stages of change:

Pre-contemplation:
1) No, I don't see this as a challenge really.
2) I don't think this impacts anyone else.
3) I see many cons of changing and very few pros.
4) I see lots of pros of staying the same and no cons.
5) Stop what? I'm not sure there is a real challenge here.
6) I don't feel ready to make any change, so I'm at 0 on the scale.
7) I won't make any changes until next year… if at all.

Contemplation:
1) Yes, I can see this situation is impacting my life.
2) It's affecting some people – friends, family, loved ones and colleagues.
3) I know there are pros for changing, but I think there are quite a few cons too.
4) I'm aware of the cons around making change. There aren't enough pros yet.
5) I definitely have mixed feelings about changing.
6) I don't feel ready, maybe a three or a four on the scale? I'm afraid I'll fail.
7) I'll make some changes next month – I just need to get myself sorted.

Preparation:
1) Yes, I'm aware of the need to change and want to start.
2) It is impacting friends, family, loved ones, colleagues… the list is long.
3) I can see many more pros to changing than there are cons.
4) I can see a lot of cons around staying the same and not making this shift.
5) Nothing very much is stopping me. I am making plans and will start soon.
6) I'm looking forward to seeing benefits – I'm at a six or seven on the scale.
7) I'll start working on this next week.

If you don't recognise there is a problem, you're unlikely to solve it until you do. If you don't accept some responsibility, you'll find it hard to shift. So, are you ready to make a change? If you're still putting off this shift, that's OK. It's actually an opportunity to work out what is blocking you from changing. I'd suggest spending some time reflecting on the pros and cons of staying where you are versus the pros and cons of making a change. You might discover something you weren't aware of, that is preventing you from moving forward in your life.

Exercise 3.2: Working with metaphors

Metaphors can be really helpful when you're trying to explore a situation, especially if the words don't come easily. It can help you to identify your emotions and think about those subtleties that may be hard to write or speak about. Using images or pictures can help you think about the past, present or future in a different way. You might enjoy this if you like images and stories, but it also can work well if you like to talk things through too.

There are a number of ways to work with metaphors. One that I use with my coaching clients is *Liminal Muse Conversation* cards. This is an exercise I've developed using my own photographs, many of which are abstract. If you'd like to try working on metaphors by using images, they are available to purchase via the swimjumpfly.com website.

Another method is by drawing with different coloured pens or pencils. This can help you imagine a new future, or way of life, once you've been through your change project. Don't worry if you're not good at drawing, even stick people are fine! It's just a way of accessing different parts of your brain. You can even take a pair of scissors to magazines or articles, picking out images that sum up what you want to say and what the future will look like.

Once you've done this you might like to share the results with a close friend or family member, explaining why you selected the *Liminal Muse Conversation* card photo, or why you drew an image, or cut out a picture from a magazine. Why not share how this image relates to your situation and what it means to you.

Exercise 3.3: Visualisation and guided imagery exercises

Guided imagery can help you relax and reduce your anxiety levels. Over time, and with practice, you can create a relaxing state fairly quickly. It can be good to do this twice a day for two weeks, at which point you will have become a pro!

1) One example of visualisation is *time projection imagery*[153] which asks you to project yourself beyond your challenge or problem. You could ask a good friend or close family member to help you, by asking the questions below or you could do this yourself.

> • First spend a moment reflecting on the event or situation that is making you stressed.
> • Then picture yourself in two weeks' time. How are you feeling now? Imagine yourself in four weeks' time. What are your stress levels at this point?
> • Now move to two months' time. How are you feeling now?
> • What about four months, or one year's time? Have things shifted, lightened, become easier for you? What else are you doing at those points? Has your life moved on from this challenge?

As you move forward in time, this situation/event/issue is likely to feel less central in your life. You will probably have fewer negative or stressful feelings about it. Asking yourself what else you might be doing at those points will help you focus on other activities. You may realise by this point that it is no longer an issue at all!

2) A second type of visualisation is *coping imagery*[154]. This can help you prepare for a challenging event by imagining yourself in the future, where you deal with the situation effectively. Let's say you have problems remembering names under stressful situations. You're worried about introducing a new person in your team to others at a work event. What you could do is this:

> • Identify which part is the most worrying and think about actions you could take. Perhaps sending the new team member photos of the team, so they have a head start before the event.
> • Or if you have a good memory for faces, spending time reviewing the organisation charts to remind yourself of your work colleagues' names.
> • You might try picturing yourself handling the introductions very well, even making a joke or two, which would relax everyone.
> • You could rehearse or practice this in your mind a few times beforehand, particularly when you're feeling anxious about the event.

3) A third type of visualisation is *relaxation imagery* which can help you to

create a relaxed state of mind and reduce thoughts and feelings that are stressful. You start by remembering a favourite location or place whilst following these steps:

- Sit or lie down in a quiet and comfortable spot.
- Shut your eyes and imagine a favourite location or scene. It could be walking your dog in a wood, sitting on a dockside breathing in the sea air, or resting in the sun in your garden.
- These can be real places in your life, situations from the past, or even imagined places.
- The next step is to focus on all your senses. What do you hear, see, smell and feel? Think about those for a while.
- Try to keep your breathing soft and slow whilst you imagine that place in your mind.
- When you are ready, slowly open your eyes.
- How do you feel? Hopefully a little calmer or happier?

Exercise 3.4: A letter from the future

If you'd like help exploring your goals and future vision, your WHY and your WHERE, then you might find this exercise useful. It can be particularly good if your plans will bring a large amount of change. It can also help if you don't believe you have the motivation to achieve your goals, or the ability to do so. By the end of this exercise you're likely to have much more clarity on your future goals/vision and what your life might be like once you've achieved them.

When you imagine a time in the future and write about it, you will be clearer about what actions you need to take. It's also useful to spend time thinking about how you might feel once you've achieved your goals. Plus, you're more likely to feel the motivation and confidence to press ahead.

Here is an exercise I've used with clients – a letter from the future. Simply think about a time in the future when you will have achieved a particular goal. Then write a letter to yourself on paper, or card. You might like to ask yourself some of these questions to help you write the letter:

- What is your life like at this point, what has changed?
- What are you thinking about or feeling?
- How was the journey to this point - the highs and the lows?

- What do you think helped you get there?
- What messages would you like to give your younger self - the things you learned, how you grew as a person?
- Where might you be heading to next, now that you've achieved this goal?

Once you've written your letter or postcard, place it in an envelope and seal it. Then, when the time is right, open the letter and read it back to yourself. Perhaps this will be when you've achieved your goal. Or maybe it might be when things are tough and you need some extra support.

Exercise 3.5: Working on WHY

If you're stuck on your WHY, your purpose, then you could ask yourself these questions. They are borrowed from Liane Hambly and Ciara Bomford's book, *Creative Career Coaching: Theory into Practice*[155]:

- If you could experience anything in your life, what would it be?
- What brings you joy?
- What/who makes you feel most alive?
- How will pursuing this goal help you express your authentic self?
- How do your beliefs and values support you in this goal?
- What does this change mean for you?
- What are you most grateful for in your life?
- What is the most important lesson that life has taught you so far? How are you using that lesson?

Chapter 8:
In chapter eight, I mentioned these exercises:
1) Assessing the advantages and disadvantages of your beliefs
2) Thinking errors (also highlighted in chapters 17 and 18)

Why not take a look at these and see if any of these are helpful to you?

Exercise 8.1 Assessing the advantages and disadvantages of your beliefs

They say that a fish is the last thing to notice the water it's swimming in. Perhaps we are the last one to notice the beliefs we hold? Often these beliefs can be about ourselves; what we're good at, not good at or where we might fail. Some of us have a nagging voice in our heads that says, "You still can't reverse park" or "Why aren't you going for a walk. You're lazy!" Since this voice and our beliefs are always there, it's like the water in the fish's bowl, hard to notice.

This exercise is the equivalent of putting dye into the fish's water. It'll help you see the colour of your beliefs about yourself and your life. It's called a *Thought Balance Sheet* and it helps you to stand back from your beliefs, then work out the advantages and the disadvantages of holding onto them. Below is an example of someone who is unhappy at work. They lack trust in others, are a perfectionist and often say, "Only I can get it right." Their beliefs make them unhappy and unwell.

Example:
1) Problem: I feel overwhelmed at how much there is to do at work but don't feel I can talk to anyone about it or delegate it. I'm not sure anyone would do it to the same quality as I would.

2) Belief: People don't take the same care and attention that I do. I have good relationships with my colleagues and I don't want to damage these by involving other people who won't produce good quality work.

3) Goal: Trusting others so I can delegate more of my work.

4) Advantages of my beliefs:
• I know what quality of work will be created because I do it.
• I don't have to spend time explaining the processes to others.
• I work hard so I know if more needs to be done, I'll work longer hours and complete it.
• I have more control.

5) Disadvantages of my beliefs:
• I am overworked and stressed all the time.
• I've let my friendships slip because I'm always working.
• My relationships with my friends aren't going so well because I'm stressed a lot of the time.
• I don't sleep much and am often tired.
• I eat convenience food because I don't have time to cook.
• I have no hobbies or things I do outside work.
• I'm not enjoying my life very much right now.

Why not use the structure in the example above so you can practice this yourself? Here are some actions you can take:

- Write down a particular challenge that you're facing at the moment.
- Then outline the beliefs you have about this situation.
- Now write out your goal around this challenge, then the advantages of this belief, plus the disadvantages.
- Then stop and reflect for a while. Do the negatives about this belief outweigh the positives?

Exercise 8.2: Thinking Errors

Having read about *Thinking Errors*, or *Thinking Traps,* you're probably keen to know if you have these thoughts yourself. Well, you're in the right place if you want to find out. Here are some examples of *Thinking Errors*:

- **Focusing on the negative,** only paying attention to what has gone wrong in the past. Whatever we think we can or can't do, we're probably right. It's helpful to shift this mindset, pivot to what has gone well and remind ourselves of these when we're feeling full of doubt.
- **Fortune Telling,** predicting how something will go (often the worst-case scenario). Try to re-imagine a change and think through all the aspects that will be successful. Athletes do this, imagining themselves in a race/playing a game, picturing how well it goes and how they win.
- **Mind-Reading,** second-guessing what someone is thinking, how they'll behave/what they'll do, without evidence. Is there a challenging conversation coming up? Maybe you're avoiding it because you're predicting how that person will react. Instead imagine different responses that are more positive. It will make you less anxious in the run up to the conversation.
- **Overgeneralisation,** taking the outcome of one event and predicting that will always happen every time. Instead remember other times when you tried something new and it went well. Be aware that we often overgeneralise on what went wrong, not what went right.
- **Magnification,** taking events and blowing them out of proportion. You might say you "make mountains out of molehills."
- **Emotional Reasoning,** assessing situations based on how you feel, rather than facts. For example, when you feel nervous getting onto a plane, you presume your anxiety is because it's not safe. In fact, it's 100 times more risky travelling in a car than in a plane.
- **Catastrophising,** imagining the worst-case scenario will happen and that

you won't be able to cope properly with the outcome. The reality is this rarely happens, but when it does, we are often able to cope with it.

- **Fallacy of Fairness,** expecting the world to be a fair place, which can lead to anger and resentment.
- **Polarised Thinking** (or all-or-nothing thinking), looking at situations in terms of extremes. Things are either good or bad, a success or a failure. In reality most are somewhere in between. One setback rarely means a whole project is a disaster.
- **Labelling,** we might talk to ourselves unkindly, sometimes using a single negative word to describe ourselves. But we can rarely be summed up in one word!
- **Perfectionism**, believing everything we do has to be 100% perfect which can lead to procrastination or self-criticism.

There are others, but that's enough to focus on right now! So, which ones do you use? Which are the most frequent? Try and check every few days whether you're telling yourself things that are unhelpful. If you're thinking one of these then pause and change what you say to yourself or others. For example, sometimes I might say, "I'm always…" or, "You're never…" but I stop myself and use these instead: "Sometimes I find that I… " or "There are times when you…" It can take the heat out of a discussion (with other people, or with myself).

Chapter 10:
These were two exercises I mentioned in chapter 10, the stress quiz and also how to reduce your stress levels, which also came up in chapter 18.

Exercise 10.1: Stress quiz

You can find out whether you're stressed by taking this quiz[156]:

1) First check how you're feeling. Have you recently felt any of these:
   - Irritable, aggressive or impatient?
   - Overburdened?
   - Anxious with a sense of dread?
   - Racing thoughts?
   - Lost interest in the things you usually do?
   - Enjoying life less than usual?
   - Lost your sense of humour?

2) Now think about your behaviours. Have you recently been:
- Indecisive?
- Avoiding challenging situations?
- Snapping at friends, family or colleagues at work?
- Biting your nails or picking at your skin?
- Finding it difficult to concentrate?
- Eating too much or too little?
- Smoking or drinking more alcohol than you usually do?
- Crying quite a lot?

3) Finally, reflect on your physical health. Are you:
- Breathing quite shallowly, hyperventilating or having panic attacks?
- Suffering from insomnia or nightmares?
- Feeling very tired?
- Grinding your teeth or clenching your jaw?
- Having more headaches than normal?
- Getting chest pains?
- Having problems with your digestion or eating?
- Showing high blood pressure levels?
- Having challenges around sex?

If you are showing signs of a few of these, then you might have mild stress. The more you are experiencing, the more stressed you are likely to be. You might be so exhausted that you find it hard to function well. This could be the extreme end of stress, which is burnout.

The signs of burnout can be emotional or physical exhaustion, feeling cut off from yourself or other people, finding it hard to work effectively, using numbing strategies like watching TV, drinking alcohol, comfort eating, playing computer games excessively, shopping or spending too much time on social media or the internet. If you are feeling severe stress then you may need to talk to your doctor or look for coaching, counselling or therapy.

Exercise 10.2: Reducing stress levels

In chapter 10, I included a number of ways that you can relax. Below are a few more exercises that you might like to try:

1) Breathing:
Breathing does far more than just supply oxygen to the brain and body. You

can change the way you think and feel with the way you breathe. It can change your heart rate, lower your blood pressure, reduce your stress levels, combat anxiety, reduce feelings of pain and even change your brain chemistry to make your mind sharper. Just a few short breaths can give our brains a reset and give us clearer thinking and a better ability to control our emotions.

But we often forget how to breathe properly. For most of us breathing isn't part of our self-care repertoire. When we're sitting at a desk, we're often not breathing fully, breathing more from our chest or shoulder area, which can lead to feelings of panic. James Nester is a science journalist who wrote a book called *Breath*[157]: *The New Science of a Lost Art*, where he explores how we've lost the art of breathing. Not breathing properly can create problems from snoring, to sleep apnoea and asthma, through to autoimmune disease and allergies. Here are two ways to improve your breathing and calm your system down:

Navy SEALs are a special operations force, part of the USA's Naval Special Warfare Command. They may not be the first people you think of for this topic, but we can learn something from them. They are taught *box breathing* as a way of staying calm. It's also called *square breathing*. This technique will slow down your heart rate and decrease your stress levels. Try doing this for a few minutes:

• Simply count to four as you breathe in.
• Then hold for four seconds.
• Now count to four seconds as you breathe out.
• Hold there for four seconds and then repeat.
• If this is too long or short lower to three seconds or increase to five seconds.

Belly breathing is another exercise that can help you relax or relieve stress.

• Sit or lie flat in a comfortable position.
• Put one hand on your stomach below your ribs and the other on your chest.
• Breathe through your nose. Use your stomach to push your hand up or down.
• Try to isolate the movement, moving only your belly and not your chest.
• Breathe out slowly through your mouth, feeling your stomach reduce in size.
• You can even use your hand on your belly to push all the air out.

- Breathe like this between three to 10 times. Take your time with each breath.

2) Mindfulness

This is a state of focused, non-judgemental attention on the present. Meditation began as a spiritual practice in Buddhist teaching, but as it has moved from East to West, many of the religious elements have been removed. It is now a practice adapted for many uses. In its simplest form it is purposefully paying attention to each moment, without judging what is happening.

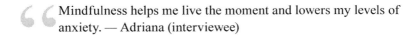

Mindfulness helps me live the moment and lowers my levels of anxiety. — Adriana (interviewee)

Both mindfulness and meditation have been shown to increase wellbeing, reduce blood pressure, improve the immune system, increase levels of self-compassion and emotional awareness, as well as increasing the potential to learn. There are plenty of apps, books and guides out there for you to try. Here are a few that have been recommended to me, although there are many more: *Buddhify, Calm, Headspace, Insight Timer, Simple Habit, Ten Percent Happier* and *Unplug*. A book that was recommended to me was *Mindfulness Pocketbook: Little Exercises for a Calmer Life*[158].

3) Taking breaks

We talked about rest in chapter 10. Here is a bit more on taking breaks. Gunther is one of the participants in my research and this is his version of taking time out and relaxing: "Motorcycling is one of my biggest therapies because I'm on my own. I'm transfixed by it and I'm completely zoning out of everything else. I don't worry about anything for those miles."

Most of us don't take enough time to step back from the busyness of our lives. Being busy can become a habit, making lists whilst we're in the shower, thinking about what we'll do the next day whilst we eat our meals. We don't leave much time to rest our minds, to just be. Instead, why not try this on for size? For a few days, set an alarm so you can take regular breaks. Each time stop what you're doing and just focus on being in the moment. Get up, walk around. Get a drink of water. Watch the birds outside. Anything that you fancy that will give your brain and body a break. At the end of this, see if you're feeling a bit less stressed.

Another way to take breaks from work is through hobbies, things that we just do for fun. It can be anything from woodwork, knitting or historical battle re-enactments to cave diving, ancestry research or stamp collecting. We lose sight of the things we used to love. We stop doing them when we're busy.

Nolan found this when he was working too hard. We heard in chapter 18 that he'd lost himself to his job and couldn't turn to interests outside of work anymore. "I've become an empty husk of a person. I've lost of all of those things. So, if I were to look back over my time again, I'd change things earlier." Lucy likes to read but stopped when she was working long hours. "I'm an avid reader, but I didn't read books for three years. I remember feeling so much enjoyment and relaxation from reading fiction again. Being able to lose myself in a different world. I didn't watch TV for a whole month and just read books."

Another way is to give ourselves a break from our own heads, the thoughts that go round and round like a dog chasing its tail. Ruby likes to write her thoughts and feelings in a journal and has been doing this for a few years. "I had never journaled before, but I found it was really helpful for me to just write out what was filling my head. I just needed to get it on paper. It was pretty cathartic for me."

4) Increasing our hormone levels
We covered hormones in chapters 10 and 17. Here are some actions you might like to take to increase your level of hormones:
- To increase dopamine (the reward chemical) you can finish a task, work on self-care activities, eat food and celebrate small wins.
- If you want to raise your endorphin levels (the pain killer) then laughter is a really good one. Dark chocolate can help too, as well as exercising.
- To increase oxytocin (the love hormone) you can play with your dog or cat (or lizard if you have one), give someone a compliment or do a good turn for your neighbour.
- You can increase serotonin (the mood stabiliser) by meditating, going for a run or taking a walk outside in nature. You can also sit in a patch of sunlight, go cycling, swimming or take part in any type of exercise.

Chapter 13:
In chapter 13 I mentioned an additional exercise which is below. This also came up in chapter 18.

Exercise 13.1: Self-affirmations exercise

I sometimes encourage my coaching clients to use self-affirmations. There are a few who take to them like a duck to water. There are others who find the exercise less comfortable. If this is you, then try to persevere because it really can make a difference. One of my clients was surprised at how much it helped him, despite finding it awkward at first.

Self-affirmations are positive statements that can help you to question and overcome your negative thinking. Repeating these positive statements frequently can help you to re-programme automatic negative thoughts (you may remember we talked about these in chapter eight). Over time, self-affirmations will help you to think and act differently.

Ways you can use self-affirmations include:
- Writing down a number of positive self-affirmations and attaching them to your fridge, putting them next to your bed or placing them somewhere on your desk when you work.
- Reflecting on your strengths and qualities before a difficult meeting, which will help you increase your confidence and reduce your levels of anxiety.
- You can also use them alongside a visualisation exercise (see exercise 3.3). If you picture a positive change with a written self-affirmation, or if you say one out loud, then it will have more impact.
- Using them when you're feeling frustrated, angry or impatient, or when you're feeling low in self-esteem. They are also really useful if you're finding it hard to start a project.
- Repeating frequently, particularly when you're in a negative thought loop.

Chapter 15:
There was just one additional exercise that I mentioned in chapter 15.

Exercise 15.1: Gratitude exercise

We tend to be better at thinking about, and dwelling on, what hasn't worked, rather than focusing on what has gone well. If we can encourage ourselves to be grateful for the good things in life, it can really help. Expressing gratitude releases dopamine and serotonin, and can increase our feelings of appreciation, generosity and compassion for others. It can even change our brain structure. Dr Melanie Greenberg[159] is a professor and clinical psychologist who writes about gratitude. She says our natural tendency is to think about concerns, problems and threats. But a regular focus on gratitude can balance this out, giving us feelings like contentment, joy and love. There are a number of ways to develop a practice of gratitude. You can:

- Set a daily timer to pause and reflect on the 2-3 things you're grateful for in that moment.
- Write a gratitude diary at the end of each day, highlighting what you're grateful for
- Send notes, emails, cards etc. to people in your life that you want to express your gratitude to.
- Demonstrate your gratitude to friends or neighbours by taking their bins out, offering to mow their lawns or baking them biscuits.

This is something I do most days, particularly if I'm in a grumpy mood or feeling sorry for myself. I pick five things I'm grateful for or appreciate in someone else. I often do this with my husband and we take turns, identifying five each. It can be the smallest of things, like the warmth of the sun on my face or how much I'm enjoying drinking a cup of tea in that moment. I find this can lift my spirits and give me a boost in the day. If you can repeat this exercise often, it will even change the way your brain fires!

Chapter 19:
Here is the exercise I mentioned in chapter 19 around working with your emotions:

Exercise 19.1: Increasing awareness of our emotions

Paying attention to your feelings is useful in any change process. It's a source of information that can help you to travel in the right direction. So being aware of your emotions is important. This exercise will help if you find it hard to express how you are feeling.

Dr Melanie Greenberg writes about emotions in her book *The Stress-Proof Brain*[160]. At one level emotions are just mental and physical events, yet we can get overwhelmed by them and try to get rid of them. Instead, she says it's better to allow ourselves to experience them, even if that is painful. Then we'll get more used to those feelings, which will help us to worry less about them. We will also start to see them as temporary and more manageable, and this will reduce the likelihood that we'll tip over into panic or anger.

Dr Ann Weiser Cornell is an expert in *Focusing*, a psychotherapeutic technique developed by Eugene Gendlin. I listened to an interesting podcast where she was interviewed by Joel Monk from *Coaches Rising*.[161] In this conversation she said that as we grow up we don't get much help with learning how to handle our feelings. We distract ourselves or try to talk ourselves out of how we're feeling and that can mean we tell ourselves stories about our emotions, which isn't very helpful. One approach she follows is to help her clients become aware of their feelings and then just sit with them in that moment and accept them.

You can become more aware of your feelings by focusing on your body. The advantage of this is that our bodies are in the present, not worrying about the past or fearful about the future. If we can tap into how our bodies are feeling, then we can engage with our emotions. Why not try this exercise:

- First sit down and make yourself comfortable, resting your arms on your legs.
- Then take in a few breaths in through your nose and out through your mouth.
- Now sense your body against the chair, or floor, becoming aware of the points of contact and how they feel.
- Then start scanning down your body, starting from the top of your head all the way down to your toes, moving your attention from one area to the next, from your head and neck, shoulders/chest/arms, to your trunk, the finally your legs, feet and toes.
- Try not to stop in any one place. You're simply paying a moment's attention to that place in your body, becoming aware of how it is feeling and where you are holding tension. Keep breathing as you are going.
- Now return to any areas where you are keeping stress or tightness. Breathe into those areas. How are those areas feeling right now? How are you and what emotions might be rising up for you? Try and be patient, sometimes they might take a while to surface.
- Once you've done this, you might like to note how you felt. This can help you map how your emotions and moods change over time. Why not look at an app called *Universe of Emotions*[162]? This can help you track your feelings and start taking steps towards working on them.
- Or you might like the *Emotional Barometer* tool by the *School of Life*, just search for their website using *the school of life*.
- You could also read *Atlas of the Heart*, by Brené Brown[163] which helps you to expand the language you have to communicate your feelings.

Right, that's it on the extra exercises. I hope you found them useful? I'd suggest coming back from time to time to see if any more might fit your needs. If you'd like further information then check out the *Swim, Jump, Fly* website at swimjumpfly.com.

APPENDIX B: ADDITIONAL MATERIAL

Have you ever been on holiday and couldn't fit everything into your suitcase? Well, this Appendix is for all the bits and pieces I couldn't fit into the chapters. There is also more material on the *Swim, Jump, Fly* website at swimjumpfly. com.

Chapter 3:

In chapter three I talked about three models of change that are worth explaining in more detail. The first two are *thinking* type exercises, which might suit some people very well. If you're more of a *feeling* type person, you may like to skip on by and head to the *Transtheoretical model of behavior change* (TTM).

The three models are:
1) SPACE
2) PRACTICE
3) TTM (*transtheoretical model of behavior change*)

3.1 SPACE model

Nick Egerton is a chartered psychologist who developed the SPACE model. Together with Professor Stephen Palmer, Egerton wrote an article about *SPACE* in 2005[164]. It stands for **S**ocial context, **P**hysical, **A**ction, **C**ognitions and **E**motions. Stephen Palmer and Kasia Symanska write about SPACE and PRACTICE in a chapter called *Cognitive Behaviour Coaching* in the *Handbook of Coaching Psychology*[165].

The SPACE framework is useful as it can help you become more aware of the relationships between your behaviour, your mind, your moods and your body. These can all be influenced by your surroundings and the context that you are in. Here is more about each aspect that makes up SPACE:

Social context: the people around you, their beliefs about the role you and others play.
Physical: this is your breathing and heart rate, your level of tension, wellbeing/ illness and how well you are sleeping.
Actions: what actions you're taking, but also what you're not doing.
Cognitions: your thoughts, your values, memories, images in your mind and expectations.

Emotions: your feelings and mood.

To work through the SPACE model, think about an event, action or change that worries you. Now reflect on what is going on for you around that action by asking yourself these questions:

Social context: who is around you, what role are they playing in making you feel anxious?

Physical: how are you feeling? How is your body reacting?

Actions: what are you doing and not doing?

Cognitions: what thoughts do you have about this? What are you telling yourself? What are you imagining will happen?

Emotions: how are you feeling? What is your mood?

The aim is to raise your awareness of what is happening to you around this event. Once you have a clearer picture, the next step is to think through some actions you could take to address any challenges you might have with the people around you, how your body is reacting, how you're feeling and what you are thinking. What could you do differently to support yourself in any of these areas? What behaviours, thoughts and actions would be more helpful?

3.2 PRACTICE model

Stephen Palmer also developed the *PRACTICE* model of *Cognitive Behavioural Coaching* in 2007[166]. The acronym which stands for **P**roblem identification, **R**ealistic and relevant goals, **A**lternative solutions generated, **C**onsider consequences, **T**arget most feasible solutions, **I**mplement solution and **C**hosen solution **E**valuation. PRACTICE is a practical, solution focused framework which has a strengths focus. It works like this:

1) **P**roblem identification. First, reflect on the area you'd like to work on. What aspects need shifting for you? When does it work well for you? What will you see that's different when this challenge has been addressed?

Ask yourself on a scale of 0 (not at all) to 10 (completely), how well you are dealing with this concern? If you woke up tomorrow and it had been addressed, what would you notice is different? How would you describe it? What has changed?

2) **R**ealistic, relevant goals. Bearing in mind the outcome you'd like to get to, what goals will you set yourself? Make sure they are SMART goals (see chapter three for a reminder about SMART goals).

3) **A**lternative solutions generated. This is the point where you develop a number of alternatives that will help you address your challenge. Then, write them all down before you work out which ones are more useful.

4) **C**onsideration of consequences. Now is the time to reflect on which ones might work well and which are less helpful. You could score them on a scale of 0 (not at all useful) to 10 (very useful).

5) **T**arget the most feasible solution. Next, you'll need to work out which one will work most effectively for you.

6) **I**mplementation of the solution. Finally, take the action you'd like to work on and separate it into smaller, easier to manage parts. Then take each one a step at a time.

7) **C**hosen solution **E**valuation. When you've completed this series of actions, it's time to review how well they went. You can do this by rating them from 0 (not at all successful) to 10 (very successful). Finally, reflect on what you have learned when you were doing this action. How has this helped you move forward?

3.3 Transtheoretical model of behavior change

John Norcross is an American professor of psychology and psychiatry, and is a clinical psychologist. He writes about the *transtheoretical model of behavior change (TTM)* for psychotherapists and practitioners, but has also written books for general population, for example *Changeology*[1]: *5 Steps to Realising Your Goals and Resolutions*[167].

There are a number of stages in TTM and below is a short summary about each one:

1) **Pre-contemplation** (not ready). The person has no intention to change, or may be unaware they have a problem, even if their friends and families do. They won't put much time aside to reflecting on themselves or thinking about their challenge, and in therapy they will be less active or more resistant than most other clients. It's often others who persuade them to seek this type of help. For pre-contemplators, the pros for change are outweighed by the cons.

2) **Contemplation** (getting ready). An individual is aware of their problem and is thinking about overcoming it in the next six months. They haven't moved to action yet. They will be aware of the pros and the cons, but they carry equal weight. So, the person may get stuck at this stage for long periods of time. Asking someone to change when they're at the pre-contemplation or contemplation stages means nothing will happen. That's unless they work on building insight about themselves.

3) **Preparation** (ready). The person is getting ready to change in the immediate future (usually seen as the next month). The pros will have started to outweigh the cons by now, so they may have already made small shifts in behaviour. The authors use examples of clients who reduced their cigarette usage or delayed their first cigarette of the day. But it can be any slight change that someone is making.

4) **Action** (changing). The person has already changed their behaviour or environment in the last six months. They are actively doing new things, behaving differently, or distancing themselves from the people or places that encouraged their behaviour in the first place.

5) **Maintenance** (continuing). Individuals will be working to prevent a relapse and consolidate gains. They are clear that the pros outweigh the cons in making this change. This helps in lowering the risk of relapse. They may need to monitor themselves, to check they are reinforcing new behaviours and removing triggers in their environment. This helps maintain change over time.

Chapters 9 and 10:
In chapters nine and 10, I mentioned how being outside can positively impact our health and our mood. According to Helen Williams, Stephen Palmer and Kristina Gyllensten[168] we are becoming more detached from the natural world and there is concern that this is affecting our wellbeing and our physical and mental health. Consequently, there has been a lot of academic interest in this issue.

In 1991, Roger Ulrich[169] and others found that people recover more quickly from stressful events when they spend time in nature. Rita Berto[170] also found that these environments have a greater calming effect than urban ones, reducing negative mood and enhancing positive emotion. In 2013 Matthew White[171] and other researchers discovered that blue coastal environments were the most restorative to people. This was followed by woodlands/forest, hills/

moorland and mountains. Urban parks were the least restorative but were still more helpful than being indoors.

In 2015, Gregory Bratman, J. Paul Hamilton and James Gross[172] posed a question: *People who live in cities have less exposure to nature so what impact does this have on mental illness?* In their research they looked at the level of rumination; when we have the same negative thoughts over and over, which is often associated with increased risk of depression and other mental health issues. The researchers found that a 90-minute walk in a natural setting decreased the time that participants ruminated. However, a 90-minute walk in an urban setting had no impact on the levels of rumination at all. So, try to make sure you get out into nature, even if it's just a small park near you.

In 2021, in the wonderfully titled *Journal of Happiness Studies,* Stefan Stieger, David Lewetz and Viren Swami published a research paper called *Emotional Well-being Under Conditions of Lockdown*[173]. They looked at the relationship between being outdoors or indoors, and the impact it had on loneliness and emotional wellbeing. They found that when participants were outside more often, they had higher emotional wellbeing, but those who spent more time inside had higher levels of loneliness, would spend more time using technology, and therefore had poorer wellbeing.

Professor Swami says, "Pre-pandemic we know that people were spending more time indoors than ever before in human history." The research shows that, "The more time spent outdoors, the more you'll feel the restorative effects. Beyond mental and physical health, being outdoors improves imagination and learning, and increases creativity and the feeling of fulfilment."
A different area of research is identifying the amount of time we spend inside. In 2001 the National Human Activity Pattern Survey[174] found that we are indoors 86.9% of the time. However, we often underestimate the time we are inside and overestimate the time outside. In 2018 YouGov ran market research that found people guessed they spent about four hours a day inside. In fact, the actual figure was more than 21 hours a day! So, time to get outside.

Over the last few years in the UK the *National Health Service* (NHS) has been placing more focus on *social prescribing.* This is when health professionals refer patients to support in the community, to help with their health and wellbeing, partly because around 20% of people in the UK visit their health professionals (like General Practitioners) for social issues, rather than health issues.

Do you remember Annette in chapter seven? You may recall that when she had depression her doctor said. "I want you to spend every day in nature." So, Annette did just that. "I literally went every day to the park, which is amazing to just throw myself into nature." The doctor knew the benefits of being outside and how this would significantly help Annette's mental health.

Right, that's it on the additional material that I couldn't fit in the suitcase. I hope you enjoyed it.

APPENDIX C: INSPIRATIONAL RESOURCES

This is a list of resources that have come from a number of sources: participants who shared books, articles or other materials they found helpful; members of my book focus group who provided examples of things they had watched/read themselves or, if they were coaches/therapists, they had used with clients; plus books I've read or other materials I've come across that I recommend.

Books:

1) *Affluenza,* Oliver James, 2007.
2) *Atlas of the Heart: Mapping Meaningful Connection and the Language of Human Experience.* Brené Brown, 2021.
3) *Atomic Habits: An Easy and Proven Way to Build Good Habits and Break Bad Ones,* James Clear, 2018.
4) *Authentic Happiness: Using the New Positive Psychology to Realise your Potential for Lasting Fulfilment.* Martin Seligman, 2017.
5) *Become What You Are.* Alan W. Watts, 1955.
6) *Bittersweet: How Sorrow and Longing Make us Whole.* Susan Cain, 2022.
7) *Breath: The New Science of a Lost Art.* James Nester, 2021.
8) *Changeology: 5 Steps to Realizing Your Goals and Resolutions.* John C. Norcross, 2012.
9) *Coaching for Performance, 3rd edition.* John Whitmore, 2002.
10) *Creative Career Coaching: Theory into Practice.* Liane Hambly and Ciara Bomford, 2019.
11) *Digital Minimalism: Choosing a Focused Life in a Noisy World.* Cal Newport, 2019.
12) *Emotional Agility: Get Unstuck, Embrace Change and Thrive in Work and Life.* Susan David, 2016.
13) *Feel The Fear And Do It Anyway: How to Turn Your Fear and Indecision into Confidence and Action.* Susan Jeffers, 2007.
14) *Flourish: A New Understanding of Happiness and Well-Being, and How To Achieve Them.* Martin Seligman, 2011.
15) *Flow: The psychology of optimal experience. Steps toward enhancing the quality of life.* Mihály Csíkszentmihályi, 1991.
16) *Happiness by Design: Finding pleasure and purpose in everyday life.* Paul Dolan, 2014.
17) *Hardwired to Learn: Leveraging the Self-Sustaining Power of Lifelong Learning.* Teri Hart, 2021.
18) *How God Becomes Real: Kindling the Presence of Invisible Others.*

Tanya Luhrmann, 2020.

19) *Ikigai: The Japanese secret to a long and happy life.* Héctor García and Francesc Miralles, 2016.

20) *Kara Goucher's Running for Women: From First Steps to Marathons.* Kara Goucher, 2011.

21) *Man's Search for Meaning.* Viktor Frankl, 1946.

22) *Mindfulness Pocketbook: Little exercises for a Calmer Life.* Gill Hasson, 2015.

23) *Mindset: The new psychology of success.* Carol Dweck, 2006.

24) *Oranges Are Not the Only Fruit.* Jeanette Winterson, 1985.

25) *The Power of Regret, How Looking Backwards Moves us Forwards.* Daniel Pink 2022.

26) *So Good They Can't Ignore You: Why Skills Trump Passion in the Quest for Work You Love.* Cal Newport, 2012.

27) *Spoon-Fed. Why Almost Everything We've Been Told About Food is Wrong.* Tim Spector, 2022.

28) *Story: Substance, Structure, Style, and the Principles of Screenwriting.* Robert McKee, 1999.

29) *Stumbling on Happiness.* Daniel Gilbert, 2007.

30) *The 5 Second Rule: Transform your Life, Work, and Confidence with Everyday Courage.* Mel Robbins, 2017.

31) *The 7 Habits of Highly Effective People.* Stephen Covey, 1989.

32) *The Art of Travel.* Alain de Botton, 2002.

33) *The Book of Joy: Lasting Happiness in a Changing World.* Dalai Lama, Desmond Tutu and Douglas Adams, 2016.

34) *The Calm Workbook: A Guide to Greater Serenity.* The School of Life, 2021.

35) *The Coaches Handbook.* Edited by Jonathan Passmore, 2021.

36) *The Goal.* Eliyahu Goldratt, Jeff Cox and David Whitford, 2012.

37) *The Little Voice.* Joss Sheldon, 2020.

38) *The Paradox of Choice: why more is less.* Barry Schwartz, 2004.

39) *The Power of Now: A Guide to Spiritual Enlightenment.* Eckhart Tolle, 1997.

40) *The School of Life – Emotional First Aid Kit.* The School of Life, 2019.

41) *The second Mountain: The Quest for a Moral Life.* David Brooks, 2020.

42) *This Too Shall Pass: Stories of Change, Crisis and Hopeful Beginnings.* Julia Samuel, 2020.

43) *Transcend: The New Science of Self-Actualization.* Scott Barry Kaufman, 2020.

44) *Visual Thinking.* Williemien Brand and Pieter Koene, 2017.
45) *When: The Scientific Secrets of Perfect Timing.* Daniel Pink, 2019.
46) *Wilding: The Return of Nature to a British Farm.* Isabella Tree, 2018.

Apps:
1) *Buddhify* (meditation)
2) *Calm* (meditation)
3) *Couch to 5K* (running)
4) *Daily Workouts Fitness Trainer* (fitness)
5) *Headspace* (meditation)
6) *Insight Timer* (fitness)
7) *MyFitness Pal* (fitness)
8) *Olio* (avoiding wasted food and other items)
9) *Simple Habit* (meditation)
10) *Sworkit* (fitness)
11) *Ten Percent Happier* (meditation)
12) *The 7 Minute Workout* (fitness)
13) *Too Good to Go* (avoiding food waste)
14) *Universe of Emotions* (understanding emotions)
15) *Unplug* (meditation)
16) *Zoe Covid Study (*Covid research and wider health studies)
17) *Zones for Training* (fitness)

Blogs, podcasts and online materials

To keep this list up-to-date, I have published the relevant links on my website swimjumpfly.com.

1) *Alfred & Shadow* (a film about emotions). Anne Hilde Vassbø Hagen and Dr Leslie Greenberg.
2) *Aspire,* Sam Collins.
3) *British Association for Counselling and Psychotherapy._*
4) *Career Change Myths and How to Avoid them.*
5) Career Shifters.
6) *Coaches Rising podcast.* Joel Monk.
7) David Cooperider and Associates website.
8) *Doing It Right* podcast, episode 7. Pandora Sykes with Alain de Botton. On Spotify, Apple and other platforms. 2020.
9) *Habits, Reactions and Letting go.* Yung Pueblo (writing name of Diego Perez). December 2021.

10) *Happiness Half Hour* podcast. Professor Bruce Hood and Emma Britton.
11) *How to Stop Procrastinating.* Christian Jarrett, Professor Tim Pychyl and Dr Fuschia Sirois.
12) *Just One Thing. How to reset your brain with breathing.* Michael Mosley – search on the BBC.
13) *Just One Thing. Drink Water.* Michael Mosley – search on the BBC.
14) Kristin Neff on self-compassion.
15) *Mind.*
16) *Power of Vulnerability* TED Talk. Brené Brown.
17) *School of Life.*
18) *Spoon-by-Spoon* blogs. Charlotte Sheridan.
19) *Stop searching for your passion* TEDx Talk. Terri Trespicio.
20) *The Flipside* podcast. *Learning to be Happy* episode. Professor Bruce Hood and Paris Lees.
21) *The Gut Microbiome: What Is It and Why Should You Care About Yours?* Jonathan Wolf, Professor Tim Spector and Dr Will Bulsiewicz.
22) *The Paradox of Choice* TED Talk. Barry Schwartz.
23) *The Psychology of Problem Solving.* Edward Oneill.
24) *The Real reason why we are tired and what you can do about it* TED Talk. Saundra Dalton-Smith.
25) *The Rebel Business School.*
26) *The Tyranny of the Shoulds* podcast. Charlotte Sheridan.
27) *Why some of us don't have one true calling* TED Talk (multipotentialites). Emilie Wapnick.
28) *Why you Feel What you Feel* TEDx Talk. Dr Alan Watkins.

APPENDIX D: INTERVIEW RESEARCH

During 2019 and 2020, I interviewed 108 people who were going through (or had been through) change. They were experiencing all sorts of shifts like changes in health, career, relationship, money worries, moving city, moving country or having an existential crisis about their lives.

What started as a few conversations, mostly focused on career, turned into a much larger research project about all sorts of changes in life. As more participants took part, it became clear these conversations were an intervention in themselves. People found comfort, and sometimes benefit, from sharing their stories with me. How often do we get to talk about ourselves for 40 minutes?

Many people came away with insights about their lives, or reflections on their behaviour, which they found useful. Some saw repeated patterns over many years. Quite a few had epiphanies. As I continued the research, more people asked to be interviewed. The topics quickly broadened from career change to all sorts of different types of change in peoples' lives. I had aimed for five, which turned into 20, then 50. I eventually ended up with 108 people.

I liked getting feedback from the participants as I went. It was useful to know the view from the other side of the fence. This is what James said about our call: "The conversation has been great. I think I could go on for another hour. I think this is a useful exercise... getting me to be a bit introspective and to start thinking about things that, quite frankly, I don't think about, because no one asks me the question... The fact that we got there in 40 minutes is testament to the quality of the conversation. So, I'm grateful, it's been constructive."

Susanne is 55 and Canadian. "I always find it very interesting to reflect back and say where were the different points in my life where I think I was happy? Where did it go sideways? It also reminds me of what I'm really proud of, what I can offer."

Morgan said this: "I enjoy talking, being able to explore my feelings. You've made me think, consider things from an angle I hadn't actually considered before. Also talking to you reminds me of some things that are important that I lose sight of sometimes."

This is from Ellen: "A big thank you for our chat. It's a long time since I have felt so listened-to and understood, you really helped me a lot. So many insights have been popping up since we spoke."

Some final words from Sarah: "I think it's always helpful to just get things out, to be asked questions. I think it's good because then you don't go blathering on wildly into nowhere. To have some kind of direction and to have questions that you have to think about, which you wouldn't normally ask yourself... It's a different way of thinking about things than you would do yourself. Sort of directed thinking."

The interviews:
- Semi-structured interview, questions below.
- 30-60 minutes, the average was around 40 minutes.
- Total time for all interviews, c. 75 hours.
- Telephone calls were all conducted in English.
- All interviews were taped and turned into transcripts using *Otter.ai* software.
- The first interview was 15/8/2019 and the last was 6/10/2020.

There were four interviews (a total of around three hours) which I didn't include in the analysis. For completeness I have included them in the number of people I interviewed and the number of hours, although they weren't analysed. The reason for leaving them out was that sound quality was poor, so it would be hard to turn them into a transcript, or the conversation wasn't as fruitful.

I ran follow-up conversations with 10% of the participants to hear about how their change projects were going and there were 11 of these in total. Of these, seven were conversations and four were surveys via email, because we didn't manage to catch up. The timings on these were anywhere between a few months and a year after the first conversation. So, for the whole project, the total number of interviews/surveys was 119.

Interview questions:

First interview:
- Can you tell me your story about what happened/how you moved away from what fits you best?
- Was there a trigger/tipping point that encouraged you to question your work/ life and decide to make some changes?
- Could you describe behaviours you saw in others that made you feel uncomfortable or didn't align with your values (work or elsewhere)?
- Can you think back to a time when you were more yourself/things were more

aligned for you? What was different then?

- What have you found helpful whilst making these work or life changes?
- What impact have the changes you've been experiencing had on your friends, family, work colleagues/co-workers, health etc?
- What would you do differently if you went through this again? What advice would your older self give your younger self?
- What haven't I asked you that is important? What else would you like to share?
- How have you found this conversation? What have you enjoyed or not enjoyed?

Second interview/survey:
- What has changed (e.g. better/worse, expected/unexpected) since we last spoke?
- What are you doing differently/how are you thinking differently?
- What specific activities have you been involved in/what's happening now in the change work you're doing?
- What have you learned about yourself?
- What advice would you give others based on your own experience?

I also ran one interview between the youngest participant Anne (who was 28) and William (who was 68) to see what insights they could share with each other over the forty years difference in their lives. See chapter 20 for more on this.

Participants profiles:
To ensure there were different voices in the research, I tried to get a balanced spread of people from different age groups, locations and backgrounds. I invited people from a career changing course I attended and my own network, and those from my network's network. Over time people outside of these groups contacted me because they'd heard about the research.

Information about the participants includes:

- Youngest 28 and oldest 68. Average age 43, median 48. Ages were at the time of the interview.
- There were fewer men (42%) and more women (58%). In the book I have offset this by using more quotes from renowned people who were male, to aim to give a balance of male and female voices.
- Participants were located in the following continents/countries:

Continents	Countries
Europe	France, Germany, Greece, Ireland, Italy, Netherlands, Norway, Poland, Portugal, Spain, Switzerland and UK
Middle East/ Asia	Hong Kong, India, Kuwait, Pakistan, Russia and Saudi Arabia
Americas	Brazil, Canada, Venezuela and USA
Africa	Ghana, Kenya and Nigeria
Australasia	Australia and New Zealand
Total	**27**

I wanted to hear from people from a range of backgrounds, so people interviewed for this book include those who are Black, Asian, Hispanic, Arabic, mixed ethnicity and those who are Muslim, Jewish, Christian, Jain and Buddhist. One participant self-declared that they were Gay and one identified as Non-Binary.

Many people lived in a *non-birth* country e.g. an Australian living in Switzerland, a British person in The Netherlands, a Kenyan in Saudi Arabia, a Greek person in the UK, a Kuwaiti living in Canada, an Indian person in the USA, an American in Sweden etc. I found this fascinating, watching people travelling all over the world to build new homes and lives.

There was a big British contingent. It's understandable because it's where I live. But I was pleased that 37% of the participants were from other countries, or British people who had been living for many years in other countries. I would have liked to get a better balance with fewer British and more African, South American, Middle Eastern and Asian participants. I would have preferred to include some non-English speakers but did not have the resources for that. I also wonder if that would have changed the project in some way; working with an interpreter would have placed me a little further from my participants and their stories than I would have wanted to be involved in.

Finally, not all the names are the originals of the people I interviewed. Quite a few participants asked me to change their name (25%) because they were well-known in their field. Or they wanted to remain anonymous because they were sharing deeply personal topics. There were also nine people who had names that duplicated other interviewee names. With the participants' permission, I changed these to make it less confusing for the reader. However, all stories are participants' own. I haven't consolidated stories to create composite participants. One other thing to include is that all the quotes have been signed off by the interviewees. However, despite a number of attempts, I was not able to reach one participant and have therefore changed their name, so they are not identifiable.

Participant stories and quotes:
A friend of mine is a General Practitioner (GP)/Primary Care doctor, who manages a programme in the UK that trains junior doctors to become GPs. She said this when I told her that *Swim, Jump, Fly* would be full of stories: "love it. Stories are fantastic and humans are naturally curious. I tell this to my trainees, that curiosity is their most powerful diagnostic tool. There is an area of study called narrative medicine that aims to use narrative competence to enhance empathy, trust and professionalism, as well as improving the diagnostic process."

My aim was always to bring many different voices into *Swim, Jump, Fly*. I wanted to include the stories of people from different countries, backgrounds, ages, religions and orientations, so picked quotes that offered a good range of ideas or thoughts. In total I have included 247 quotes from interviewees in the book, which came from 97% of the participants.

Since there were 75 hours of interviews, many of the quotes didn't make the final cut. I tried to bring all of the participants into the book at least once, so they felt included and part of the conversation. I wasn't able to do that for everyone though. Despite this, all interviews were useful, bringing greater depth to my understanding of the topic. If you are one of the participants who hasn't been quoted, or was only quoted briefly, please be assured that you brought great value to my thinking and to the development of this book.

Thematic Analysis:
This is a fancy academic name for working out what themes can be pulled out of the research. It's one of the most common forms of analysis in qualitative research. This is one type of research used in psychology, sociology, education, and is based on collecting data through interviews or questionnaires. This means the data is mostly word based and not numerical. *Thematic Analysis* is aptly named as it looks at themes or patterns in the data. It uses a process to identify potential themes by using codes, labels and tags. It's iterative because you start off with a larger number of codes and combine these over time to create groups of themes.

I used an *inductive* approach which means I created themes from the data. This is the opposite of *deductive*, which is having a view of what you will find before you start, then trying to match the data to your ideas. I had no theory of change in mind, just a curiosity to see what people experienced. Experts in this area say it's not possible for a researcher to be completely free from assumptions as we all bring our own background and experiences to situations. So, research will always be shaped by the researcher's views and philosophies on life.

I found the *Thematic Analysis* hard work at times, surrounded by mounds of paper, realms of codes and a pulsing head for weeks at a time. It was a long process from end to end. It took around three to four hours per hour of interview to edit the transcripts and align them to the audio recordings, plus the four different stages in the coding process (see below for more on this). So, all in, this was about 60 days of effort.

I am incredibly grateful for the help I received from two researchers Zeenat and Helen who helped me turn 32 of the 115 recorded interviews into useable transcripts that properly matched the original conversations.

Coding stages:
The following are the stages I went through when coding.

1) Number all transcripts from 1 – 119 (including the four I didn't use). Create a spreadsheet with all the names, dates of interview, numbers and demographic data for each interviewee (e.g. age, country of birth/where they live now), plus source of interviewee etc.

2) Write a summary of key narrative points from each interview and put them into the spreadsheet.

3) Read through the transcripts and surveys and highlight topics (codes) in green and code them 1, 2, 3…. etc. List code names and numbers on a separate sheet. This produced 120 codes.

4) Go through transcripts and highlight quotes in orange. Assign to a code topic e.g. 1.1, 1.2, 1.3; 2.1, 2.2 etc. List quote number/quote topic and transcript number on a separate sheet.

5) Go through all transcripts and identify potential blog topics, many of which I turned into the 73 blog posts in my *Spoon-by-Spoon* blog and additional writing for others, e.g. *The Rebel Business School.*

6) Review 120 initial codes and combine overlapping codes to create 112 codes. Then consolidate these codes into 25 broader themes. I did some final work to consolidate those 25 themes into the final 18 themes. There were a few tiny stragglers left over at the end. Codes which only had one or two mentions throughout the 108 interviews.

Here are the most frequently identified themes. Each theme is made up of multiple codes that I think are connected in terms of subject matter. They are in order from the most frequent at the start, to least frequent at the end:

- Happiness (248 instances)
- Self-awareness (239)
- Values Alignment (208)
- Mindset (202)
- Work Culture and Leadership (200)*
- Authenticity (187)
- Clarity (152)
- Direction (146)
- Moving to Action (120)
- Control (116)
- Stress (106)
- Resources (100)

Some of the less frequent themes were:

- Snap Response (85)
- Balance (76)
- Pressure to Conform (72)
- Triggers for Change (56)
- Money (41)
- Time (28)

*I don't refer to the theme *work culture and leadership* in the book. Many of the conversations were about work, so it's understandable that this came up as a theme. I'm not sure it's so useful for a book that's about broader change and I couldn't find a natural place for it to fit.

Below I've listed some of the topics that came up under this theme, which included: leaders who encourage people to stay because they are role models. Negative behaviours that persuaded people to leave. Lack of trust/loss of trust over time. Organisational culture, such as long hours, bullying, politics, overly demanding clients. Unfairness, injustice and conflict at work. Increased pressure due to the changing nature of work that we are all experiencing, with leaner teams, fewer resources and less loyalty to organisations.

7) I did intend to review the most frequently used words, but then discovered I could do this using my *Otter.ai* account; simply type in a word and it'll show the frequency of use. So, I stopped doing this by hand.

I've mentioned before that I started using the data from this project as content for a blog series that I wrote called *Spoon-by-Spoon*. You can read it on my website swimjumpfly.com. I created one blog post a week for 18 months, so the research project provided wonderful content for my posts. One of my readers asked me if I could summarise what I had learned from all the interviews I had run.

Clearly it would have been impossible to condense 75 hours of interviews into a few words, but I had a go! This is the blog post below:

Seventy-five hours in one hundred words

Last week a friend forwarded me the 100-word *Microfiction Challenge*. It's a competition that challenges writers around the world to create very short stories, 100 words max. The email languished in my inbox for days and when I turned my attention to it, I'd missed the deadline.

Instead, I thought, "Why not write just 100 words for my next post?" Could I continue my journey to greater succinctness? Like a good stock, better when reduced? It can't be that hard to summarise 75 hours of my *Spoon-by-Spoon* interviews. Can it? A Twitter-blog. A super skinny *Spoon-lite*.

So, here goes:

"Don't listen to your parents. What was good for them (then) isn't good for you (now). Life is short. Do it now. Better to try and fail than not bother. People don't think about you as much as you think they do (or think they should). They do however quite like you to stay where you are. We judge ourselves harder than we judge others. What comes easily is a good start for a career (or career change). Happiness is under-rated. Stuff is over-rated. Money won't make you happy.

Well, it will for a while and then it won't."

Apparently, there were thousands of cash prizes available to the winners of the *Microfiction* competition. But as they say, you have to be in it to win it. So, no money for me then… but didn't I say money won't make you happy?

After I posted this someone suggested it would look great on a poster. Another wondered whether I could ask the people on the career change course if anyone would like to create one – there were a number of course participants who were thinking of switching to become graphic designers. I duly set up a competition and got the cohort (over 1,000 people) to vote on which they liked best. The winner was Ana Marta. To see what she created have a look on the *Swim, Jump, Fly* website at swimjumpfly.com.

So, that's it, my research in a nutshell. I hope you found that interesting or useful.

Notes

1. If you'd like to read my *Spoon-by-Spoon* blog, you'll find it via the website at swimjumpfly.com

2. You may know the statement, *"All models are wrong, but some are useful."* Life is complex and change models are simple versions of reality. I suggest holding them lightly, as they'll all be flawed in one way or another, including mine!

3. Brené Brown offers an integration index on her website - search for brenebrown.com/resources.

4. *Coaching for Performance, 3*rd edition. John Whitmore, 2002.

5. *Become What You Are*, Alan W. Watts, 1955.

6. *Stumbling on Happiness*. Daniel Gilbert, 2007.

7. *Possible Selves*. Markus, H., and Nurius, P. American Psychologist, 41, 954-969, 1986.

8. Dr Alan Watkins Ted Talk called *Why you Feel What you Feel* is available to find on the internet.

9. *Atomic Habits: An Easy and Proven Way to Build Good Habits and Break Bad Ones*. James Clear, 2018.

10. Ayurveda is a system of alternative medicine with origins in India, including herbal medicines, diets, meditation, and yoga.

11. *PRACTICE: A model suitable for coaching, counselling, psychotherapy and stress management*. Stephen Palmer, The Coaching Psychologist. 3, 2, 72-77, 2007.

12. *Changeology: 5 Steps to Realizing Your Goals and Resolutions*. John C. Norcross, 2012.

13. There is a view in some circles that this can be a bit 'old school' - seeing resistance as something to overcome. Some suggest focusing on root causes for resistance and what needs attention. Alex Boulting writes about this on his website ebbnflow.

14. *Alice in Wonderland* is by Lewis Carroll (a pseudonym of Charles Dodgson). He wrote about Alice's adventures in 1865, where she falls through a rabbit hole into a fantasy world full of animals that walk, talk and act like humans (and are all slightly mad).

15. *Ikigai: The Japanese secret to a long and happy life*. Héctor García and Francesc Miralles, 2016.

16. *Transcend: The New Science of Self-Actualization*. Scott Barry Kaufman, 2020.

17. Search for *Habits, Reactions and Letting go,* Yung Pueblo (the writing name of Diego Perez), December 2021.

18   *The pen is mightier than the keyboard: Advantages of longhand over laptop note taking.* Mueller, P. A. and Oppenheimer, D. M. *Psychological Science*, 25, 1159–1168, 2014.

19.   *The importance of Cursive Handwriting Over Typewriting for Learning in the Classroom.* Eva One Askvik, F. R (Ruud) van de Weel and Audrey L. H. Van der Meer. Frontiers in Psychology, 2020.

20.   *The 7 Habits of Highly Effective People.* Stephen Covey, 1989.

21.   *Solution Focused Coaching* chapter, Jonathan Passmore. *The Coaches Handbook,* Edited by Jonathan Passmore, 2021.

22.   *The development of goal-setting theory: A half-century retrospective.* Locke, E. A., & Latham, G. P. Motivation Science, 2019.

23.   Michelle Obama's Democratic Convention speech, August 2008.

24.   *Finding Our Way: Leadership For an Uncertain Time*, Margaret J. Wheatley, 2005.

25.   *The School of Life* has many interesting articles - search for *School of Life The Book of Life.*

26.   You may remember the stages were pre-contemplation, contemplation, preparation, action, maintenance and termination.

27.   *Changeology: 5 Steps to Realizing Your Goals and Resolutions.* John C. Norcross,2012.

28.   *Creative Career Coaching: Theory into Practice.* Liane Hambly and Ciara Bomford. 2019.

29.   *How God Becomes Real: Kindling the Presence of Invisible Others.* Tanya Luhrmann, 2020.

30.   *The effectiveness of a hope intervention in coping with cold pressor pain*, Carla J Berg, C R Snyder, Nancy Hamilton. Journal of Health Psychology. 13(6): 804-9, 2008.

31.   *Creative Career Coaching: Theory into Practice.* Liane Hambly and Ciara Bomford, 2019.

32.   *Mindset: The new psychology of success.* Carol Dweck, 2006.

33.   *Why do beliefs about intelligence influence learning success? A social cognitive neuroscience model.* Mangels, J.A, Butterfield, B, Lamb, J, Good, C. and Dweck C.S. Social Cognitive and Affective Neuroscience. 1, 75-86, 2006.

34.   *Theories of intelligence and achievement across the junior high school transition: A longitudinal study and an intervention.* Blackwell, L.A, Trzesniewski, K. H, and Dweck, C.S. Child Development. 78, 246-263, 2007.

35.   *The far-reaching effects of believing people can change: Implicit theories of personality shape stress, health and achievement during adolescence.* Yeager, D, Johnson, R., Spitzer, B., Trzesniewski,

K, Powers, J., and Dweck, C.S. Journal of Personality and Social Psychology. 106, 867-884, 2014.

36.   *Hardwired to Learn: Leveraging the Self-Sustaining Power of Lifelong Learning*. Teri Hart, 2021.

37.   *How Art Changes Your Brain: Differential Effects of Visual Art Production and Cognitive Art Evaluation on Functional Brain Connectivity*. Anne Bolwerk, Jessica Mack-Andrick, Frieder R. Lang, Arnd Dörfler and Christian Maihöfner. PLOS ONE 9 (12), 2014.

38.   *Happiness by Design: Finding pleasure and purpose in everyday life*. Paul Dolan, 2014.

39.   *The Book of Joy: Lasting Happiness in a Changing World*. Dalai Lama, Desmond Tutu, Douglas Adams, 2016.

40.   *Transcend: The New Science of Self-Actualization*. Scott Barry Kaufman, 2020.

41.   Tim Anstiss, *Acceptance and Commitment Coaching*, chapter in *The Coaches' Handbook*. Edited by Jonathan Passmore, 2021.

42.   *Character strengths and virtues: A handbook and classification*. Peterson, C., & Seligman, M. E. P. (2004).

43.   *Teaching Positive Psychology*. Nick Baylis. In Positive Psychology in Practice. Edited by P. Alex Linley and Stephen Joseph, 2004.

44.   Professor Bruce Hood was co-hosting the *Happiness Half Hour* podcast with Emma Britton. Search for this on BBC programmes.

45.   *Thinking and Depression. 1. Idiosyncratic content and cognitive distortions*. Archives of General Psychiatry. Aaron T Beck, 1963; 9 (4): 324-333.

46.   *Master Mentors, 30 Transformative Insights from Our Greatest Minds*. Scott Jeffrey Miller, 2021.

47.   You can find this CBT guide on the MIND website at mind.org.uk.

48.   *Cognitive Behavioural Coaching*. Neenan, M. and Palmer, S. Stress News, 13, 3, 15-18, (2001).

49.   A schema is a pattern of thought or behaviour. It organises categories of information/data and the relationships between them.

50.   Search out *The Psychology of Problem Solving* on YouTube for an easy eight-minute guide.

51.   *The Book on the Taboo Against Knowing Who You Are*. Alan Watts, 2009.

52.   Raffia palms in Guinea contain sugars that ferment in the tropical heat. This creates a sweet, mildly alcoholic beverage that wild chimpanzees love to drink.

53.   YouTube's CEO Susan Wojcicki's speech to the Johns Hopkins University class of 2014. Search for this on YouTube.

54. *Hardwired to Learn: Leveraging the Self-Sustaining Power of Lifelong Learning.* Teri Hart, 2021.

55. Find all 70+ blogs via the *Swim, Jump, Fly* website at swimjumpfly.com.

56. Alain de Botton was a guest on Pandora Syke's *Doing It Right* podcast, August 2020.

57. *Le Petit Prince (The Little Prince).* Antoine de Saint-Exupéry, 1943.

58. *To a Mouse, on Turning Her Up In Her Nest With The Plough.* Robert Burns, 1785.

59. *Your Job is to make art,* Seth Godin presentation at Convertkit Craft and Commerce, 2017. He cites Kurt Vonnegut as the originator of the phrase "throwing ourselves off the cliff and growing wings on the way down", but others say it is the science fiction writer, Ray Bradbury.

60. *Wilding: The Return of Nature to a British Farm.* Isabella Tree, 2018.

61. *Creative Career Coaching: Theory into Practice.* Liane Hambly and Ciara Bomford, 2019.

62. You can find *The Rebel Business School* at therebelschool.com.

63. *Is neural development Darwinian?* Purves, D., Voyvodic, J.T, Magrassi, L., and Yawo, H. Trends in Neuroscience. 19, 460-464, 1987.

64. *The dynamic brain. Neuroplasticity and mental health.* Kays, J.L, Hurley, R.A., and Taber, K.H. Journal of Neuropsychiatry and Clinical Neurosciences. 24, 118-124, 2012.

65. You can watch their conversation on YouTube. Search for *The Gut Microbiome: What Is It and Why Should You Care About Yours?*

66. *Spoon-Fed. Why Almost Everything We've Been Told About Food is Wrong.* Tim Spector, 2022.

67. *The Fiber Fueled Cookbook.* Will Bulsiewicz, 2022.

68. Professor Christopher Gardner in conversation with Jonathan Wolf, on a podcast called *Why Starting That New Year's Diet Might Actually Be Bad for Your Health.* January 2022.

69. *How to banish brain fog and boost energy this winter,* BBC Food.

70. *Drink Water,* episode on BBC Radio Four series, *Just One Thing,* Michael Mosley. October 2021.

71. You can search online for Saundra Dalton's TED talk called *The Real reason why we are tired and what you can do about it.*

72. You can find this on the *Swim, Jump, Fly* website at swimjumpfly.com.

73. *Why We All Need Quiet Days,* School of Life at the theschooloflife.com, August 2021.

74. *When: The Scientific Secrets of Perfect Timing.* Daniel Pink, 2019.

75. WHO, United Global Mental Health and World Federation for Mental Health press release, August 2020.

76. A book I've been recommended is *Mindfulness Pocketbook: Little*

exercises for a Calmer Life. Gill Hasson, 2015.

77. There are plenty of meditation apps you can use, including Calm, Headspace, Insight Timer, Ten Percent Happier, Buddhify, Unplug and Simple Habit.

78. *The Power of Now: A Guide to Spiritual Enlightenment*. Eckhart Tolle, 1997.

79. This is also referenced in *Restructuring for Caring and Effective Education: Piecing the Puzzle Together*, 2000. This refers to Mary Lippit's 1987 *The Managing Complex Change Model*. D Ambrose (1987) is also sometimes referenced.

80. *Developmental Coaching: Life Transitions and Generational Perspectives*. Palmer, S, and Panchal, S., 2011.

81. *Affluenza*. Oliver James, 2007.

82. *Stumbling on Happiness*. Daniel Gilbert, 2007.

83. *Self-control and compulsive buying*. Faber, R. J. In T. Kasser and A. D. Kanner (Eds.), *Psychology and consumer culture. The struggle for a good life in a materialistic world*. pp. 169-187, 2004.

84. Professor Bruce Hood was co-hosting the *Happiness Half Hour* podcast with Emma Britton. Search for this on BBC Programmes website.

85. Ann Weiser Cornell talking to Joel Monk on *Focusing and the Forward Movement of Life* episode of Coaches Rising podcast, January 2022.

86. *Emotional Agility: Get Unstuck, Embrace Change and Thrive in Work and Life*. Susan David, 2016.

87. *Strategies for Accentuating Hope*, Shane J. Lopez, C. R. Snyder, Jeana L. Magyar-Moe, Lisa M. Edwards, Jennifer Teramoto Pedroot, Kelly Janowski, Jerri L. Turner, Cindy Pressgrove. Chapter 24 of *Positive Psychology in Practice: Promoting Human Flourishing in Work, Health, Education, and Everyday Life*, Stephen Joseph, 2015.

88. Sam Collins' *Aspire* is a networking and development organisation. Check it out on the internet.

89. *Overly shallow?: Mis-calibrated expectations create a barrier to deeper conversation*. Kardas, M., Kumar, A., & Epley, N. *Journal of Personality and Social Psychology*. 122(3), 367–398, 2022.

90. *Visual Thinking*. Williemien Brand and Pieter Koene, 2017.

91. *When: The Scientific Secrets of Perfect Timing*. Daniel Pink, 2019.

92. *Implementation Intentions and Goal Achievement: A Meta analysis of Effects and Processes,* Peter M. Gollwitzer and Paschal Sheeran. Advances in Experimental Social Psychology. volume 38, pp 69-119, 2006.

93. *Atomic Habits: An Easy and Proven Way to Build Good Habits and Break Bad Ones*. James Clear, 2018.

94. *How to Stop Procrastinating,* Christian Jarrett podcast on the BPS (British Psychological Society) website.

95. Take a look at Escape the City's *Career Change Myths and How to Avoid them* ebook on escapethecity.org.

96. *The happenstance learning theory.* Krumboltz, J. D. Journal of Career Assessment. 17, p 135, 2019.

97. *Flow: The psychology of optimal experience. Steps toward enhancing the quality of life.* Mihály Csíkszentmihályi, 1991.

98. *Changeology: 5 Steps to Realizing Your Goals and Resolutions.* John C. Norcross, 2012.

99. Find the Swim Jump Fly website at swimjumpfly.com.

100. You can find out more on David Cooperider's website. Just search for davidcooperider.com.

101. *The Zeigarnik Effect* was named after Russian psychologist Bluma Zeigarnik.

102. *Brené Brown on Empathy* - RSA Shorts on YouTube, December 2013.

103. *Thich Nhat Hanh on Compassionate Listening,* Oprah Talks to Thich Nhat Hanh. Search YouTube, May 2012.

104. *How are habits formed: Modelling habit formation in the real world,* Phillippa Lally, Cornelia H. M. van Jaarsveld, Henry W. W. Potts and Jane Wardle. European Journal of Social Psychology. July 2009.

105. Steven joined *Launch Pad*, run by an organisation called *Career Shifters*. You can find them on the internet.

106. *Little Women,* Louisa May Alcott, first published 1868.

107. *Talent, Effort Or Luck: Which Matters More For Career Success?* Tomas Chamorro-Premuzic, Forbes, September 2021.

108. *The Power of Regret, How Looking Backwards Moves us Forwards.* Daniel Pink, 2022.

109. Professor Bruce Hood was talking to Paris Lees on her podcast, *The Flipside,* in an episode called *Learning to be Happy*, December 2021.

110. *The Art of Travel.* Alain de Botton, 2002.

111. Find out more about Multipotentialites by watching Emilie Wapnick's TED Talk: *Why some of us don't have one true calling.*

112. *The Paradox of Choice: why more is less.* Barry Schwartz 2004. Or search for his TED Talk from 2005.

113. *Using attachment theory in coaching leaders: The search for a coherent narrative,* David B Drake. International Coaching Psychology Review. Volume. 4 No. 1. The British Psychological Society, 2009.

114. David Drake, *Narrative Coaching* in *The Coaches' Handbook*. Edited by Jonathan Passmore, 2021.

115. *Enhancing Transition Resilience: Using the INSIGHT coaching and*

counselling model to assist in coping with COVID-19, Panchal, S., Palmer, S. and O'Riordan, S. International Journal of Stress Prevention and Wellbeing, Vol 4, Article 3, 2020.

116. *Feel The Fear And Do It Anyway: How to Turn Your Fear and Indecision into Confidence and Action.* Susan Jeffers, 2007.

117. *Anatomically distinct dopamine release during anticipation and experience of peak emotion to music*, Salimpoor, V. N, Benovoy, M, Larcher, K, Dagher, A and Zatorre, R. J. Nature Neuroscience, February 2011.

118. *Why Be Happy When You Could Be Normal?* Jeanette Winterson, 2011.

119. *Ex-Facebook president Sean Parker: site made to exploit human 'vulnerability'.* Olivia Solon, The Guardian, November 2017.

120. *So Good They Can't Ignore You: Why Skills Trump Passion in the Quest for Work You Love.* Cal Newport, 2012.

121. *Stop searching for your passion.* Terri Trespicio, 2015.

122. Elizabeth Kübler-Ross was a Swiss-American psychiatrist who studied death and dying, including people going through bereavement.

123. These ideas come from *Compassion Focused Therapy*, which uses elements of CBT and mindfulness.

124. There are many useful resources on Kristin Neff's website - self-compassion.org.

125. *Self-control and grit: related by separable determinants of success.* Duckworth A. and Gross, J. *Current Directions in Psychological Science.* 23, pp. 319-325, 2014.

126. *Atomic Habits: An Easy and Proven Way to Build Good Habits and Break Bad Ones.* James Clear, 2018.

127. *Kara Goucher's Running for Women: From First Steps to Marathons,* Kara Goucher, 2011.

128. Alain de Botton was a guest on Pandora Syke's *Doing It Right* podcast, August 2020.

129. Search for the app *Headspace* on the internet.

130. *Feelings Into Words: Contributions of Language to Exposure Therapy.* K. Kircanski, M. D. Lieberman, M. G. Craske. Psychological Science, 2012.

131. *Bittersweet: How Sorrow and Longing Make us Whole.* Susan Cain, 2022.

132. *Stumbling on Happiness.* Daniel Gilbert, 2007.

133. *Alfred & Shadow - A short story about emotions,* was created by psychologist Anne Hilde Vassbø Hagen and Dr Leslie Greenberg. The foundation to it is Emotion-focused therapy (EFT).

134. You can find the *Universe of Emotions* app in your app stores or online.

135. *The Power of Now: A Guide to Spiritual Enlightenment.* Eckhart Tolle, 1997.

136. Search for *What is Cognitive Behavioural Therapy* on the APA website.

137. *An Interview with Maya Angelou.* Psychology Today website. February, 2009

138. *Man's Search For Meaning.* Viktor Frankl, 1946.

139. *A clinical approach to post-traumatic growth.* Richard G Tedeschi and Lawrence G Calhoun. In Positive Psychology in Practice. Edited by P. Alex Linley and Stephen Joseph, 2004.

140. *Coronavirus: Why surviving the virus may be just the beginning.* Chris Morris, BBC News, July 2020.

141. Search on YouTube for *Transformation through Adversity,* Steve Taylor, 2020.

142. *Post-Traumatic Growth: Finding Meaning and Creativity in Adversity,* Scott Barry Kaufman, Scientific American, April 2020.

143. *Transcend: The New Science of Self-Actualization.* Scott Barry Kaufman, 2020.

144. *Man's Search for Meaning.* Viktor Frankl, 1946.

145. *In Over Our Heads: Mental Demands of Modern Life.* Robert Kegan, 1995.

146. *Story: Substance, Structure, Style, and the Principles of Screenwriting.* Robert McKee, 1997.

147. *I am Malala: The Girl Who Stood Up for Education and Was Shot by the Taliban,* Malala Yousafzai, 2014.

148. Victor Frankl founded a movement in Germany called *Logotherapy,* focused on finding meaning in our lives. This approach came out of his experiences in a Nazi death camp, which is in his book, *Man's Search for Meaning,* 1946.

149. This quote was popularised by Steven Covey in his book *The 7 Habits of Highly Effective People.* He was inspired by reading a book (but couldn't remember the name). Researchers suggest it may not have been Frankl's, but possibly psychologist Rollo May.

150. *When: The Scientific Secrets of Perfect Timing.* Daniel Pink, 2019.

151. *Authentic Happiness: Using the New Positive Psychology to Realise your Potential for Lasting Fulfilment.* Martin Seligman, 2017.

152. *Flourish: A New Understanding of Happiness and Well-Being - and How To Achieve Them.* Martin Seligman, 2011.

153. *How to deal with Stress.* Palmer, S. and Cooper, C. 2007 and 2013.

154. *Double Imagery Procedure. The Rational Emotive Behaviour Therapist,* Palmer, S. and Neenan, M. 6, 2. 89-92. 1998.

155. *Creative Career Coaching: Theory into Practice.* Liane Hambly and

Ciara Bomford. 2019.

156. Adapted from *Signs of Stress* in *Creative Career Coaching: Theory into Practice*. Liane Hambly and Ciara Bomford, 2019.

157. *Breath: The New Science of a Lost Art*. James Nester, 2021.

158. *Mindfulness Pocketbook: Little Exercises for a Calmer Life*. Gill Hasson, 2015.

159. *How Gratitude Leads to a Happier Life. The benefits of being grateful and how to harness them*. Melanie Greenberg, Psychology Today, 2015.

160. *The Stress-Proof Brain: Master Your Emotional Response to Stress Using Mindfulness and Neuroplasticity*. Melanie Greenberg, 2016.

161. *Focusing and The Forward Movement of Life*. Ann Weiser Cornell in conversation with Joel Monk. Episode 116 of Coaches Rising podcast, January 2022.

162. You can find the *Universe of Emotions* app in your app stores or online.

163. *Atlas of the Heart: Mapping Meaningful Connection and the Language of Human Experience*. Brené Brown, 2021.

164. *SPACE: a psychological model for use within cognitive behavioural coaching, therapy and stress management*. Edgerton N. Palmer S. The Coaching Psychologist. 2(2): 25–31, 2005.

165. *Handbook of Coaching Psychology: A guide for practitioners*. Edited by Stephen Palmer and Alison Whybrow, 2019.

166. *PRACTICE: A model suitable for coaching, counselling, psychotherapy and stress management*. Stephen Palmer, The Coaching Psychologist. 3, 2, 72-77, 2007.

167. *Changeology: 5 Steps to Realizing Your Goals and Resolutions*. John C. Norcross, 2012.

168. *Stress, resilience, health and wellbeing coaching,* Williams, H., Palmer, S., Gyllensten, K. Handbook of Coaching Psychology. Edited by Stephen Palmer and Alison Whybrow, 2019.

169. *Stress recovery during exposure to natural and urban environments*. Ulrich, R.S, Simons, R.F, Losito, B.D, Fiorito, E, Miles, M.A & Zelson, M. Journal of Environmental Psychology, 11, 201-230, 1991.

170. *The Role of Nature in Coping with Psycho-Physiological Stress: A Literature Review on Restorativeness*. Rita Berto. Behavioural Science, 4, 394-409, 2014.

171. *Feelings of restoration from recent nature visits*. White, M.P, Pahl, S, Ashbullby, K, Herbert, S & Depledge, M.H. Journal of Environmental Psychology, 35, 40-51, 2013.

172. *Nature experience reduces rumination and subgenual prefrontal cortex activation*. Gregory Bratman, J. Paul Hamilton and James Gross. Psychological and Cognitive Sciences. 2015.

173. *Emotional Well-Being Under Conditions of Lockdown: An Experience Sampling Study in Austria During the COVID-19 Pandemic.* Stefan Stieger, David Lewetz and Viren Swami, Journal of Happiness Studies, 22 2703 - 2720, January 2021.

174. *The National Human Activity Pattern Survey (NHAPS): a resource for assessing exposure to environmental pollutants.* Klepeis, N.E, Nelson, W.C, Ott, W.R, Robinson, J.P, Tsang, A.M, Switzer, P, Behar, J.V, Hern, S.C & Engelmann, W.H. Journal of Exposure Analysis and Environmental Epidemiology, 11, 231-252, 2001.